The Official

SAT
Subject Tests
in Mathematics Levels 1 & 2

Study Guide™

The College Board
New York, NY

The College Board

The College Board is a not-for-profit membership association whose mission is to connect students to college success and opportunity. Founded in 1900, the College Board is composed of more than 5,700 schools, colleges, universities and other educational organizations. Each year, the College Board serves seven million students and their parents, 23,000 high schools, and 3,800 colleges through major programs and services in college readiness, college admission, guidance, assessment, financial aid and enrollment. Among its widely recognized programs are the SAT®, the PSAT/NMSQT®, the Advanced Placement Program® (AP®), SpringBoard® and ACCUPLACER®. The College Board is committed to the principles of excellence and equity, and that commitment is embodied in all of its programs, services, activities and concerns.

For further information, visit www.collegeboard.org.

Copies of this book are available from your bookseller or may be ordered from College Board Publications, P.O. Box 86900, Plano, TX 86901. 800 323-7155. The price is $18.99.

Editorial inquiries concerning this book should be addressed to the College Board, SAT Program, 45 Columbus Avenue, New York, New York 10023-6992.

ISBN 13: 978-0-87447-772-6

ISBN 10: 0-87447-772-7

Library of Congress Card Catalog Number: 2006016434

Printed in the United States of America

10 9 8 7 6 5

Distributed by Macmillan

CONTENTS

The SAT Subject Tests™

About SAT Subject Tests

SAT Subject Tests™ are a valuable way to help you show colleges a more complete picture of your academic background and interests. Each year, nearly one million Subject Tests are taken by students throughout the country and around the world to gain admission to the leading colleges and universities in the U.S.

SAT Subject Tests are one-hour exams that give you the opportunity to demonstrate knowledge and showcase achievement in specific subjects. They provide a fair and reliable measure of your achievement in high school — information that can help enhance your college admission portfolio. The Mathematics Levels 1 and 2 Subject Tests are a great way to highlight your understanding, skills and strengths in mathematics.

This book provides information and guidance to help you study for and familiarize yourself with the Mathematics Levels 1 and 2 Subject Tests. It contains actual, previously administered tests and official answer sheets that will help you get comfortable with the tests' format, so you feel better prepared on test day.

The Benefits of SAT Subject Tests

SAT Subject Tests let you to put your best foot forward, allowing you to focus on subjects that you know well and enjoy. They can help you differentiate yourself in a competitive admission environment by providing additional information about your skills and knowledge of particular subjects. Many colleges also use Subject Tests for course placement and selection; some schools allow you to place out of introductory courses by taking certain Subject Tests.

Subject Tests are flexible and can be tailored to your strengths and areas of interest. These are the **only** national admission tests where **you** choose the tests that best showcase your achievements and interests. You select the Subject Test(s) and can take up to three tests in one sitting. With the exception of listening tests, you can even decide to change the subject or number of tests you want to take on the day of the test. This flexibility can help you be more relaxed on test day.

Who Should Consider Subject Tests?

Anyone can take an SAT Subject Test to highlight his or her knowledge of a specific subject. SAT Subject Tests may be especially beneficial for certain students:

REMEMBER

. . . .
Subject Tests are
a valuable way
to help you show
colleges a more
complete picture
of your academic
achievements.
. . . .

- Students applying to colleges that require or recommend Subject Tests — be aware that some schools have additional Subject Test requirements for certain students, majors or programs of study
- Students who wish to demonstrate strength in specific subject areas
- Students who wish to demonstrate knowledge obtained outside a traditional classroom environment (e.g., summer enrichment, distance learning, weekend study, etc.)
- Students looking to place out of certain classes in college
- Students enrolled in dual-enrollment programs
- Home-schooled students or students taking courses online
- Students who feel that their course grade may not be a true reflection of their knowledge of the subject matter

The SAT Subject Tests in Mathematics are particularly useful for students interested in majors with a quantitative focus, including Economics and STEM (Science, Technology, Engineering and Math) majors.

Who Requires the SAT Subject Tests?

Most college websites and catalogs include information about admission requirements, including which Subject Tests are needed or recommended for admission. Schools have varying policies regarding Subject Tests, but they generally fall into one or more of the following categories:

- Required for admission
- Recommended for admission
- Required or recommended for certain majors or programs of study (e.g., engineering, honors, etc.)
- Required or recommended for certain groups of students (e.g., home-schooled students)
- Required, recommended or accepted for course placement
- Accepted for course credit

- Accepted as an alternative to fulfill certain college admission requirements
- Accepted as an alternative to fulfill certain high school subject competencies
- Accepted and considered, especially if Subject Tests improve or enhance a student's application

In addition, the College Board provides a number of resources where you can search for information about Subject Test requirements at specific colleges.

- Visit the websites of the colleges and universities that interest you.
- Visit College Search at www.collegeboard.org.
- Purchase a copy of *The College Board College Handbook*.

Some colleges require specific tests, such as mathematics or science, so it's important to make sure you understand the policies prior to choosing which Subject Test(s) to take. If you have questions or concerns about admission policies, contact college admission officers at individual schools. They are usually pleased to meet with students interested in their schools.

Subject Tests Offered

SAT Subject Tests measure how well you know a particular subject area and your ability to apply that knowledge. SAT Subject Tests aren't connected to specific textbooks or teaching methods. The content of each test evolves to reflect the latest trends in what is taught in typical high school courses in the corresponding subject.

The tests fall into five general subject areas:

English	Languages	
Literature	**Reading Only**	**Language with Listening**
History	French	Chinese
United States History	German	French
World History	Italian	German
Mathematics	Latin	Japanese
Mathematics Level 1	Modern Hebrew	Korean
Mathematics Level 2	Spanish	Spanish
Science		
Biology E/M		
Chemistry		
Physics		

Who Develops the Tests

The SAT Subject Tests are part of the SAT Program of the College Board, a not-for-profit membership association of more than 5,700 schools, colleges, universities and other educational associations. Every year, the College Board serves seven million students and their parents, 23,000 high schools, and 3,800 colleges through major programs and services in college readiness, college admission, guidance, assessment, financial aid and enrollment.

Each subject has its own test development committee, typically composed of teachers and college professors appointed for the different Subject Tests. The test questions are written and reviewed by each Subject Test Committee, under the guidance of professional test developers. The tests are rigorously developed, highly reliable assessments of knowledge and skills taught in high school classrooms.

Deciding to Take an SAT Subject Test

Which Tests Should You Take?

The SAT Subject Test(s) that you take should be based on your interests and academic strengths. The tests are a great way to indicate interest in specific majors or programs of study (e.g., engineering, pre-med, cultural studies).

You should also consider whether the colleges that you're interested in require or recommend Subject Tests. Some colleges will grant an exemption from or credit for a freshman course requirement if a student does well on a particular SAT Subject Test. Below are some things for you to consider as you decide which test(s) to take.

Think through your strengths and interests

- List the subjects in which you do well and that truly interest you.
- Think through what you might like to study in college.
- Consider whether your current admission credentials (high school grades, SAT® scores, etc.) highlight your strengths.

Consider the colleges that you're interested in

- Make a list of the colleges you're considering.
- Take some time to look into what these colleges require or what may help you stand out in the admission process.
- Use College Search to look up colleges' test requirements.

- If the colleges you're interested in require or recommend SAT Subject Tests, find out how many tests are required or recommended and in which subjects.

Take a look at your current and recent course load

- Have you completed the required course work? The best time to take SAT Subject Tests is at the end of the course, when the material is still fresh in your mind.
- Check the recommended preparation guidelines for the Subject Tests that interest you to see if you've completed the recommended course work.
- Try your hand at some SAT Subject Test practice questions on collegeboard.org or in this book.

Don't forget, regardless of admission requirements, you can enhance your college portfolio by taking Subject Tests in subject areas that you know very well.

If you're still unsure about which SAT Subject Test(s) to take, talk to your teacher or counselor about your specific situation. You can also find more information about SAT Subject Tests on collegeboard.org.

When to Take the Tests

We generally recommend that you take the Mathematics Levels 1 or 2 Subject Test after you complete three years of college-preparatory mathematics, prior to your senior year of high school, if possible. This way, you will already have your Subject Test credentials complete, allowing you focus on your college applications in the fall of your senior year. Try to take the test soon after your courses end, when the content is still fresh in your mind. More information about the topics covered on each of the Mathematics Subject Tests can be found later in this book.

Since not all Subject Tests are offered on every test date, be sure to check when the Subject Tests that you're interested in are offered and plan accordingly.

You should also balance this with college application deadlines. If you're interested in applying Early Decision or Early Action to any college, many colleges advise that you take the SAT Subject Tests by October or November of your senior year. For regular decision applications, some colleges will accept SAT Subject Test scores through the December or January administration. Use College Search to look up policies for specific colleges.

This book suggests ways you can prepare for the Subject Tests in Mathematics Levels 1 and 2. Before taking a test in a subject you haven't studied recently, ask your teacher for advice about the best time to take the test. Then review the course material thoroughly over several weeks.

How to Register for the Tests

There are several ways to register for the SAT Subject Tests.

- Visit the College Board's website at www.collegeboard.org. Most students choose to register for Subject Tests on the College Board website.

- Register by telephone (for a fee) if you have registered previously for the SAT or an SAT Subject Test. Call, toll free from anywhere in the United States, 866-756-7346. From outside the United States, call 212-713-7789.

- If you do not have access to the Internet, find registration forms in *The Paper Registration Guide for the SAT and SAT Subject Tests*. You can find the booklet in a guidance office at any high school or by writing to:

  The College Board
  SAT Program
  P.O. Box 025505
  Miami, FL 33102

When you register for the SAT Subject Tests, you will have to indicate the specific Subject Tests you plan to take on the test date you select. You may take one, two or three tests on any given test date; your testing fee will vary accordingly. Except for the Language Tests with Listening, you may change your mind on the day of the test and instead select from any of the other Subject Tests offered that day.

You will be asked to fill out or update a Student Questionnaire when you register for the test. Although it is optional, the questionnaire can benefit you. Your answers can help connect you with colleges that match your interests and scholarship agencies that can help you pay for college. Your answers will *not* influence your test score, and the information will be provided to colleges only with your permission.

Keep the Tests in Perspective

Colleges that require Subject Test scores do so because the scores are useful in making admission or placement decisions. Schools that don't have specific Subject Test policies generally review them during the application process because the scores can give a fuller picture of your academic achievement. The Subject Tests are a particularly helpful tool for admission and placement programs because the tests aren't tied to specific textbooks, grading procedures or instruction methods but are still tied to curricula. The tests provide level ground on which colleges can compare your scores with those of students who come from schools and backgrounds that may be far different from yours.

It's important to remember that test scores are just one of several factors that colleges consider in the admission process. Admission officers also look at your high school grades, letters of recommendation, extracurricular activities, essays and other criteria. Try to keep this in mind when you are preparing for and taking Subject Tests.

Score Choice™

In March 2009, the College Board introduced Score Choice™, a feature that gives you the option to choose the scores you send to colleges by test date for the SAT and by individual test for the SAT Subject Tests — at no additional cost. Designed to reduce your test day stress, Score Choice gives you an opportunity to show colleges the scores you feel best represent your abilities. Score Choice is optional, so if you don't actively choose to use it, all of your scores will be sent automatically with your score report. Since most colleges only consider your best scores, you should still feel comfortable reporting scores from all of your tests.

> **REMEMBER**
>
> Score Choice gives you an opportunity to show colleges the scores you feel best represent your abilities.

More about collegeboard.org

collegeboard.org is a comprehensive tool that can help you be prepared, connected and informed throughout the college planning and admission process. In addition to registering for the SAT and SAT Subject Tests, you can find information about other tests and services, try The Official SAT Question of the Day™, browse the College Board Store (where you can order *The College Board College Handbook* and *The Official Study Guide for all SAT Subject Tests*™ or *The Official SAT Subject Tests in U.S. and World History Study Guide*™), and send e-mails with your questions and concerns. collegeboard.org also contains free practice questions for each of the 20 SAT Subject Tests. These are an excellent supplement to this Study Guide and can help you be even more prepared on test day.

Once you create a free online account, you can print your SAT admission ticket, see your scores and send them to schools.

Which colleges are right for you? College Search at www.collegeboard.org has two ways to help you. The College MatchMaker lists colleges that meet all of your needs. If you are already familiar with a school, use College QuickFinder for updates of essential information. Both methods help you find the latest information on more than 3,800 colleges, as well as easy access to related tools.

How will you pay for college? While you're at the College Board website, look at the Financial Aid EasyPlanner, to help you organize your finances. It can help you find answers to such questions as: What does the school of your choice cost? How much can you save? How much can you and your family afford to pay? How much can your family afford to borrow for your education? What scholarships are available to you?

SAT Subject Tests Schedule

Subject	Date					
	October	November	December	January	May	June
Literature	*	*	*	*	*	*
United States History	*	*	*	*	*	*
World History			*			*
Mathematics Level 1	*	*	*	*	*	*
Mathematics Level 2	*	*	*	*	*	*
Biology E/M	*	*	*	*	*	*
Chemistry	*	*	*	*	*	*
Physics	*	*	*	*	*	*
Languages: Reading Only						
French	*		*	*	*	*
German						*
Modern Hebrew						*
Italian			*			
Latin			*			*
Spanish	*		*	*	*	*
Languages with Listening						
Chinese		*				
French		*				
German		*				
Japanese		*				
Korean		*				
Spanish		*				

NOTES
1. You can take up to three SAT Subject Tests on a single day.
2. On test day you can change which tests you actually take except for the Language Tests with Listening.
3. You may only use a calculator for Mathematics Level 1 and Mathematics Level 2 Subject Tests. Some questions on these tests cannot be solved without a scientific or a graphing calculator. You do not need to use a calculator to solve every question, but it is important to know how and when to use one. We recommend a graphing calculator rather than a scientific calculator because a graphing calculator may provide an advantage on some questions.
4. You must bring an acceptable CD player if you are taking a Language with Listening test.

How to Do Your Best on the SAT Subject Test

Get Ready

Give yourself plenty of time to review the material in this book before test day. The rules for the SAT Subject Tests may be different than the rules for most of the tests you've taken in high school. You're probably used to answering questions in order, spending more time answering the hard questions and, in the hopes of getting at least partial credit, showing all your work.

When you take the SAT Subject Tests, it's OK to move around within the test section and to answer questions in any order you wish. Keep in mind that the questions go from easier to harder. You receive one point for each question answered correctly. No partial credit is given, and only those answers entered on the answer sheet are scored. For each question that you try, but answer incorrectly, a fraction of a point is subtracted from the total number of correct answers. No points are added or subtracted for unanswered questions. If your final raw score includes a fraction, the score is rounded to the nearest whole number.

Avoid Surprises

Know what to expect. Become familiar with the test and test-day procedures. You'll boost your confidence and feel a lot more relaxed.

- **Know how the tests are set up.** All SAT Subject Tests are one-hour multiple-choice tests. The first page of each Subject Test includes a background questionnaire. You will be asked to fill it out before taking the test. The information is for statistical purposes only. It will not influence your test score. Your answers to the questionnaire will assist us in developing future versions of the test. You can see a sample of the background questionnaire for the Mathematics Level 1 and Mathematics Level 2 Subject Tests at the start of each test in this book.

- **Learn the test directions.** The directions for answering the questions in this book are the same as those on the actual test. If you become familiar with the directions now, you'll leave yourself more time to answer the questions when you take the test.

- **Study the sample questions.** The more familiar you are with question formats, the more comfortable you'll feel when you see similar questions on the actual test.

- **Get to know the answer sheet.** At the back of this book, you'll find a set of sample answer sheets. The appearance of the answer sheets in this book may differ from the answer sheets you see on test day.

- **Understand how the tests are scored.** You get one point for each right answer and lose a fraction of a point for each wrong answer. You neither gain nor lose points for omitting an answer. Hard questions count the same amount as easier questions.

A Practice Test Can Help

Find out where your strengths lie and which areas you need to work on. Do a run-through of a Subject Test under conditions that are close to what they will be on test day.

- **Set aside an hour so you can take the test without interruption.** You will be given one hour to take each SAT Subject Test.
- **Prepare a desk or table that has no books or papers on it.** No books, including dictionaries, are allowed in the test room.
- **Read the instructions that precede the practice test.** On test day, you will be asked to do this before you answer the questions.
- **Remove and fill in an answer sheet from the back of this book.** You can use one answer sheet for up to three Subject Tests.
- **For the mathematics tests,** use the calculator that you plan to use on test day.
- **Use a clock or kitchen timer to time yourself.** This will help you to pace yourself and to get used to taking a test in 60 minutes.

The Day Before the Test

It's natural to be nervous. A bit of a nervous edge can keep you sharp and focused. Below are a few suggestions to help you be more relaxed as the test approaches.

Do a brief review on the day before the test. Look through the sample questions, answer explanations, and test directions in this book, or on the College Board website. Keep the review brief; cramming the night before the test is unlikely to help your performance and might even make you more anxious.

The night before test day, prepare everything you need to take with you. You will need:

- your admission ticket
- an acceptable photo ID (see page 12)
- two No. 2 pencils with soft erasers. Do not bring pens or mechanical pencils.
- a watch without an audible alarm
- an approved calculator with fresh batteries
- a snack

REMEMBER

You are in control.

Come prepared.

Pace yourself.

Guess wisely.

Know the route to the test center and any instructions for finding the entrance.

Check the time your admission ticket specifies for arrival. Arrive a little early to give yourself time to settle in.

Get a good night's sleep.

Acceptable Photo IDs

- Driver's license (with your photo)

- State-issued ID

- Valid passport

- School ID card

- Student ID form that has been prepared by your school on school stationery and includes a recognizable photo and the school seal, which overlaps the photo (go to www.collegeboard.org for more information)

The most up-to-date information about acceptable photo IDs can be found on collegeboard.org.

REMINDER   **What I Need on Test Day**

Make a copy of this box and post it somewhere noticeable.

I Need   **I Have**

Appropriate photo ID

Admission ticket   _____

Two No. 2 pencils with clean soft erasers   _____

Watch (without an audible alarm)   _____

Calculator with fresh batteries   _____

Snack   _____

Bottled water   _____

Directions to the test center   _____

Instructions for finding the entrance on weekends   _____

I am leaving the house at _____ a.m.

Be on time or you can't take the test.

On Test Day

You have good reason to feel confident. You're thoroughly prepared. You're familiar with what this day will bring. You are in control.

Keep in Mind

You must be on time or you can't take the test. Leave yourself plenty of time for mishaps and emergencies.

Think positively. If you are worrying about not doing well, then your mind isn't on the test. Be as positive as possible.

Stay focused. Think only about the question in front of you. Letting your mind wander will cost you time.

Concentrate on your own test. The first thing some students do when they get stuck on a question is to look around to see how everyone else is doing. What they usually see is that others seem busy filling in their answer sheets. Instead of being concerned that you are not doing as well as everyone else, keep in mind that everyone works at a different pace. Your neighbors may not be working on the question that puzzled you. They may not even be taking the same test. Thinking about what others are doing takes you away from working on your own test.

Making an Educated Guess

Educated guesses are helpful when it comes to taking tests with multiple-choice questions; however, making random guesses is not a good idea. To correct for random guessing, a fraction of a point is subtracted for each incorrect answer. That means random guessing — guessing with no idea of an answer that might be correct — could lower your score. The best approach is to eliminate all the choices that you know are wrong. Make an educated guess from the remaining choices. If you can't eliminate any choice, move on.

> **REMEMBER**
>
> All correct answers are worth one point, regardless of the question's difficulty level.

IMPORTANT

Cell phones are not allowed to be used in the test center or the testing room. If your cell phone is on, your scores will be canceled.

10 **Tips**
FOR TAKING THE TEST

1. **Read carefully.** Consider all the choices in each question. Avoid careless mistakes that will cause you to lose points.

2. **Answer the easier questions first.** Work on less time-consuming questions before moving on to the more difficult ones.

3. **Eliminate choices that you know are wrong.** Cross them out in your test book so that you can clearly see which choices are left.

4. **Make educated guesses or skip the question.** If you have eliminated the choices that you know are wrong, guessing is your best strategy. However, if you cannot eliminate any of the answer choices, it is best to skip the question.

5. **Keep your answer sheet neat.** The answer sheet is scored by a machine, which can't tell the difference between an answer and a doodle. If the machine mistakenly reads two answers for one question, it will consider the question unanswered.

6. **Use your test booklet as scrap paper.** Use it to make notes or write down ideas. No one else will look at what you write.

7. **Check off questions as you work on them.** This will save time and help you to know which questions you've skipped.

8. **Check your answer sheet regularly.** Make sure you are in the right place. Check the number of the question and the number on the answer sheet every few questions. This is especially important when you skip a question. Losing your place on the answer sheet will cost you time and may cost you points.

9. **Work at an even, steady pace and keep moving.** Each question on the test takes a certain amount of time to read and answer. Good test-takers develop a sense of timing to help them complete the test. Your goal is to spend time on the questions that you are most likely to answer correctly.

10. **Keep track of time.** During the hour that each Subject Test takes, check your progress occasionally so that you know how much of the test you have completed and how much time is left. Leave a few minutes for review toward the end of the testing period.

IMPORTANT

If you erase all your answers to a Subject Test, that's the same as a request to cancel the test. All Subject Tests taken with the erased test will also be canceled.

7 Ways
TO PACE YOURSELF

1. Set up a schedule. Know when you should be one-quarter of the way through and halfway through. Every now and then, check your progress against your schedule.

2. Begin to work as soon as the testing time begins. Reading the instructions and getting to know the test directions in this book ahead of time will allow you to do that.

3. Work at an even, steady pace. After you answer the questions you are sure of, move on to those for which you'll need more time.

4. Skip questions you can't answer. You might have time to return to them. Remember to mark them in your test booklet, so you'll be able to find them later.

5. As you work on a question, cross out the answers you can eliminate in your test book.

6. Go back to the questions you skipped. If you can, eliminate some of the answer choices, then make an educated guess.

7. Leave time in the last few minutes to check your answers to avoid mistakes.

Check your answer sheet. Make sure your answers are dark and completely filled in. Erase completely.

REMEMBER

After the Tests

Most, but not all, scores will be reported online several weeks after the test date. A few days later, a full score report will be available to you online. Your score report will also be mailed to your high school, and to the colleges, universities, and scholarship programs that you indicated on your registration form or on the correction form attached to your admission ticket. The score report includes your scores, percentiles, and interpretive information. You will only receive a paper score report if you indicate that you would like one.

What's Your Score?

Scores are available for free at www.collegeboard.org several weeks after each SAT is given. You can also get your scores — for a fee — by telephone. Call Customer Service at 866 756-7346 in the U.S. From outside the U.S., dial 212 713-7789.

Some scores may take longer to report. If your score report is not available online when expected, check back the following week. If you have not received your mailed score report by eight weeks after the test date (by five weeks for online reports), contact Customer Service by phone at 866 756-7346 or by e-mail at sat@info.collegeboard.org.

Should You Take the Tests Again?

Before you decide whether or not to retest, you need to evaluate your scores. The best way to evaluate how you really did on a Subject Test is to compare your scores to the admissions or placement requirements, or average scores, of the colleges to which you are applying. You may decide that with additional work you could do better taking the test again.

Contacting the College Board

If you have comments or questions about the tests, please write to us at the College Board SAT Program, P.O. Box 025505, Miami, FL 33102, or e-mail us at sat@info.collegeboard.org.

The Mathematics Subject Tests

Purpose

There are two, one-hour SAT Subject Tests in Mathematics: Mathematics Level 1 and Mathematics Level 2. The purpose of these tests is to measure your knowledge of mathematics through the first three years of college-preparatory mathematics for Level 1 and through precalculus for Level 2.

Mathematics Level 1 Subject Test

Format

Mathematics Level 1 is a one-hour broad survey test that consists of 50 multiple-choice questions. The test has questions in the following areas:

- Number and Operations
- Algebra and Functions
- Geometry and Measurement (plane Euclidean/measurement, coordinate, three-dimensional, and trigonometry)
- Data Analysis, Statistics, and Probability

How to Prepare

The Mathematics Level 1 Subject Test is intended for students who have taken three years of college-preparatory mathematics, including two years of algebra and one year of geometry. You are not expected to have studied every topic on the test. Familiarize yourself with the test directions in advance. The directions in this book are identical to those that appear on the test.

Calculator Use

It is NOT necessary to use a calculator to solve every question on the Level 1 test, but it is important to know when and how to use one. **Students who take the test without a calculator will be at a disadvantage.** For about 50 to 60 percent of the questions, there is no advantage, perhaps even a disadvantage, to using a calculator. For about 40 to 50 percent of the questions, a calculator may be useful or necessary.

A graphing calculator may provide an advantage over a scientific calculator on some questions. However, you should bring the calculator with which you are most familiar. If you are comfortable with both a scientific calculator and a graphing calculator, you should bring the graphing calculator.

Mathematics Level 2 Subject Test

Format

Mathematics Level 2 is also a one-hour test that contains 50 multiple-choice questions that cover the following areas:

- Number and Operations
- Algebra and Functions
- Geometry and Measurement (coordinate geometry, three-dimensional geometry, and trigonometry)
- Data Analysis, Statistics, and Probability

How to Prepare

The Mathematics Level 2 Subject Test is intended for students who have taken college-preparatory mathematics for more than three years, including two years of algebra, one year of geometry, and elementary functions (precalculus) and/or trigonometry. You are not expected to have studied every topic on the test.

Choosing Between Mathematics Levels 1 and 2

If you have taken trigonometry and/or elementary functions (pre-calculus), received grades of B or better in these courses, and are comfortable knowing when and how to use a scientific or a graphing calculator, you should select the Level 2 test. If you are sufficiently prepared to take Level 2, but elect to take Level 1 in hopes of receiving a higher score, you may not do as well as you expect. You may want to consider taking the test that covers the topics you learned most recently, since the material will be fresh in your mind. You should also consider the requirements of the colleges and/or programs you are interested in.

Pages 21 and 22 explain in greater detail the similarities and differences between the two Mathematics tests. Take the time to review this information prior to deciding which Mathematics test to take. Seek advice from your high school math teacher if you are still unsure of which test to take. Keep in mind you can choose to take either test on test day, regardless of what test you registered for.

Calculator Use

It is NOT necessary to use a calculator to solve every question on the Level 2 test, but it is important to know when and how to use one. For about 35 to 45 percent of the questions, there is no advantage, and perhaps even a disadvantage, to using a calculator. For about 55 to 65 percent of the questions, a calculator may be useful or necessary.

As with the Level 1 test, a graphing calculator may provide an advantage over a scientific calculator on some questions. However, you should bring the calculator with which you are most familiar. If you are comfortable with both a scientific calculator and a graphing calculator, you should bring the graphing calculator.

Calculator Policy: You may NOT use a calculator on any Subject Test other than the Mathematics Level 1 and Level 2 Tests.

What Calculator to Bring

- Bring a calculator that you are used to using. If you're comfortable with both a scientific calculator and a graphing calculator, bring the graphing calculator.

- Before you take the test, make sure that your calculator is in good working order. You may bring batteries and a backup calculator to the test center.

- The test center will not have substitute calculators or batteries on hand. Students may not share calculators.

- If your calculator malfunctions during one of the Mathematics Level 1 or Level 2 Tests and you do not have a backup calculator, you must tell your test supervisor when the malfunction occurs. The supervisor will then cancel the scores on that test only, if you desire to do so.

What Is NOT Permitted

- calculators that have QWERTY keypads (e.g., TI-92 Plus, Voyage 200) or have pen-input, stylus,* or touch-screen capability (e.g., PDAs, Casio Class Pad)

- calculators that have wireless, Bluetooth, cellular, audio/video recording and playing, camera, or any other cell-phone type feature

- calculators that make noise or "talk," require an electrical outlet, or use paper tape

- calculators that can access the Internet

- laptops, portable handheld computers, electronic writing pads, or pocket organizers

  * The use of the stylus with the Sharp EL-9600 calculator will not be permitted. The Sharp EL-9600 remains on the list of approved graphing calculators.

Additional information about calculator usage can be found on collegeboard.org.

Using Your Calculator

- Only some questions on these tests require the use of a calculator. First decide how you will solve a problem, then determine if you need a calculator. For many of the questions, there's more than one way to solve the problem. **Don't pick up a calculator if you don't need to**—you might waste time.

- **The answer choices are often rounded**, so the answer you get might not match the answer in the test book. Since the choices are rounded, plugging the choices into the problem might not produce an exact answer.

- **Don't round any intermediate calculations**. For example, if you get a result from your calculator for the first step of a solution, keep the result in the calculator and use it for the second step. If you round the result from the first step and the answer choices are close to each other, you might choose the wrong answer.

- **Read the question carefully** so that you know what you are being asked to do. Sometimes a result that you may get from your calculator is NOT the final answer. If an answer you get is not one of the choices in the question, it may be that you didn't answer the question being asked. You should read the question again. It may also be that you rounded at an intermediate step in solving the problem, and that's why your answer doesn't match any of the choices in the question.

- **Think about how you are going to solve the question** before picking up your calculator. It may be that you only need the calculator for the final step or two and can do the rest in your test book or in your head. Don't waste time by using the calculator more than necessary.

- If you are taking the **Level 1 test, make sure your calculator is in degree mode** ahead of time so you won't have to worry about it during the test. If you're taking the Level 2 test, make sure your calculator is in the correct mode (degree or radian) for the question being asked.

- For some questions on these tests, a **graphing calculator** may provide an advantage. If you use a graphing calculator, you should know how to perform calculations (e.g., exponents, roots, trigonometric values, logarithms), graph functions and analyze the graphs, find zeros of functions, find points of intersection of graphs of functions, find minima/maxima of functions, find numerical solutions to equations, generate a table of values for a function, and perform data analysis features, including finding a regression equation.

- **You will not be allowed to share calculators.** You will be dismissed and your scores canceled if you use your calculator to share information during the test, or to remove test questions or answers from the test room.

Comparing the Two Tests

Although there is some overlap between Mathematics Levels 1 and 2, the emphasis for Level 2 is on more advanced content. Here are the differences in the two tests.

Topics Covered*	Approximate Percentage of Test	
	Level 1	Level 2
Number and Operations	**10–14**	**10–14**
Operations, ratio and proportion, complex numbers, counting, elementary number theory, matrices, sequences, *series, vectors*		
Algebra and Functions	**38–42**	**48–52**
Expressions, equations, inequalities, representation and modeling, properties of functions (linear, polynomial, rational, exponential, *logarithmic, trigonometric, inverse trigonometric, periodic, piecewise, recursive, parametric*)		
Geometry and Measurement	**38–42**	**28–32**
Plane Euclidean/Measurement	18–22	—
Coordinate	8–12	10–14
Lines, parabolas, circles, *ellipses, hyperbolas*, symmetry, transformations, *polar coordinates*		
Three-dimensional	4–6	4–6
Solids, surface area and volume (cylinders, cones, pyramids, spheres, prisms), *coordinates in three dimensions*		
Trigonometry	6–8	12–16
Right triangles, identities, *radian measure, law of cosines, law of sines, equations, double angle formulas*		
Data Analysis, Statistics, and Probability	**8–12**	**8–12**
Mean, median, mode, range, interquartile range, *standard deviation*, graphs and plots, least-squares regression (linear, *quadratic, exponential*), probability		

* Topics in italics are tested on Level 2 only. The content of Level 1 overlaps somewhat with that on Level 2, but the emphasis on 2 is on more advanced content. Plane Euclidean Geometry is not tested directly on Level 2.

Areas of Overlap

The content of Level 1 has some overlap with Level 2, especially in the following areas:

- elementary algebra
- three-dimensional geometry
- coordinate geometry
- statistics
- basic trigonometry

How Test Content Differs

Although some questions may be appropriate for both tests, the emphasis for Level 2 is on more advanced content. The tests differ significantly in the following areas:

Number and Operations. Level 1 measures a more basic understanding of the topics than Level 2. For example, Level 1 covers the *arithmetic of complex numbers*, but Level 2 also covers *graphical and other properties of complex numbers*. Level 2 also includes *series* and *vectors*.

Algebra and Functions. Level 1 contains mainly *algebraic* equations and functions, whereas Level 2 also contains more advanced equations and functions, such as *exponential*, *logarithmic*, and *trigonometric*.

Geometry and Measurement. A significant percentage of the questions on Level 1 is devoted to *plane Euclidean geometry and measurement*, which is not tested directly on Level 2. On Level 2, the concepts learned in plane geometry are applied in the questions on *coordinate geometry* and *three-dimensional geometry*.

The trigonometry questions on Level 1 are primarily limited to *right triangle trigonometry* (*sine, cosine, tangent*) and *the fundamental relationships among the trigonometric ratios*. Level 2 includes questions about *ellipses, hyperbolas, polar coordinates*, and *coordinates in three dimensions*. The trigonometry questions on Level 2 place more emphasis on *the properties and graphs of trigonometric functions*, *the inverse trigonometric functions*, *trigonometric equations and identities*, and *the laws of sines and cosines*.

Data Analysis, Statistics, and Probability. Both Level 1 and Level 2 include *mean, median, mode, range, interquartile range, data interpretation*, and *probability*. Level 2 also includes *standard deviation*. Both include *least-squares linear regression*, but Level 2 also includes *quadratic and exponential regression*.

Scores

The total score for each test is reported on the 200 to 800 point scale. Because the content measured by Level 1 and Level 2 differs considerably, you should not use your score on one test to predict your score on the other.

Note: Geometric Figures

Figures that accompany problems are intended to provide information useful in solving the problems. They are drawn as accurately as possible EXCEPT when it is stated in a particular problem that the figure is not drawn to scale. Even when figures are not drawn to scale, the relative positions of points and angles may be assumed to be in the order shown. Also, line segments that extend through points and appear to lie on the same line *may be assumed to be* on the same line.

When "Note: Figure not drawn to scale," appears below a figure in a question, it means that degree measures may not be accurately shown and specific lengths may not be drawn proportionately.

Mathematics Level 1

Sample Questions

All questions in the Mathematics Level 1 Test are multiple-choice questions in which you must choose the BEST response from the five choices offered. The directions that follow are the same as those on the Mathematics Level 1 Test.

Directions: For each of the following problems, decide which is the BEST of the choices given. If the exact numerical value is not one of the choices, select the choice that best approximates this value. Then fill in the corresponding circle on the answer sheet.

Notes: (1) A scientific or graphing calculator will be necessary for answering some (but not all) of the questions in this test. For each question you will have to decide whether or not you should use a calculator.

(2) The only angle measure used on this test is degree measure. Make sure your calculator is in the degree mode.

(3) Figures that accompany problems in this test are intended to provide information useful in solving the problems. They are drawn as accurately as possible EXCEPT when it is stated in a specific problem that its figure is not drawn to scale. All figures lie in a plane unless otherwise indicated.

(4) Unless otherwise specified, the domain of any function f is assumed to be the set of all real numbers x for which $f(x)$ is a real number. The range of f is assumed to be the set of all real numbers $f(x)$, where x is in the domain of f.

(5) Reference information that may be useful in answering the questions in this test can be found on the following page.

Reference Information: The following information is for your reference in answering some of the questions in this test.

Volume of a right circular cone with radius r and height h: $V = \frac{1}{3}\pi r^2 h$

Volume of a sphere with radius r: $V = \frac{4}{3}\pi r^3$

Volume of a pyramid with base area B and height h: $V = \frac{1}{3}Bh$

Surface Area of a sphere with radius r: $S = 4\pi r^2$

Number and Operations

1. How many of the first 200 positive integers are multiples of neither 6 nor 15?

   (A)   154
   (B)   156
   (C)   160
   (D)   164
   (E)   166

Choice (C) is the correct answer. Of the first 200 positive integers, the integers 6, 12, 18, …, 198, or (1)(6), (2)(6), (3)(6), …, (33)(6), are the multiples of 6. Thus, there are 33 multiples of 6. Of the first 200 positive integers, the integers 15, 30, 45, …, 195, or (1)(15), (2)(15), (3)(15), …, (13)(15) are the multiples of 15. Thus, there are 13 multiples of 15.

An integer is a multiple of 6 and 15 if and only if it is a multiple of 30. Of the first 200 positive integers, the integers 30, 60, 90, 120, 150, and 180 are the multiples of 30. Thus, there are 6 multiples of 30.

Therefore, of the first 200 positive integers, $33 + 13 - 6 = 40$ are multiples of 6 or 15 or both 6 and 15. In choice (C), $200 - 40 = 160$ of these integers are multiples of neither 6 nor 15, making it the correct answer.

2. The 3rd term of an arithmetic sequence is 14 and the 17th term is 63. What is the sum of the first 10 terms of the sequence?
   (A)   227.5
   (B)   245
   (C)   262.5
   (D)   297.5
   (E)   385

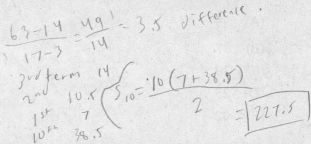

Choice (A) is the correct answer. In an arithmetic sequence, the difference between consecutive terms is constant. Since the 3rd term of the sequence is 14 and the 17th term is 63, the common difference is $\frac{63-14}{17-3} = 3.5$.

If the 3rd term of the sequence is 14, the 2nd term is $14 - 3.5 = 10.5$, and the 1st term is 7. Likewise, the 10th term is equal to $7 + 9(3.5) = 38.5$. The sum of the first 10 terms of the sequence is given by $S_{10} = \frac{10(7+38.5)}{2} = 227.5$.

Algebra and Functions

3. For a school trip to the circus, each bus costs b dollars and holds 30 passengers. Two of the passengers on each bus must be adults. If each child and each adult must pay x dollars for admission to the circus, what is the minimum total cost, in dollars, for 75 children to go on the trip?
   (A) $69x + 2b$
   (B) $75x + 3b$
   (C) $75x + 9b$
   (D) $81x + 3b$
   (E) $81x + 30b$

Choice (D) is the correct answer. Since each bus holds 30 passengers and 2 of these passengers must be adults, each bus can take a maximum of 28 children. Therefore, a minimum of 3 buses are required, at a total cost of $3b$ dollars. On the 3 buses, a total of at least 6 adults must accompany the 75 children. Therefore, there will be a total of at least 81 people on the trip, and the total cost for admission to the circus will be at least $81x$ dollars. Thus, the minimum total cost, in dollars, for 75 children to go on the trip is $81x + 3b$.

4. If $\log_a x^2 = 5$, what is the value of $\log_a x$?

   (A) $\dfrac{5}{2}$

   (B) 7

   (C) 10

   (D) 25

   (E) 32

[handwritten: $\log_a x^2 = 5$; $2\log_a x = 5$; $\log_a x = \dfrac{5}{2}$]

Choice (A) is the correct answer. By the properties of logarithms, $\log_a x^2 = 2(\log_a x)$. Thus, $\log_a x = \dfrac{\log_a x^2}{2} = \dfrac{5}{2}$.

5.
$$y > x^2 + 1$$
$$y < x + 3$$

If $(1, t)$ is a solution to the system of inequalities above, which of the following could be the value of t?

   (A) 0.1

   (B) 1.1

   (C) 1.9

   (D) 3.9

   (E) 4.6

[handwritten: $t > (1)^2 + 1$ → $t > 2$; $t < (1) + 3$ → $t < 4$; $3.9 > 2$, $3.9 < 4$]

Choice (D) is the correct answer. One way to solve the problem is to substitute 1 for x and t for y in the given inequalities. This gives $t > 2$ and $t < 4$. Only the value of t in choice (D) satisfies both of these inequalities.

Another way to solve this problem is to use a graphing calculator to graph or make tables for $Y1 = x^2 + 1$ and $Y2 = x + 3$. Since $(1, t)$ is a solution to the system, look at the graph or table for the value of $Y1$ and $Y2$ when $x = 1$. You can see that when $x = 1$, $Y1 = 2$ and $Y2 = 4$. Thus, we need $Y1 > 2$ and $Y2 < 4$. Therefore, t could be any value between 2 and 4. Of the given choices, only choice (D) could be the value of t.

6. If $f(g(x)) = x$ and $f(x) = 3x + 1$, which of the following is $g(x)$?

(A) $g(x) = \frac{1}{3}x - \frac{1}{9}$

(B) $g(x) = \frac{1}{3}x - \frac{1}{3}$

(C) $g(x) = \frac{1}{3}x + 1$

(D) $g(x) = \frac{1}{3}x - 1$

(E) $g(x) = 3x - 1$

Choice (B) is the correct answer. If $f(g(x)) = x$ and $f(x) = 3x + 1$, then $f(g(x)) = 3g(x) + 1 = x$. Solving this equation for $g(x)$ yields $x - 1 = 3g(x)$ and $g(x) = \frac{x-1}{3}$ or $\frac{1}{3}x - \frac{1}{3}$.

$$F(g(x)) = 3g(x) + 1 = x$$

$$\frac{3g(x)}{3} = \frac{x-1}{3}$$

$$g(x) = \frac{x-1}{3} = \frac{1}{3}x - \frac{1}{3}$$

B.

7.

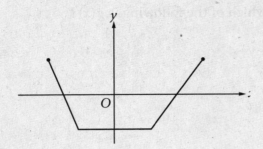

The graph of the function $y = f(x)$ is shown in the figure above. Which of the following could be the graph of $y = |f(x)|$?

(A)

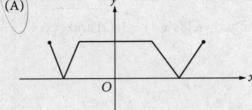

(B)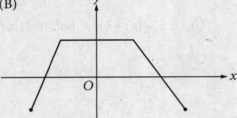

(C)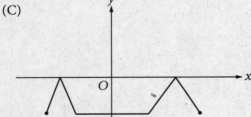

(D)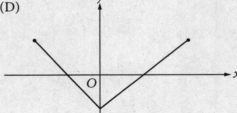

(E)

Choice (A) is the correct answer. The graph of $|y|$ is equal to the graph of y for $y \geq 0$ and to the graph of $-y$ for $y < 0$. The graph of $y = |f(x)|$ is the same as the graph of $y = f(x)$ for all values of x where $y \geq 0$ (points on or above the x-axis; those in quadrants I and II). For values of x where $y < 0$ (points below the x-axis; those in quadrants III and IV), the graph of $y = |f(x)|$ consists of the reflection of the graph of $y = f(x)$ about the x-axis.

8. The managers of Eagle Groceries project the price, in dollars, of a certain product from the year 2005 through the year 2013 by using the function P, defined by $P(t) = -0.11t^3 + 0.71t^2 + 2.1t + 9.3$, where t is the number of years after the beginning of 2005. What is the maximum price projected for the product during this period?

(A) $5.47
(B) $15.22
(C) $24.03
(D $69.30
(E) $211.30

Choice (C) is the correct answer. One way to solve this is to use a graphing calculator to graph the function, and look for a maximum between $t = 0$ and $t = 8$. The maximum value on this interval is about 24.03 and occurs at $t \approx 5.47$. Thus, the maximum price projected is $24.03.

Geometry and Measurement: Plane Euclidean Geometry

9.

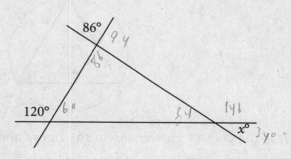

In the figure above, three lines intersect as shown. What is the value of x ?

(A) 33
(B) 34
(C) 35
(D) 36
(E) 37

Choice (B) is the correct answer. The interior angles of the triangle in the figure have measures 60° (supplementary angle to the angle marked 120°), 86° (vertical angle to the angle marked 86°), and $x°$ (vertical angle to the angle marked $x°$). Thus, $60 + 86 + x = 180$, and $x = 34$.

10.

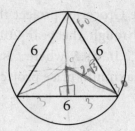

In the figure above, the equilateral triangle is inscribed in the circle. What is the area of the circle?

(A) 6π

(B) 9π

(C) 10π

(D) 12π

(E) $6\sqrt{3}\pi$

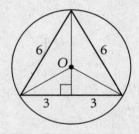

Choice (D) is the correct answer. As in the figure above, let O be the center of the circle, and draw the radii from O to the three vertices of the equilateral triangle; these radii divide the equilateral triangle into three congruent triangles with interior angles of measures 30°, 30°, and 120°. Then draw the perpendicular from O to one of the sides of the equilateral triangle, which yields two 30° – 60° – 90° triangles. The side opposite the 60° angle is half of one side of the equilateral triangle and, thus, has length 3. Thus, the hypotenuse of each 30° – 60° – 90° triangle has length $2\sqrt{3}$. Since each hypotenuse is a radius of the circle, the area of the circle is $\pi\left(2\sqrt{3}\right)^2 = 12\pi$.

Geometry and Measurement: Coordinate Geometry

11.

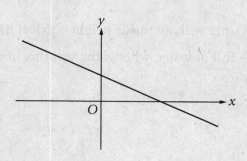

The line with equation $y = mx + b$ is graphed above. Which of the following <u>must</u> be true?

(A) $m + b = 0$

(B) $m + b < 0$

(C) $m - b = 0$

(D) $m - b > 0$

(E) $m - b < 0$

negative slope
positive y-intercept

Choice (E) is the correct answer. The slope of the line is m, and the y-intercept of the line is b. By the direction of the line in the figure, you can tell that the slope of the line is negative. Also, from the figure you can tell that the y-intercept is positive. Thus, $m < 0$ and $b > 0$. You can use this information to evaluate each option. Choice (A) does not have to be true since we cannot conclude that $m = -b$. Choice (B) does not have to be true since the value of $m + b$ could be positive, negative, or zero. Choice (C) is not true since $m \neq b$. The value of $m - b$ must be negative since m is negative and b is positive. Choice (D) cannot be true.

Geometry and Measurement: Three-Dimensional Geometry

12. A cylindrical container with an inside height of 6 feet has an inside radius of 2 feet. If the container is $\frac{2}{3}$ full of water, what is the volume, in cubic feet, of the water in the container?

    (A) 25.1
    (B) 37.7
    (C) 50.3
    (D) 62.3
    (E) 75.4

    Choice (C) is the correct answer. The volume V of a cylinder with radius r and height h is given by $V = \pi r^2 h$. Thus, the volume, in cubic feet, of the container is $\pi \cdot 2^2 \cdot 6 = 24\pi$. Since the container is $\frac{2}{3}$ full of water, the volume of the water in the container is $\frac{2}{3} \cdot 24\pi \approx 50.3$.

Geometry and Measurement: Trigonometry

13. In the xy-plane, points $D(1,0)$, $E(1,6)$, and $F(r, s)$ are the vertices of a right triangle. If $\overline{DE}$ is the hypotenuse of the triangle, which of the following CANNOT be the area of the triangle?

    (A) 0.6
    (B) 4.7
    (C) 7.5
    (D) 8.8
    (E) 9.2

    Choice (E) is the correct answer. Since $\overline{DE}$ is the hypotenuse of the right triangle DEF, this triangle can be inscribed in the circle with diameter $\overline{DE}$, as shown in the figure on the following page. The area of the triangle is $A = \frac{1}{2}bh$, where $b = 6$, and h could be any value greater than 0 and less than or equal to the radius of the circle. That is, $0 < h \le 3$. Therefore, the area A of $\triangle DEF$ could be any value that satisfies $0 < A \le 9$. Of the choices, only 9.2 *cannot* be the value of A.

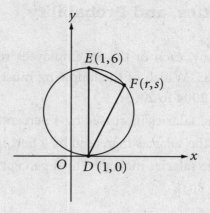

14. In triangle ABC, the measure of $\angle B$ is 90°. Which of the following <u>must</u> be true?

    I. $\sin A < \sin C$

    II. $\sin A = \cos C$

    III. $\sin^2 A + \cos^2 C = 1$

(A) None

(B) II only

(C) I and II

(D) I and III

(E) II and III

Choice (B) is the correct answer. Statement I need not be true. For example, if the measure of $\angle A$ is 60°, then the measure of $\angle C$ is 30°. Then $\sin A = \sin 60° = \dfrac{\sqrt{3}}{2}$ and $\sin C = \sin 30° = \dfrac{1}{2}$, so $\sin A > \sin C$. Statement II must be true. Since $m\angle B = 90°$, it follows that $m\angle A + m\angle C = 90°$, which implies that $\sin A = \cos C$. Statement III need not be true. For example, if the measure of $\angle A$ is 60°, then the measure of $\angle C$ is 30°. Then $\sin^2 A + \cos^2 C = \dfrac{3}{4} + \dfrac{3}{4} \ne 1$. Since only statement II must be true, the correct answer is (B).

Data Analysis, Statistics, and Probability

15. At a small design company, each of the 89 employees received a 4 percent salary increase from 2004 to 2005. Which of the following must be true about the salaries of the 89 employees from 2004 to 2005?

      I.   The mean of the salaries increased by 4 percent.

      II.   The median of the salaries increased by 4 percent.

      III.   The range of the salaries increased by 4 percent.

(A) None

(B) II only

(C) I and II only

(D) II and III only

(E) I, II, and III

Choice (E) is the correct answer. Since each 2004 salary is increased by 4 percent to get the corresponding 2005 salary, the total of all 89 salaries also increased by 4 percent. Thus, the average salary, which is the total divided by 89, also increased by 4 percent. Therefore, statement I must be true.

If the 89 salaries for 2004 are listed in order from lowest to highest, the middle (45th) number in the list is the median salary for 2004. If each salary is increased by 4 percent, and the new salaries are listed in order from lowest to highest, the median salary for 2005 will again be the middle (45th) number, which is 4 percent greater than the median number for 2004. Therefore, statement II must be true.

The range of salaries for 2004 is $H - L$, where H is the highest salary among the 89 employees and L is the lowest salary. Since each salary increased by 4 percent, the highest salary for 2005 is $(1.04)H$ and the lowest salary is $(1.04)L$. Thus, the range of salaries for 2005 is $1.04(H - L)$. Therefore, statement III must be true.

Since statements I, II, and III must all be true, the correct answer is choice (E).

Mathematics Level 1 – Practice Test 1

Practice Helps

The test that follows is an actual, previously administered SAT Subject Test in Mathematics Level 1. To get an idea of what it's like to take this test, practice under conditions that are much like those of an actual test administration.

- Set aside an hour when you can take the test uninterrupted.

- Sit at a desk or table with no other books or papers. Dictionaries, other books, or notes are not allowed in the test room.

- Remember to have a scientific or graphing calculator with you.

- Tear out an answer sheet from the back of this book and fill it in just as you would on the day of the test. One answer sheet can be used for up to three Subject Tests.

- Read the instructions that precede the practice test. During the actual administration you will be asked to read them before answering test questions.

- Use a clock or kitchen timer to time yourself.

- After you finish the practice test, read the sections "How to Score the SAT Subject Test in Mathematics Level 1" and "How Did You Do on the Subject Test in Mathematics Level 1?"

- The appearance of the answer sheet in this book may differ from the answer sheet you see on test day.

- The Reference Information at the start of the practice test is slightly different from what appeared on the original test. It has been modified to reflect the language included on tests administered at the time of this book's printing. These changes are minor and will not affect how you answer the questions.

MATHEMATICS LEVEL 1 TEST

The top portion of the page of the answer sheet that you will use to take the Mathematics Level 1 Test must be filled in exactly as illustrated below. When your supervisor tells you to fill in the circle next to the name of the test you are about to take, mark your answer sheet as shown.

○ Literature	● Mathematics Level 1	○ German	○ Chinese Listening	○ Japanese Listening
○ Biology E	○ Mathematics Level 2	○ Italian	○ French Listening	○ Korean Listening
○ Biology M	○ U.S. History	○ Latin	○ German Listening	○ Spanish Listening
○ Chemistry	○ World History	○ Modern Hebrew		
○ Physics	○ French	○ Spanish	**Background Questions:** ①②③④⑤⑥⑦⑧⑨	

After filling in the circle next to the name of the test you are taking, locate the Background Questions section, which also appears at the top of your answer sheet (as shown above). This is where you will answer the following Background Questions on your answer sheet.

BACKGROUND QUESTIONS

Please answer Part I and Part II below by filling in the appropriate circle in the Background Questions box on your answer sheet. The information you provide is for statistical purposes only and will not affect your test score.

<u>Part I.</u> Which of the following describes a mathematics course you have taken or are currently taking? (FILL IN **ALL** CIRCLES THAT APPLY.)

- Algebra I or Elementary Algebra **OR** Course I of a college preparatory mathematics sequence   —Fill in circle 1.

- Geometry **OR** Course II of a college preparatory mathematics sequence   —Fill in circle 2.

- Algebra II or Intermediate Algebra **OR** Course III of a college preparatory mathematics sequence   —Fill in circle 3.

- Elementary Functions (Precalculus) and/or Trigonometry **OR** beyond Course III of a college preparatory mathematics sequence   —Fill in circle 4.

- Advanced Placement Mathematics (Calculus AB or Calculus BC)   —Fill in circle 5.

<u>Part II.</u> What type of calculator did you bring to use for this test? (FILL IN THE **ONE** CIRCLE THAT APPLIES. If you did not bring a scientific or graphing calculator, do not fill in any of circles 6-9.)

- Scientific   —Fill in circle 6.
- Graphing (Fill in the circle corresponding to the model you used.)

  Casio 9700, Casio 9750, Casio 9800, Casio 9850, Casio 9860, Casio FX 1.0, Casio CG-10, Sharp 9200, Sharp 9300, Sharp 9600, Sharp 9900, TI-82, TI-83, TI-83 Plus, TI-83 Plus Silver, TI-84 Plus, TI-84 Plus Silver, TI-85, TI-86, or TI-Nspire   —Fill in circle 7.

  Casio 9970, Casio Algebra FX 2.0, HP 38G, HP 39 series, HP 40 series, HP 48 series, HP 49 series, HP 50 series, TI-89, TI-89 Titanium, or TI-Nspire CAS   —Fill in circle 8.

  Some other graphing calculator   —Fill in circle 9.

When the supervisor gives the signal, turn the page and begin the Mathematics Level 1 Test. There are 100 numbered circles on the answer sheet and 50 questions in the Mathematics Level 1 Test. Therefore, use only circles 1 to 50 for recording your answers.

MATHEMATICS LEVEL 1 TEST

REFERENCE INFORMATION

THE FOLLOWING INFORMATION IS FOR YOUR REFERENCE IN ANSWERING SOME OF THE QUESTIONS IN THIS TEST.

Volume of a right circular cone with radius r and height h: $V = \frac{1}{3}\pi r^2 h$

Volume of a sphere with radius r: $V = \frac{4}{3}\pi r^3$

Volume of a pyramid with base area B and height h: $V = \frac{1}{3}Bh$

Surface Area of a sphere with radius r: $S = 4\pi r^2$

DO NOT DETACH FROM BOOK.

GO ON TO THE NEXT PAGE

MATHEMATICS LEVEL 1 TEST

For each of the following problems, decide which is the BEST of the choices given. If the exact numerical value is not one of the choices, select the choice that best approximates this value. Then fill in the corresponding circle on the answer sheet.

Notes: (1) A scientific or graphing calculator will be necessary for answering some (but not all) of the questions in this test. For each question you will have to decide whether or not you should use a calculator.

(2) The only angle measure used on this test is degree measure. Make sure your calculator is in the degree mode.

(3) Figures that accompany problems in this test are intended to provide information useful in solving the problems. They are drawn as accurately as possible EXCEPT when it is stated in a specific problem that its figure is not drawn to scale. All figures lie in a plane unless otherwise indicated.

(4) Unless otherwise specified, the domain of any function f is assumed to be the set of all real numbers x for which $f(x)$ is a real number. The range of f is assumed to be the set of all real numbers $f(x)$, where x is in the domain of f.

(5) Reference information that may be useful in answering the questions in this test can be found on the page preceding Question 1.

USE THIS SPACE FOR SCRATCHWORK.

1. If $xy + 7y = 84$ and $x + 7 = 3$, what is the value of y ?

(A) -4
(B) 4.9
(C) 8.4
(D) 12
(E) 28

GO ON TO THE NEXT PAGE

MATHEMATICS LEVEL 1 TEST—*Continued*

USE THIS SPACE FOR SCRATCHWORK.

2. When four given numbers are multiplied together, the product is negative. Which of the following could be true about the four numbers?

   (A) One is negative, two are positive, and one is zero.
   (B) Two are negative, one is positive, and one is zero.
   (C) Two are negative and two are positive.
   (D) Three are negative and one is positive.
   (E) Four are negative.

3. If $x + y = 5$ and $x - y = 3$, then $x^2 - y^2 =$

   (A) 9   (B) 15   (C) 16   (D) 25   (E) 34

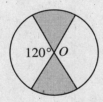

4. In the figure above, what fraction of the circular region with center O is shaded?

   (A) $\frac{1}{6}$ (B) $\frac{1}{5}$ (C) $\frac{1}{4}$ (D) $\frac{1}{3}$ (E) $\frac{3}{5}$

GO ON TO THE NEXT PAGE

MATHEMATICS LEVEL 1 TEST—*Continued*

5. Which of the following is the graph of a linear function with both a negative slope and a negative *y*-intercept?

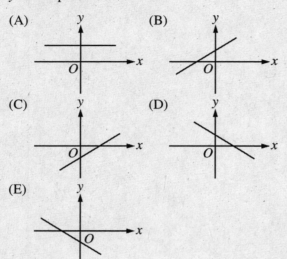

(A)

(B)

(C)

(D)

(E)

6. If $k^2 - 4 = 4 - k^2$, what are all possible values of k ?

(A) 0 only
(B) 2 only
(C) 4 only
(D) −2 and 2 only
(E) −2, 0, and 2

7. If $b^{2x+1} = b^{3x-1}$ for all values of b, what is the value of x ?

(A) 2   (B) $\frac{3}{2}$ (C) $\frac{2}{3}$ (D) −2   (E) −3

GO ON TO THE NEXT PAGE

MATHEMATICS LEVEL 1 TEST—*Continued*

8. At North High School, the number of students taking French is decreasing by 20 students per year and the number of students taking Spanish is increasing by 10 students per year. This year 250 students are taking French, and 100 students are taking Spanish. Which of the following equations could be used to find the number of years n until the number of students is the same in both courses?

(A) $250 - 20n = 100 + 10n$
(B) $250 + 10n = 100 - 20n$
(C) $250 + 20n = 100 - 10n$
(D) $20n - 250 = 100 + 10n$
(E) $n(250 - 20) = n(100 + 10)$

9. If $y = x^3 - 1.5$, for what value of x is $y = 2$?

(A) 0.79
(B) 1.14
(C) 1.52
(D) 1.87
(E) 6.50

10. The length of a rectangle is four times its width. If the perimeter of the rectangle is 40 centimeters, what is its area?

(A) 4 cm^2
(B) 16 cm^2
(C) 20 cm^2
(D) 40 cm^2
(E) 64 cm^2

GO ON TO THE NEXT PAGE

MATHEMATICS LEVEL 1 TEST—*Continued*

11. The function g, where $g(t) = 0.066t + 0.96$, can be used to represent the relation between grade point average $g(t)$ and the number of hours t spent studying each week. Based on this function, a student with a grade point average of 3.5 studied how many hours per week?

   (A) 0.96
   (B) 1.2
   (C) 14.5
   (D) 38.5
   (E) 67.8

12. $x^2 - 2x + 3 = x^3 + 2x + x^2$ is equivalent to

   (A) 0

   (B) $2x^2 - 4x = 0$

   (C) $-x^3 + 4x - 3 = 0$

   (D) $x^3 - 2x^2 - 3 = 0$

   (E) $x^3 + 4x - 3 = 0$

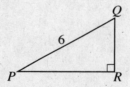

13. In right triangle PQR in the figure above, $\sin P = 0.5$. What is the length of side QR ?

   (A) 2
   (B) 3
   (C) 5
   (D) 6
   (E) 12

GO ON TO THE NEXT PAGE

MATHEMATICS LEVEL 1 TEST—*Continued*

USE THIS SPACE FOR SCRATCHWORK.

14. Which of the following numbers is a COUNTEREXAMPLE to the statement "All odd numbers greater than 2 are prime numbers" ?

    (A) 2   (B) 3   (C) 5   (D) 7   (E) 9

15. If $f(x) = \dfrac{2x - 1}{x^2}$, what is the value of $f(-0.1)$?

    (A) -120
    (B) -100
    (C) 100
    (D) 120
    (E) 220

16. On a blueprint, 0.4 inch represents 6 feet. If the actual distance between two buildings is 76 feet, what would be the distance between the corresponding buildings on the blueprint?

    (A)   3.2 in
    (B)   5.1 in
    (C)   12.7 in
    (D)   30.4 in
    (E)   31.7 in

GO ON TO THE NEXT PAGE

MATHEMATICS LEVEL 1 TEST—Continued

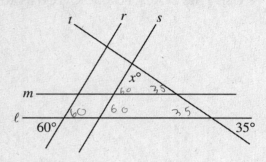

17. In the figure above, if $\ell \parallel m$ and $r \parallel s$, what is the value of x?

(A) 65
(B) 80
(C) 85
(D) 95
(E) 115

18. For what value of x is $\dfrac{2x}{3x-1}$ undefined?

(A) $-\dfrac{1}{3}$ (B) 0 (C) $\dfrac{1}{3}$ (D) $\dfrac{1}{2}$ (E) 1

19. A sales team sold an average (arithmetic mean) of 10.375 mobile phones per week during the first 8 weeks of the last quarter of the year. The members of the sales team will receive a bonus if they sell a total of 185 phones for the quarter. What must their average sales, in phones per week, be for the remaining 5 weeks of the quarter if they are to receive the bonus?

(A)   4.2
(B) 20.4
(C) 83
(D) 102
(E) 174.6

GO ON TO THE NEXT PAGE

MATHEMATICS LEVEL 1 TEST—*Continued*

USE THIS SPACE FOR SCRATCHWORK.

20. What is the y-coordinate of the point at which the line whose equation is $3x - 2y - 7 = 0$ crosses the y-axis?

    (A) $-\dfrac{7}{2}$

    (B) $-\dfrac{7}{3}$

    (C) $\dfrac{7}{3}$

    (D) $\dfrac{7}{2}$

    (E) 7

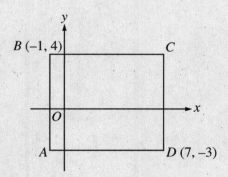

21. In the figure above, the sides of rectangle $ABCD$ are parallel to the axes. What is the distance between point A and point C?

    (A) 6.07
    (B) 7
    (C) 10.1
    (D) 10.6
    (E) 15

GO ON TO THE NEXT PAGE ⇨

MATHEMATICS LEVEL 1 TEST—*Continued*

22. Four signal flags — one red, one blue, one yellow, and one green — can be arranged from top to bottom on a signal pole. Every arrangement of the four flags is a different signal. How many different signals using all four flags have the red flag at the top?

    (A) 3   (B) 4   (C) 6   (D) 16   (E) 24

23. Triangle *FGH* is similar to triangle *JKL*. The length of side *GH* is 2.1 meters, the length of corresponding side *KL* is 1.4 meters, and the perimeter of $\triangle JKL$ is 3.6 meters. What is the perimeter of $\triangle FGH$?

    (A) 2.4 m
    (B) 3.3 m
    (C) 4.3 m
    (D) 5.1 m
    (E) 5.4 m

24. Which of the following is an equation of a line that is parallel to the line with equation $2x - y = 7$?

    (A) $y = -2x - 7$

    (B) $y = -2x + 7$

    (C) $y = -\frac{1}{2}x - 7$

    (D) $y = \frac{1}{2}x - 7$

    (E) $y = 2x + 7$

GO ON TO THE NEXT PAGE

MATHEMATICS LEVEL 1 TEST—*Continued*

USE THIS SPACE FOR SCRATCHWORK.

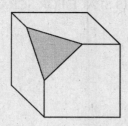

25. A tetrahedron was cut from the corner of the cube shown above, with three of its vertices at the midpoints of three edges of the cube. If tetrahedrons of the same size are cut from the remaining seven corners of the cube, how many faces will the resulting solid have?

    (A) 6   (B) 8   (C) 12   (D) 14   (E) 16

26. The consecutive vertices of a certain parallelogram are A, B, C, and D. Which of the following are NOT necessarily congruent?

    (A) $\angle A$ and $\angle C$
    (B) $\angle B$ and $\angle D$
    (C) $\overline{AC}$ and $\overline{BD}$
    (D) $\overline{AB}$ and $\overline{CD}$
    (E) $\overline{AD}$ and $\overline{BC}$

GO ON TO THE NEXT PAGE

MATHEMATICS LEVEL 1 TEST—*Continued*

USE THIS SPACE FOR SCRATCHWORK.

27. A car traveled 200 miles at an average speed of 45 miles per hour. Of the following, which is the closest approximation to the amount of time that could be saved on this 200-mile trip if the average speed had increased 20 percent?

(A) 1 hour

(B) $\frac{3}{4}$ hour

(C) $\frac{1}{2}$ hour

(D) $\frac{1}{4}$ hour

(E) $\frac{1}{5}$ hour

28. If c is a negative integer, for which of the following values of d is $|c - d|$ greatest?

(A) −10   (B) −4   (C) 0   (D) 4   (E) 10

29. In $\triangle PQR$, $\angle Q$ is a right angle. Which of the following is equal to cos P ?

(A) $\dfrac{PQ}{PR}$

(B) $\dfrac{PR}{PQ}$

(C) $\dfrac{PR}{QR}$

(D) $\dfrac{QR}{PQ}$

(E) $\dfrac{QR}{PR}$

GO ON TO THE NEXT PAGE

MATHEMATICS LEVEL 1 TEST—*Continued*

USE THIS SPACE FOR SCRATCHWORK.

30. The junior class is sponsoring a drama production to raise funds and plans to charge the same price for all admission tickets. The class has $700 in expenses for this production. If 300 tickets are sold, the class will make a profit of $1,100. What will be the profit for the class if 500 tickets are sold?

(A) $1,133
(B) $1,833
(C) $2,300
(D) $3,000
(E) $3,700

31. In the xy-plane, the point $(6, 3)$ is the midpoint of the line segment with endpoints $(x, 5)$ and $(9, y)$. What is the value of $x + y$?

(A) 4   (B) 9   (C) 14   (D) 18   (E) 32

32. If $\frac{1}{2}$ is $\frac{3}{4}$ of $\frac{4}{5}$ of a certain number, what is that number?

(A) $\frac{3}{10}$

(B) $\frac{5}{6}$

(C) $\frac{11}{10}$

(D) $\frac{6}{5}$

(E) $\frac{10}{3}$

GO ON TO THE NEXT PAGE

MATHEMATICS LEVEL 1 TEST—*Continued*

USE THIS SPACE FOR SCRATCHWORK.

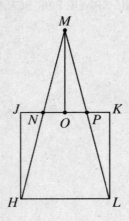

33. In the figure above, *HJKL* is a square and
   $JN = NO = OP = PK$. What is the ratio of the
   area of $\triangle MNP$ to the area of square *HJKL* ?

   (A) $\dfrac{1}{8}$ (B) $\dfrac{1}{4}$ (C) $\dfrac{1}{3}$ (D) $\dfrac{3}{8}$ (E) $\dfrac{1}{2}$

34. Which of the following numbers is NOT
   contained in the domain of the function *f*
   if $f(x) = \dfrac{x+2}{x+3} - \dfrac{1}{x}$?

   (A) −3   (B) −2   (C) 1   (D) $\sqrt{3}$ (E) 3

35. Which of the following is the graph of all values
   of *x* for which $1 \leq x^2 \leq 4$?

   (A) ![number line from −2 to 2, closed dots at 1 and 2 with segment between]

   (B) ![number line, closed dots at −2 and −1 with segment between]

   (C) ![number line, closed dots at −2 and 2 with segment between]

   (D) ![number line, segment between −2 and 2]

   (E) ![number line, segments from −2 to −1 and 1 to 2]

GO ON TO THE NEXT PAGE ⟩

USE THIS SPACE FOR SCRATCHWORK.

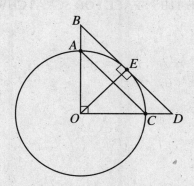

36. The circle in the figure above has center O and radius r. If $OB = OD$, how many of the line segments shown (with labeled endpoints) have length r ?

   (A) Two
   (B) Three
   (C) Four
   (D) Five
   (E) Six

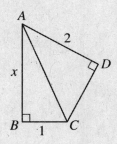

37. In the figure above, if $\triangle ABC$ and $\triangle ADC$ are right triangles, then $CD =$

   (A) $\sqrt{x^2 - 3}$

   (B) $\sqrt{x^2 + 1}$

   (C) $\sqrt{x^2 + 1} + 2$

   (D) $\sqrt{x^2 + 3}$

   (E) $x^2 + 5$

GO ON TO THE NEXT PAGE

USE THIS SPACE FOR SCRATCHWORK.

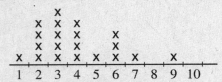

Number of red candies in sample

38. Each of 20 students in a class took a sample of 10 candies from a large bag and counted the number of red candies in the sample. The distribution of red candies in their samples is shown above. If one of the students were chosen at random, what is the probability that the student's sample would have at least 5 red candies?

(A) $\dfrac{3}{5}$

(B) $\dfrac{3}{10}$

(C) $\dfrac{1}{4}$

(D) $\dfrac{3}{20}$

(E) $\dfrac{1}{20}$

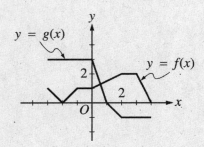

39. The figure above shows the graphs of functions f and g. What is the value of $f(g(3))$?

(A) -2 (B) -1 (C) 0 (D) 1 (E) 2

GO ON TO THE NEXT PAGE

MATHEMATICS LEVEL 1 TEST—*Continued*

USE THIS SPACE FOR SCRATCHWORK.

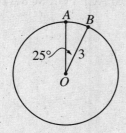

40. If O is the center of the circle in the figure above, what is the length of minor arc AB ?

    (A) 0.65
    (B) 1.27
    (C) 1.31
    (D) 1.40
    (E) 1.96

41. In the xy-plane, which of the following are the points of intersection of the circles whose equations are $x^2 + y^2 = 4$ and $(x - 2)^2 + y^2 = 4$?

    (A) $(-1, \sqrt{3}), (-1, -\sqrt{3})$

    (B) $(1, \sqrt{3}), (1, -\sqrt{3})$

    (C) $(1, \sqrt{3}), (-1, \sqrt{3})$

    (D) $(1, 1), (-1, 1)$

    (E) $(1, 1), (1, -2)$

GO ON TO THE NEXT PAGE

MATHEMATICS LEVEL 1 TEST—*Continued*

USE THIS SPACE FOR SCRATCHWORK.

42. The area of one face of a cube is x square meters. Which of the following gives an expression for the volume of this cube, in cubic meters?

(A) $x\sqrt{x}$

(B) $3\sqrt{x}$

(C) $x^2\sqrt{x}$

(D) x^3

(E) $3x^3$

43. For which of the following equations is it true that the sum of the roots equals the product of the roots?

(A) $x^2 - 4 = 0$
(B) $x^2 - 2x + 1 = 0$
(C) $x^2 - 4x + 4 = 0$
(D) $x^2 - 5x + 6 = 0$
(E) $x^2 + 4x + 4 = 0$

44. If the positive integers, starting with 1, are written consecutively, what will be the 90th digit written?

(A) 0   (B) 1   (C) 5   (D) 8   (E) 9

GO ON TO THE NEXT PAGE

MATHEMATICS LEVEL 1 TEST—*Continued*

USE THIS SPACE FOR SCRATCHWORK.

45. The function f is defined by
$f(x) = x^4 - 4x^2 + x + 1$ for $-5 \le x \le 5$.
In which of the following intervals does the minimum value of f occur?

(A) $-5 < x < -3$
(B) $-3 < x < -1$
(C) $-1 < x < 1$
(D) $\ \ 1 < x < 3$
(E) $\ \ 3 < x < 5$

46. In convex polygon P, the sum of the measures of the interior angles is $1,800°$. How many sides does P have?

(A) 8   (B) 10   (C) 12   (D) 14   (E) 18

47. What is the least integer value of k such that $x^2(3k + 1) - 6x + 2 = 0$ has no real roots?

(A) 5   (B) 2   (C) 1   (D) −1   (E) −2

48. If $\angle A$ is an acute angle and $\dfrac{\sin^2 A}{\cos^2 A} = 2.468$,

what is the value of $\tan A$?

(A) 1.234
(B) 1.571
(C) 2.468
(D) 4.936
(E) 6.091

GO ON TO THE NEXT PAGE

MATHEMATICS LEVEL 1 TEST—*Continued*

USE THIS SPACE FOR SCRATCHWORK.

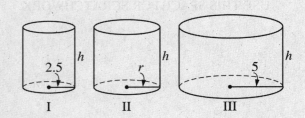

I II III

49. In the figure above, all of the right circular cylinders have height h. Cylinders I and III have a base radius of 2.5 and 5, respectively. If the volume of cylinder II is the mean of the volumes of cylinders I and III, what is the radius r of cylinder II?

(A) 1.98
(B) 3.75
(C) 3.95
(D) 4.00
(E) 15.63

50. If f and g are functions, where
$f(x) = x^3 - 10x^2 + 27x - 18$ and
$g(x) = x^3 - x^2 - 6x$, which of the following
gives a relationship between f and g ?

(A) $g(x) = 3f(x)$
(B) $g(x) = f(x) - 3$
(C) $g(x) = f(x) + 3$
(D) $g(x) = f(x - 3)$
(E) $g(x) = f(x + 3)$

S T O P

**IF YOU FINISH BEFORE TIME IS CALLED, YOU MAY CHECK YOUR WORK ON THIS TEST ONLY.
DO NOT TURN TO ANY OTHER TEST IN THIS BOOK.**

How to Score the SAT Subject Test in Mathematics Level 1

When you take an actual SAT Subject Test in Mathematics Level 1, your answer sheet will be "read" by a scanning machine that will record your responses to each question. Then a computer will compare your answers with the correct answers and produce your raw score. You get one point for each correct answer. For each wrong answer, you lose one-quarter of a point. Questions you omit (and any for which you mark more than one answer) are not counted. This raw score is converted to a scaled score that is reported to you and to the colleges you specify.

Worksheet 1. Finding Your Raw Test Score

STEP 1: Table A on the following page lists the correct answers for all the questions on the Subject Test in Mathematics Level 1 that is reproduced in this book. It also serves as a worksheet for you to calculate your raw score.

- Compare your answers with those given in the table.
- Put a check in the column marked "Right" if your answer is correct.
- Put a check in the column marked "Wrong" if your answer is incorrect.
- Leave both columns blank if you omitted the question.

STEP 2: Count the number of right answers.

Enter the total here: _____

STEP 3: Count the number of wrong answers.

Enter the total here: _____

STEP 4: Multiply the number of wrong answers by .250.

Enter the product here: _____

STEP 5: Subtract the result obtained in Step 4 from the total you obtained in Step 2.

Enter the result here: _____

STEP 6: Round the number obtained in Step 5 to the nearest whole number.

Enter the result here: _____

The number you obtained in Step 6 is your raw score.

TABLE A

Answers to the Subject Test in Mathematics Level 1 – Practice Test 1 and Percentage of Students Answering Each Question Correctly

Question Number	Correct Answer	Right	Wrong	Percentage of Students Answering the Question Correctly*	Question Number	Correct Answer	Right	Wrong	Percentage of Students Answering the Question Correctly*
1	E			92	26	C			64
2	D			95	27	B			68
3	B			83	28	E			59
4	D			91	29	A			71
5	E			91	30	C			53
6	D			83	31	A			59
7	A			90	32	B			56
8	A			83	33	B			53
9	C			88	34	A			66
10	E			85	35	B			45
11	D			84	36	D			49
12	E			84	37	A			41
13	B			81	38	B			49
14	E			89	39	D			41
15	A			70	40	C			42
16	B			87	41	B			36
17	C			89	42	A			33
18	C			81	43	C			29
19	B			78	44	C			29
20	A			75	45	B			30
21	D			77	46	C			28
22	C			63	47	B			18
23	E			75	48	B			46
24	E			78	49	C			37
25	D			70	50	E			41

* These percentages are based on an analysis of the answer sheets of a representative sample of 21,848 students who took the original administration of this test and whose mean score was 605. They may be used as an indication of the relative difficulty of a particular question.

Finding Your Scaled Score

When you take SAT Subject Tests, the scores sent to the colleges you specify are reported on the College Board scale, which ranges from 200 to 800. You can convert your practice test raw score to a scaled score by using Table B. To find your scaled score, locate your raw score in the left-hand column of Table B; the corresponding score in the right-hand column is your scaled score. For example, a raw score of 28 on this particular edition of the Subject Test in Mathematics Level 1 corresponds to a scaled score of 600.

Raw scores are converted to scaled scores to ensure that a score earned on any one edition of a particular Subject Test is comparable to the same scaled score earned on any other edition of the same Subject Test. Because some editions of the tests may be slightly easier or more difficult than others, College Board scaled scores are adjusted so that they indicate the same level of performance regardless of the edition of the test taken and the ability of the group that takes it. Thus, for example, a score of 400 on one edition of a test taken at a particular administration indicates the same level of achievement as a score of 400 on a different edition of the test taken at a different administration.

When you take the SAT Subject Tests during a national administration, your scores are likely to differ somewhat from the scores you obtain on the tests in this book. People perform at different levels at different times for reasons unrelated to the tests themselves. The precision of any test is also limited because it represents only a sample of all the possible questions that could be asked.

Table B

Scaled Score Conversion Table Subject Test in Mathematics Level 1 – Practice Test 1					
Raw Score	Scaled Score	Raw Score	Scaled Score	Raw Score	Scaled Score
50	800	28	600	6	390
49	800	27	580	5	390
48	790	26	570	4	380
47	780	25	560	3	370
46	770	24	550	2	360
45	760	23	540	1	360
44	750	22	530	0	350
43	740	21	520	-1	340
42	730	20	510	-2	330
41	720	19	500	-3	330
40	720	18	490	-4	320
39	710	17	490	-5	310
38	700	16	480	-6	300
37	690	15	470	-7	290
36	680	14	460	-8	280
35	670	13	450	-9	270
34	660	12	440	-10	260
33	650	11	440	-11	260
32	640	10	430	-12	250
31	630	9	420		
30	620	8	410		
29	610	7	400		

How Did You Do on the Subject Test in Mathematics Level 1?

After you score your test and analyze your performance, think about the following questions:

Did you run out of time before reaching the end of the test?

If so, you may need to pace yourself better. For example, maybe you spent too much time on one or two hard questions. A better approach might be to skip the ones you can't answer right away and try answering all the remaining questions on the test. Then if there's time, go back to the questions you skipped.

Did you take a long time reading the directions?

You will save time when you take the test by learning the directions to the Subject Test in Mathematics Level 1 ahead of time. Each minute you spend reading directions during the test is a minute that you could use to answer questions.

How did you handle questions you were unsure of?

If you were able to eliminate one or more of the answer choices as wrong and guess from the remaining ones, your approach probably worked to your advantage. On the other hand, making haphazard guesses or omitting questions without trying to eliminate choices could cost you valuable points.

How difficult were the questions for you compared with other students who took the test?

Table A shows you how difficult the multiple-choice questions were for the group of students who took this test during its national administration. The right-hand column gives the percentage of students that answered each question correctly.

A question answered correctly by almost everyone in the group is obviously an easier question. For example, 89 percent of the students answered question 14 correctly. However, only 29 percent answered question 43 correctly.

Keep in mind that these percentages are based on just one group of students. They would probably be different with another group of students taking the test.

If you missed several easier questions, go back and try to find out why: Did the questions cover material you haven't yet reviewed? Did you misunderstand the directions?

Answer Explanations for Mathematics Level 1 – Practice Test 1

<hr>

The solutions presented here provide one method for solving each of the problems on this test. Other mathematically correct approaches are possible.

1. Choice (E) is the correct answer. Since $x + 7 = 3$, $x = -4$. Thus,
$$-4y + 7y = 84$$
$$3y = 84$$
$$y = 28$$

2. Choice (D) is the correct answer. For the product of the numbers to be negative, an odd number of them must be negative, and none of the numbers can be zero. This is true for choice (D) only.

3. Choice (B) is the correct answer. Since $x^2 - y^2 = (x+y)(x-y)$, $x^2 - y^2 = (5)(3) = 15$.

4. Choice (D) is the correct answer. Two diameters of the circle are drawn. The central angle of each of the shaded sectors is 60°. Each shaded sector is $\frac{60}{360}$ or $\frac{1}{6}$ of the circular region. Therefore, $\frac{1}{3}$ of the circular region is shaded.

5. Choice (E) is the correct answer. A line with a negative slope slants downward from left to right, and a line with a negative y-intercept crosses the negative y-axis. Only choice (E) satisfies both of these conditions. Choice (A) is incorrect. The line is horizontal so its slope is 0, and the y-intercept is positive. Choice (B) is incorrect. The slope of the line is positive, and the y-intercept is positive. Choice (C) is incorrect. Although the y-intercept is negative, the slope of the line is positive. Choice (D) is incorrect. Although the slope of the line is negative, the y-intercept is positive.

6. Choice (D) is the correct answer. The left and right sides of the equation are opposites of each other. The only number equal to its opposite is 0, so you should find the values of k for which $k^2 - 4 = 0$. These are 2 and –2, which is choice (D). You could also solve the equation by combining like terms. If $k^2 - 4 = 4 - k^2$, then $2k^2 - 8 = 0$ or $k^2 = 4$.

7. Choice (A) is the correct answer. Since $b^{2x+1} = b^{3x-1}$, $2x + 1 = 3x - 1$ and $x = 2$.

8. Choice (A) is the correct answer. The number of students taking French is decreasing by 20 students per year. After n years, there will be $20n$ fewer students taking French. Currently, there are 250 students taking French. Thus, after n years, there will be $250 - 20n$ students taking French. The number of students taking Spanish is increasing by 10 students per year. After n years, there will be $10n$ more students taking Spanish. Currently, there are 100 students taking Spanish. Thus, after n years, there will be $100 + 10n$ students taking Spanish. To find when the number of students is the same in both courses, set the two expressions equal to each other; $250 - 20n = 100 + 10n$.

9. Choice (C) is the correct answer. To find the value of x when $y = 2$, you need to solve the equation $2 = x^3 - 1.5$, which is equivalent to $3.5 = x^3$. Taking the cube root of both sides of the equation yields $x \approx 1.52$.

10. Choice (E) is the correct answer. If the width of the rectangle is w, then the length of the rectangle is $4w$, and the perimeter is $w + 4w + w + 4w = 10w = 40$. Thus, the width of the rectangle is 4 centimeters, and the length is 16 centimeters. Therefore, the area is equal to $4 \cdot 16 = 64$ cm^2. Choice (A) is incorrect. This is the width of the rectangle. Choice (B) is incorrect. This is the length of the rectangle. Choice (D) is incorrect. This is the perimeter of the rectangle.

11. Choice (D) is the correct answer. According to the function, if a student has a grade point average of 3.5, then $3.5 = 0.066t + 0.96$ and $2.54 = 0.066t$. Thus, $t \approx 38.48$, meaning that a student with a grade point average of 3.5 studied approximately 38.5 hours per week.

12. Choice (E) is the correct answer. Since x^2 is on both sides of the equation, the equation can be written as

$$-2x + 3 = x^3 + 2x$$
$$3 = x^3 + 4x$$
$$0 = x^3 + 4x - 3$$

13. Choice (B) is the correct answer. In a right triangle, the sine of an angle is equal to the ratio of the length of the opposite side to the length of the hypotenuse. If $\sin P = 0.5$, then $\dfrac{QR}{PQ} = \dfrac{1}{2}$. So, $\dfrac{QR}{6} = \dfrac{1}{2}$ and $QR = 3$.

14. Choice (E) is the correct answer. A counterexample to the statement "All odd numbers greater than 2 are prime numbers" would be an odd number greater than 2 that is <u>not</u> a prime number. Choice (A) is not odd, so it cannot be a counterexample. Choices (B), (C), and (D) are odd numbers greater than 2, but they are prime numbers, so they are not counterexamples. Choice (E) is odd and it is greater than 2. However, since 9 is equal to 3×3, it is not a prime number. Therefore 9 is a counterexample to the statement.

15. Choice (A) is the correct answer. $f(-0.1) = \dfrac{2(-0.1) - 1}{(-0.1)^2} = \dfrac{-0.2 - 1}{0.01} = -120$.

16. Choice (B) is the correct answer. To solve the problem, set up a proportion, where x represents the distance between the buildings on the blueprint.

$$\frac{0.4 \text{ in}}{6 \text{ ft}} = \frac{x \text{ in}}{76 \text{ ft}}$$
$$\frac{76(0.4)}{6} = x$$
$$x = 5.0\overline{6} \approx 5.1$$

17.

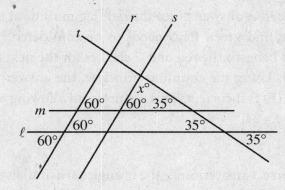

Choice (C) is the correct answer. Using the fact that vertical angles are congruent and corresponding angles are congruent, you can determine the measures of five additional angles as shown in the figure above. Since the sum of the degree measures of the interior angles in a triangle is 180, $x = 180 - (60 + 35) = 85$.

18. Choice (C) is the correct answer. The expression $\dfrac{2x}{3x-1}$ is undefined when $3x - 1$ is equal to 0. If $3x - 1 = 0$, then $x = \dfrac{1}{3}$.

19. Choice (B) is the correct answer. The total number of phones sold in the first 8 weeks of the last quarter is equal to $8 \cdot 10.375 = 83$. In order to sell 185 phones for the quarter, the team must sell 102 phones during the last five weeks, resulting in an average of 20.4 [$102 \div 5$] phones to be sold per week for the last five weeks. Choice (C) is incorrect. This is the total number of phones sold in the first 8 weeks. Choice (D) is incorrect. This is the total number of phones the team needs to sell for the remaining 5 weeks.

20. Choice (A) is the correct answer. At the point where a line crosses the y-axis, the value of the x-coordinate will be 0. When 0 is substituted into the equation, the result is $-2y - 7 = 0$. Solving for y produces a value of $-\dfrac{7}{2}$ for the y-coordinate.

21. Choice (D) is the correct answer. Because $ABCD$ is a rectangle, it has congruent diagonals. The distance from A to C is the same as the distance from B to D. You can use the distance formula to get $BD = \sqrt{(-1 - 7)^2 + (4 - (-3))^2} = \sqrt{64 + 49} = \sqrt{113} \approx 10.6$.

22. Choice (C) is the correct answer. Since the red flag must be at the top, only the order of the blue, yellow, and green flags needs to be considered. Thus, there are three choices for the flag beneath the red one, 2 choices for the next position, and 1 choice for the lowest spot. Using the counting principle, the answer is $3 \cdot 2 \cdot 1 = 6$, which is choice (C). Choice (E) is incorrect. This results from allowing any flag at the top and computing $4 \cdot 3 \cdot 2 \cdot 1 = 24$.

23. Choice (E) is the correct answer. Since the triangles are similar, the lengths of the sides and the perimeters are in proportion. If $\dfrac{GH}{KL} = \dfrac{2.1}{1.4} = 1.5$, then $\dfrac{\text{perimeter of } \triangle FGH}{\text{perimeter of } \triangle JKL} = 1.5$. Thus, $\dfrac{\text{perimeter of } \triangle FGH}{3.6} = 1.5$, so the perimeter of $\triangle FGH$ is $(3.6)(1.5) = 5.4$ meters, which is choice (E). Choice (A) is incorrect. This results from recognizing that KL is $\dfrac{2}{3}$ of GH and multiplying 3.6 by $\dfrac{2}{3}$ instead of $\dfrac{3}{2}$. Choice (C) is incorrect. This results from reasoning that since $GH - KL = 0.7$, the perimeter of $\triangle FGH$ is $3.6 + 0.7 = 4.3$.

24. Choice (E) is the correct answer. The line with equation $2x - y = 7$ can be written in $y = mx + b$ form as $y = 2x - 7$. The slope of the line is 2, and any line parallel to the line will also have a slope of 2.

25. Choice (D) is the correct answer. Since the original cube has 6 faces and 8 corners, placing a new face on each corner will add 8 faces to the resulting solid for a total of 14 faces.

26.

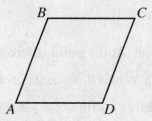

Choice (C) is the correct answer. It is helpful to draw and label a parallelogram to answer this question. In a parallelogram, opposite angles are congruent, so $\angle A$ and $\angle C$ are congruent, and $\angle B$ and $\angle D$ are congruent. Opposite sides are also congruent, so $\overline{AB} \cong \overline{CD}$ and $\overline{BC} \cong \overline{AD}$. However, $\overline{AC}$ and $\overline{BD}$ are <u>not</u> necessarily congruent, as shown in the figure.

27. Choice (B) is the correct answer. At a rate of 45 miles per hour, the time it takes to go 200 miles is $\frac{200}{45} \approx 4.44$ hours. If the speed increases by 20 percent, the new speed will be $45 \cdot 1.2 = 54$ miles per hour. At 54 miles per hour, it would take $\frac{200}{54} \approx 3.70$ hours to travel 200 miles. The time saved by going at the faster speed would be approximately $4.44 - 3.70 = 0.74$ hour, or approximately $\frac{3}{4}$ of an hour, which is choice (B). Choice (E) is incorrect. It results from assuming that an increase in speed of 20 percent yields a reduction in time of 20 percent of an hour.

28. Choice (E) is the correct answer. To solve the problem, it is helpful to think of the absolute value of the difference of two quantities as the distance between their corresponding points on the number line. Thus, you have to determine which of the five choices is furthest from c. Since c is negative, c is to the left of 0, 4, and 10 on the number line. Therefore, c is further from 10 than from either 0 or 4. To see that c is also further from 10 than -10 and -4, consider two cases. Case (1): c is between -10 and 0. Then, c is less than 10 units from -10 and -4. Since c is more than 10 units from 10, c is further from 10 than from either -10 or -4. Case (2): c is less than -10. Then, it is obvious that c is further from 10 than from either -10 or -4. Thus, in all cases, c is furthest from 10 than it is from -10, -4, 0, and 4.

29.

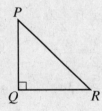

Choice (A) is the correct answer. It is helpful to draw and label $\triangle PQR$

$\cos P = \dfrac{\text{length of adjacent side}}{\text{length of hypotenuse}} = \dfrac{PQ}{PR}$, which is choice (A).

Choice (B) is incorrect.

$\dfrac{PR}{PQ} = \dfrac{\text{length of hypotenuse}}{\text{length of adjacent side}}$ and $\cos P = \dfrac{\text{length of adjacent side}}{\text{length of hypotenuse}}$.

This is the reciprocal of the correct answer, or sec P.

Choice (C) is incorrect.

$\dfrac{PR}{QR} = \dfrac{\text{length of hypotenuse}}{\text{length of opposite side}}$ and $\cos P = \dfrac{\text{length of adjacent side}}{\text{length of hypotenuse}}$ $\cdot$ $\dfrac{PR}{QR} = \csc P$.

Choice (D) is incorrect.

$\dfrac{QR}{PQ} = \dfrac{\text{length of opposite side}}{\text{length of adjacent side}}$ and $\cos P = \dfrac{\text{length of adjacent side}}{\text{length of hypotenuse}} \cdot \dfrac{QR}{PQ} = \tan P.$

Choice (E) is incorrect.

$\dfrac{QR}{PR} = \dfrac{\text{length of opposite side}}{\text{length of hypotenuse}}$ and $\cos P = \dfrac{\text{length of adjacent side}}{\text{length of hypotenuse}} \cdot \dfrac{QR}{PR} = \sin P.$

30. Choice (C) is the correct answer. To answer this question, you must use the fact that profit is equal to revenue minus expenses. The class has \$700 in expenses. The problem gives the profit when 300 tickets are sold. If x represents the price per ticket, in dollars, the revenue for this sale is $300x$. Therefore, $\$1{,}100 = 300x - 700$, which implies that the price per ticket is \$6. If 500 tickets are sold at the same price, the revenue is $500 \cdot \$6 = \$3{,}000$. The profit on the sale of the 500 tickets would be $\$3{,}000 - \$700 = \$2{,}300$.

31. Choice (A) is the correct answer. The midpoint of the line segment that has endpoints $(x, 5)$ and $(9, y)$ is given by $\left(\dfrac{x+9}{2}, \dfrac{5+y}{2}\right)$. Thus, $\dfrac{x+9}{2} = 6$ yielding $x = 3$, and $\dfrac{5+y}{2} = 3$ yielding $y = 1$. The sum of x and y is 4.

32. Choice (B) is the correct answer. If $\dfrac{1}{2}$ is $\dfrac{3}{4}$ of $\dfrac{4}{5}$ of a number n, then $\dfrac{1}{2} = \dfrac{3}{4} \cdot \dfrac{4}{5} n$.

$$\frac{1}{2} = \frac{3}{5}n$$

$$\frac{5}{2} = 3n$$

$$\frac{5}{6} = n$$

33. Choice (B) is the correct answer. In $\triangle MHL$, $\overline{NP}$ is a midsegment because $\overline{NP} \parallel \overline{HL}$ and $NP = \dfrac{1}{2}HL$. Because $\overline{NP}$ is a midsegment of $\triangle MHL$, $HN = NM$. Since vertical angles are congruent, $\angle JNH \cong \angle ONM$. Together with the given information that $JN = NO$, you can conclude that $\triangle HJN \cong \triangle MON$ by side-angle-side congruence. Corresponding parts of congruent triangles are congruent, so $JH = MO$.

$$\text{Area of } \triangle MNP = \frac{1}{2}(NP)(MO)$$

$$= \frac{1}{2}\left(\frac{1}{2}HL\right)(JH)$$

$$= \left(\frac{1}{4}\right)(HL)(JH)$$

$$= \frac{1}{4}\text{ (area of square } HJKL)$$

This shows that the area of $\triangle MNP$ is $\dfrac{1}{4}$ the area of square $HJKL$.

34. Choice (A) is the correct answer. The function f given by $f(x) = \dfrac{x+2}{x+3} - \dfrac{1}{x}$ is not defined for values of x that result in a denominator of 0. The value $x = -3$ results in a denominator of 0 in $\dfrac{x+2}{x+3}$, and the value $x = 0$ results in a denominator of 0 in $\dfrac{1}{x}$. The only choice given that is not contained in the domain of f is -3.

35. Choice (B) is the correct answer. If x^2 must be between 1 and 4, then the absolute value of x must be between 1 and 2. If x is positive, then $1 \leq x \leq 2$. If x is negative, then $-2 \leq x \leq -1$. Choice (B) shows the graph of all numbers x such that $-2 \leq x \leq -1$ or $1 \leq x \leq 2$.

36. Choice (D) is the correct answer. $\overline{OA}$, $\overline{OE}$, and $\overline{OC}$ are radii of the circle, so they all have length r. Since $OB = OD$, angles B and D are each 45°. Thus, $OE = ED$ and $OE = BE$. So, there are five labeled segments with length r: $\overline{OA}$, $\overline{OE}$, $\overline{OC}$, $\overline{BE}$, and $\overline{ED}$.

37. Choice (A) is the correct answer. To solve the problem, you will need to use the Pythagorean theorem twice. In right triangle ABC,

$$(AC)^2 = (AB)^2 + (BC)^2$$
$$(AC)^2 = x^2 + 1^2 = x^2 + 1$$
$$AC = \sqrt{x^2 + 1}$$

In right triangle ADC,

$$(AC)^2 = (AD)^2 + (CD)^2$$
$$(\sqrt{x^2 + 1})^2 = 2^2 + (CD)^2$$

$$x^2 + 1 = 4 + (CD)^2$$
$$x^2 - 3 = (CD)^2$$
$$CD = \sqrt{x^2 - 3}$$

Choice (B) is incorrect. $\sqrt{x^2 + 1} = AC$, not CD. Choice (D) is incorrect It results from using 3 instead of −3 in the solution. Choice (E) is incorrect. If you added 4 instead of subtracting 4 from both sides of the equation, and you also forgot to take the square root of both sides, you would have chosen choice (E).

38. Choice (B) is the correct answer. To answer this question, you need to determine the number of students that have at least 5 red candies. From the distribution, there are 6 students who each had at least 5 red candies. Therefore, the probability that the student's sample would have at least 5 red candies is equal to $\dfrac{6}{20}$ or $\dfrac{3}{10}$.

39. Choice (D) is the correct answer. From the graph, you can determine $g(3) = -1$. Thus, $f(g(3)) = f(-1)$. From the graph, you can determine that $f(-1)$ is 1.

40. Choice (C) is the correct answer. The measure of $\angle AOB$ is 25°, which is $\dfrac{25}{360}$ of the circle, so the length of $\overparen{AB}$ is $\dfrac{25}{360}$ of the circumference of the circle. Since the radius of the circle is 3, the circumference of the circle is $2\pi r = 6\pi$. Thus, the length of $\overparen{AB}$ is $\dfrac{25}{360}(6\pi) \approx 1.31$.

41. Choice (B) is the correct answer. To find the points of intersection, you need to solve the system $\begin{cases} x^2 + y^2 = 4 \\ (x-2)^2 + y^2 = 4 \end{cases}$ for x and y. One way to solve the system is to subtract the second equation from the first and solve for x and y.

$$x^2 + y^2 = 4$$
$$-\left[(x-2)^2 + y^2 = 4\right]$$
$$x^2 - (x-2)^2 = 0$$
$$x^2 - (x^2 - 4x + 4) = 0$$
$$4x - 4 = 0$$
$$x = 1$$

If $x = 1$, then $1^2 + y^2 = 4$. Thus, $y^2 = 3$ and $y = \pm\sqrt{3}$. The points of intersection are $\left(1, \sqrt{3}\right)$ and $\left(1, -\sqrt{3}\right)$.

42. Choice (A) is the correct answer. If the area of one face of the cube is x, then the length of each edge of the cube is $\sqrt{x}$. Therefore, the volume of the cube is equal to $\left(\sqrt{x}\right)^3 = x\sqrt{x}$.

43. Choice (C) is the correct answer. The quadratic equation $ax^2 + bx + c = 0$ with $a \neq 0$ has solutions $x = \dfrac{-b + \sqrt{b^2 - 4ac}}{2a}$ and $\dfrac{-b - \sqrt{b^2 - 4ac}}{2a}$, so the sum of the two roots is $-\dfrac{b}{a}$, and their product is $\dfrac{c}{a}$. Therefore, you need an equation in which $-\dfrac{b}{a} = \dfrac{c}{a}$, or $-b = c$. The only choice satisfying this condition is choice (C).

    You could also solve this problem by finding the actual roots of each of the five given equations, either by factoring, using the quadratic formula, or using a graphing calculator. After you find the two roots of an equation, find their sum and product and compare them. Choice (A) is incorrect. The roots of the equation are -2 and 2. The sum of the roots is 0, and the product is -4. Choice (B) is incorrect. $x^2 - 2x + 1 = (x - 1)^2$, so there is a double root at $x = 1$. The sum of the roots is 2, and the product is 1. Choice (D) is incorrect. $x^2 - 5x + 6 = (x - 3)(x - 2)$, so the roots are 3 and 2. The sum of the roots is 5, and the product is 6. Choice (E) is incorrect. $x^2 + 4x + 4 = (x + 2)^2$, so there is a double root at $x = -2$. The sum of the roots is -4, and the product is 4.

44. Choice (C) is the correct answer. Of the 90 digits you need to write, the first 9 digits correspond to the integers 1–9, and the next 81 digits come from two-digit positive integers (10, 11, ...). Because each of these are two-digit positive integers, there will be 40 complete two-digit positive integers written, and the 90th digit will be the tens digit of the 41st two-digit positive integer. Since 10 is the first two-digit positive integer, 50 is the 41st two-digit positive integer. Thus, the 90th digit will be 5.

45. Choice (B) is the correct answer. In this question, it is helpful to use a graphing calculator to graph $y = x^4 - 4x^2 + x + 1$. Since the domain of the function is $-5 \leq x \leq 5$, set the viewing window to go from $x = -5$ to $x = 5$, and graph the function. The minimum value of the function occurs when $x \approx -1.473$, which is in the interval $-3 < x < -1$. Choice (A) is incorrect. The minimum value of the function is $y \approx -4.444$,

which is $f(-1.473)$. The question asks for the interval in which the minimum value of f occurs. Choice (A) results from confusing x with y, since the minimum value of the function is $y \approx -4.444$.

46. Choice (C) is the correct answer. The sum of the measures of the interior angles of a convex polygon with n sides is equal to $(n-2)180°$. Thus, $(n-2)180° = 1,800°$ and $n - 2 = 10$, so $n = 12$.

47. Choice (B) is the correct answer. The quadratic equation $ax^2 + bx + c = 0$ has no real roots if $b^2 - 4ac < 0$. Thus, the equation $x^2(3k+1) - 6x + 2 = 0$ has no real roots if $(-6)^2 - 4(3k+1)(2) < 0$. This simplifies to $28 - 24k < 0$. The least integer value of k that satisfies this inequality is 2.

48. Choice (B) is the correct answer. Since $\dfrac{\sin^2 A}{\cos^2 A} = \tan^2 A = 2.468$, $\tan A = \sqrt{2.468} \approx 1.571$.

49. Choice (C) is the correct answer. The volume of a cylinder with radius r and height h is equal to $\pi r^2 h$. Thus, the volume of cylinder I is $\pi(2.5)^2 h = 6.25\pi h$, and the volume of cylinder III is $25\pi h$. The volume of cylinder II is the mean of the volumes of cylinders I and III. Thus, $\pi r^2 h = \dfrac{6.25\pi h + 25\pi h}{2} = 15.625\pi h$ and $r^2 = 15.625$. The value of r is $\sqrt{15.625}$, which is approximately 3.95. Choice (B) is incorrect. This is the mean of the radii of cylinders I and III. Using this value for r will not give a volume for cylinder II that is the mean of the volumes of cylinders I and III. Choice (E) is incorrect. This is the value of r^2. You need to take the square root of this value to find the radius of cylinder II.

50. Choice (E) is the correct answer. A graphing calculator is helpful for this problem. If you graph functions f and g in a standard viewing window of $[-10, 10]$ by $[-10, 10]$, you can see that the graph of g is identical to the graph of f, but it is shifted 3 units to the left. Thus, $g(x) = f(x+3)$.

Mathematics Level 1 – Practice Test 2

Practice Helps

The test that follows is an actual, previously administered SAT Subject Test in Mathematics Level 1. To get an idea of what it's like to take this test, practice under conditions that are much like those of an actual test administration.

- Set aside an hour when you can take the test uninterrupted.

- Sit at a desk or table with no other books or papers. Dictionaries, other books, or notes are not allowed in the test room.

- Remember to have a scientific or graphing calculator with you.

- Tear out an answer sheet from the back of this book and fill it in just as you would on the day of the test. One answer sheet can be used for up to three Subject Tests.

- Read the instructions that precede the practice test. During the actual administration you will be asked to read them before answering test questions.

- Use a clock or kitchen timer to time yourself.

- After you finish the practice test, read the sections "How to Score the SAT Subject Test in Mathematics Level 1" and "How Did You Do on the Subject Test in Mathematics Level 1?"

- The appearance of the answer sheet in this book may differ from the answer sheet you see on test day.

MATHEMATICS LEVEL 1 TEST

The top portion of the page of the answer sheet that you will use to take the Mathematics Level 1 Test must be filled in exactly as illustrated below. When your supervisor tells you to fill in the circle next to the name of the test you are about to take, mark your answer sheet as shown.

○ Literature	● Mathematics Level 1	○ German	○ Chinese Listening	○ Japanese Listening
○ Biology E	○ Mathematics Level 2	○ Italian	○ French Listening	○ Korean Listening
○ Biology M	○ U.S. History	○ Latin	○ German Listening	○ Spanish Listening
○ Chemistry	○ World History	○ Modern Hebrew		
○ Physics	○ French	○ Spanish	Background Questions: ① ② ③ ④ ⑤ ⑥ ⑦ ⑧ ⑨	

After filling in the circle next to the name of the test you are taking, locate the Background Questions section, which also appears at the top of your answer sheet (as shown above). This is where you will answer the following Background Questions on your answer sheet.

BACKGROUND QUESTIONS

Please answer Part I and Part II below by filling in the appropriate circle in the Background Questions box on your answer sheet. The information you provide is for statistical purposes only and will not affect your test score.

Part I. Which of the following describes a mathematics course you have taken or are currently taking? (FILL IN **ALL** CIRCLES THAT APPLY.)

- Algebra I or Elementary Algebra **OR** Course I of a college preparatory mathematics sequence   —Fill in circle 1.

- Geometry **OR** Course II of a college preparatory mathematics sequence   —Fill in circle 2.

- Algebra II or Intermediate Algebra **OR** Course III of a college preparatory mathematics sequence   —Fill in circle 3.

- Elementary Functions (Precalculus) and/or Trigonometry **OR** beyond Course III of a college preparatory mathematics sequence   —Fill in circle 4.

- Advanced Placement Mathematics (Calculus AB or Calculus BC)   —Fill in circle 5.

Part II. What type of calculator did you bring to use for this test? (FILL IN THE **ONE** CIRCLE THAT APPLIES. If you did not bring a scientific or graphing calculator, do not fill in any of circles 6-9.)

- Scientific   —Fill in circle 6.

- Graphing (Fill in the circle corresponding to the model you used.)

  Casio 9700, Casio 9750, Casio 9800, Casio 9850, Casio 9860, Casio FX 1.0, Casio CG-10, Sharp 9200, Sharp 9300, Sharp 9600, Sharp 9900, TI-82, TI-83, TI-83 Plus, TI-83 Plus Silver, TI-84 Plus, TI-84 Plus Silver, TI-85, TI-86, or TI-Nspire   —Fill in circle 7.

  Casio 9970, Casio Algebra FX 2.0, HP 38G, HP 39 series, HP 40 series, HP 48 series, HP 49 series, HP 50 series, TI-89, TI-89 Titanium, or TI-Nspire CAS   —Fill in circle 8.

  Some other graphing calculator   —Fill in circle 9.

When the supervisor gives the signal, turn the page and begin the Mathematics Level 1 Test. There are 100 numbered circles on the answer sheet and 50 questions in the Mathematics Level 1 Test. Therefore, use only circles 1 to 50 for recording your answers.

MATHEMATICS LEVEL 1 TEST

REFERENCE INFORMATION

THE FOLLOWING INFORMATION IS FOR YOUR REFERENCE IN ANSWERING SOME OF THE QUESTIONS IN THIS TEST.

Volume of a right circular cone with radius r and height h: $V = \dfrac{1}{3}\pi r^2 h$

Volume of a sphere with radius r: $V = \dfrac{4}{3}\pi r^3$

Volume of a pyramid with base area B and height h: $V = \dfrac{1}{3}Bh$

Surface Area of a sphere with radius r: $S = 4\pi r^2$

DO NOT DETACH FROM BOOK.

GO ON TO THE NEXT PAGE

MATHEMATICS LEVEL 1 TEST

For each of the following problems, decide which is the BEST of the choices given. If the exact numerical value is not one of the choices, select the choice that best approximates this value. Then fill in the corresponding circle on the answer sheet.

Notes: (1) A scientific or graphing calculator will be necessary for answering some (but not all) of the questions in this test. For each question you will have to decide whether or not you should use a calculator.

(2) The only angle measure used on this test is degree measure. Make sure your calculator is in the degree mode.

(3) Figures that accompany problems in this test are intended to provide information useful in solving the problems. They are drawn as accurately as possible EXCEPT when it is stated in a specific problem that its figure is not drawn to scale. All figures lie in a plane unless otherwise indicated.

(4) Unless otherwise specified, the domain of any function f is assumed to be the set of all real numbers x for which $f(x)$ is a real number. The range of f is assumed to be the set of all real numbers $f(x)$, where x is in the domain of f.

(5) Reference information that may be useful in answering the questions in this test can be found on the page preceding Question 1.

1. If $2t + 3t = 4t + 6t - 10$, then $t =$

    (A) -1 (B) 0 (C) $\frac{1}{2}$ (D) 1 (E) 2

2. For all $x \neq 0$, $\dfrac{1}{\left(\dfrac{2}{x^2}\right)} =$

    (A) $\dfrac{x^2}{2}$ (B) $\dfrac{x^2}{4}$ (C) $\dfrac{2}{x^2}$ (D) $\dfrac{1}{2x^2}$ (E) $2x^2$

3. If $x = 1$, then $(x - 5)(x + 2) =$

    (A) -12 (B) -3 (C) -1 (D) 3 (E) 12

GO ON TO THE NEXT PAGE

USE THIS SPACE FOR SCRATCHWORK.

4. In rectangle *ABCD* in Figure 1, what are the coordinates of vertex *C* ?

   (A) (1, 4)
   (B) (1, 5)
   (C) (5, 7)
   (D) (7, 4)
   (E) (7, 5)

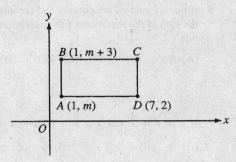

Figure 1

5.　$(a + b + 2)(a + b + 2) =$

   (A) $(a + b)^2 + 4$
   (B) $(a + b)^2 + 4(a + b)$
   (C) $(a + b)^2 + 4(a + b) + 4$
   (D) $a^2 + b^2 + 4$
   (E) $a^2 + b^2 + 4ab$

6. At what point does the graph of $2x + 3y = 12$ intersect the *y*-axis?

   (A) $(0, -6)$
   (B) $(0, -2)$
   (C) $(0, 3)$
   (D) $(0, 4)$
   (E) $(0, 12)$

7. If $12x^2 = 7$, then $7\left(12x^2\right)^2 =$

   (A) 49
   (B) 84
   (C) 98
   (D) 144
   (E) 343

GO ON TO THE NEXT PAGE

MATHEMATICS LEVEL 1 TEST—*Continued*

USE THIS SPACE FOR SCRATCH WORK.

8. If lines ℓ and m are parallel and are intersected by line t, what is the sum of the measures of the interior angles on the same side of line t ?

(A) 90°   (B) 180°   (C) 270°   (D) 360°   (E) 540°

9. If $x + y = 5$ and $x - y = 3$, then $x =$

(A) 4   (B) 2   (C) 1   (D) 0   (E) –1

10. If the cube root of the square root of a number is 2, what is the number?

(A) 16
(B) 32
(C) 36
(D) 64
(E) 256

11. Each face of the cube in Figure 2 consists of nine small squares. The shading on three of the faces is shown, and the shading on the other three faces is such that on opposite faces the reverse squares are shaded. For example, if one face has only the center square shaded, its opposite face will have eight of the nine squares shaded (the center square will not be shaded). What is the total number of shaded squares on all six faces of the cube?

(A) 12   (B) 16   (C) 18   (D) 27   (E) 54

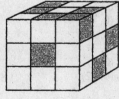

Figure 2

12. For three bins, A, B, and C, the volume of A is one-half that of B and the volume of B is two-thirds that of C. If A has a volume of 210 cubic meters, what is the volume of C, in cubic meters?

(A) 630   (B) 315   (C) 280   (D) 140   (E) 70

GO ON TO THE NEXT PAGE

USE THIS SPACE FOR SCRATCH WORK.

13. In Figure 3, when ray *OA* is rotated clockwise 7 degrees about point *O*, ray *OA* will be perpendicular to ray *OB*. What is the measure of ∠*AOB* before this rotation?

(A) 97°　(B) 90°　(C) 87°　(D) 83°　(E) 80°

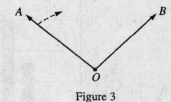

Figure 3

14. If $x + x + x = y$, then $x - y =$

(A) $-3x$　(B) $-2x$　(C) $-\dfrac{x}{2}$　(D) $\dfrac{2}{3}x$　(E) $2x$

15. If $f(x) = \dfrac{1}{x}$ for $x > 0$, then $f(1.5) =$

(A) $\dfrac{3}{4}$　(B) $\dfrac{2}{3}$　(C) $\dfrac{1}{2}$　(D) $\dfrac{1}{3}$　(E) $\dfrac{1}{4}$

16. If $15^m = 3^4 \cdot 5^4$, what is the value of m ?

(A) 4　(B) 8　(C) 16　(D) 32　(E) 128

17. What are all values of x for which $\left| x - 2 \right| < 3$?

(A) $x < -1$ or $x > 5$
(B) $x < -1$
(C) $x > 5$
(D) $-5 < x < 1$
(E) $-1 < x < 5$

GO ON TO THE NEXT PAGE

MATHEMATICS LEVEL 1 TEST—*Continued*

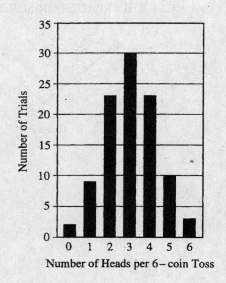

Number of Heads per 6–coin Toss

18. An algebra class conducted a coin-tossing experiment. Each trial of the experiment consisted of tossing 6 coins and counting the number of heads that resulted. The results for 100 trials are pictured in the graph above. In approximately what percent of the trials were there 3 <u>or more</u> heads?

    (A) 32%   (B) 36%   (C) 50%   (D) 60%   (E) 66%

19. The circle in Figure 4 has center *J* and radius 6. What is the length of chord *GH* ?

    (A) 6   (B) 8.49   (C) 10.39   (D) 12   (E) 16.97

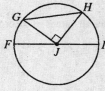

Figure 4

GO ON TO THE NEXT PAGE

MATHEMATICS LEVEL 1 TEST—*Continued*

USE THIS SPACE FOR SCRATCH WORK.

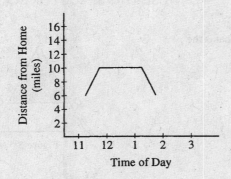

Time of Day

20. The graph above shows the distance of Janet's car from her home over a period of time on a given day. Which of the following situations best fits the information?

(A) Janet leaves her workplace, drives to a restaurant for lunch, and then returns to her workplace.
(B) Janet leaves her workplace, drives home, and stays at home.
(C) Janet leaves home, drives to a friend's house, and stays at the friend's house.
(D) Janet drives from home to the grocery store and then returns home.
(E) Janet is at the grocery store, takes the groceries home, and then drives back to the grocery store.

$$X = \{2, 3, 4, 5, 6, 7, 8, 9\}$$
$$Y = \{0, 1\}$$
$$Z = \{0, 1, 2, 3, 4, 5, 6, 7, 8, 9\}$$

21. Before 1990, telephone area codes in the United States were three-digit numbers of the form xyz. Shown above are sets X, Y, and Z from which the digits x, y, and z, respectively, were chosen. How many possible area codes were there?

(A) 919   (B) 160   (C) 144   (D) 126   (E) 20

GO ON TO THE NEXT PAGE

MATHEMATICS LEVEL 1 TEST—*Continued*

USE THIS SPACE FOR SCRATCH WORK.

22. In Figure 5, $\triangle ABC$ is equilateral and $EF \parallel DG \parallel AC$. What is the perimeter of the shaded region?

(A) 4 (B) 6 (C) 8 (D) 9 (E) 10

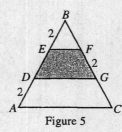

Figure 5

23. In Figure 6, two congruent circles are tangent to the number line at points 5 and 10, respectively, and tangent to rays from points 0 and 8, respectively. The circle at 10 is to be moved to the right along the number line, and the ray from point 8 is to be rotated so that it is tangent to the circle at its new position and tan $x° = $ tan $y°$. How many units to the right must the circle be moved?

(A) 1 (B) 2 (C) 3 (D) 4 (E) 5

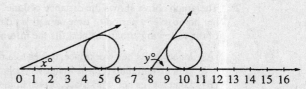

Figure 6

GO ON TO THE NEXT PAGE

USE THIS SPACE FOR SCRATCH WORK.

24. A beacon that rotates in a complete circle at a constant rate throws a single beam of light that is seen every 9 seconds at a point four miles away. How many degrees does the beacon turn in 1 second?

    (A) 6°   (B) 20°   (C) 40°   (D) 54°   (E) 60°

25. If $i^2 = -1$ and if $\left(\left(i^2 \right)^3 \right)^k = 1$, then the least positive integer value of k is

    (A) 1   (B) 2   (C) 4   (D) 6   (E) 8

26. In Figure 7, if $\theta = 44°$, what is the value of c ?

    (A) 6.94   (B) 7.19   (C) 9.66   (D) 10.36   (E) 13.90

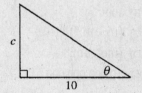

Note: Figure not drawn to scale.

Figure 7

GO ON TO THE NEXT PAGE ⟩

MATHEMATICS LEVEL 1 TEST—*Continued*

USE THIS SPACE FOR SCRATCH WORK.

27. The thickness of concrete that lines a swimming pool is a function of the depth of the pool. If d represents the depth, in feet, of the pool and $t(d)$ represents the thickness, in inches, of the concrete, then $t(d) = \frac{1}{12}\left(d^2 - 2d + 6\right)$.

Of the following, which is the closest approximation to the thickness, in inches, of the concrete at a depth of 10 feet?

(A) 0.5   (B) 1.5   (C) 6.2   (D) 7.2   (E) 10.5

28. Of the following, which has the greatest value?

(A) 10^{100}

(B) 100^{10}

(C) $\left(10 \cdot 10^{10}\right)^{10}$

(D) $(100 \cdot 10)^{10}$

(E) 10,000,000,000

29. In the xy-plane, the points $O(0, 0)$, $P(-6, 0)$, $R(-7, 5)$, and $S(-1, 1)$ can be connected to form line segments. Which two segments have the same length?

(A) OP and OR
(B) OP and OS
(C) OR and RS
(D) OS and PR
(E) PR and PS

30. A total of 9 students took a test and their average (arithmetic mean) score was 86. If the average score for 4 of the students was 81, what was the average score for the remaining 5 students?

(A) 87   (B) 88   (C) 89   (D) 90   (E) 91

GO ON TO THE NEXT PAGE

USE THIS SPACE FOR SCRATCH WORK.

31. Line ℓ has a positive slope and a negative y-intercept.
    Line m is parallel to ℓ and has a positive y-intercept.
    The x-intercept of m must be

    (A) negative and greater than the x-intercept of ℓ
    (B) negative and less than the x-intercept of ℓ
    (C) zero
    (D) positive and greater than the x-intercept of ℓ
    (E) positive and less than the x-intercept of ℓ

32. Figure 8 is a right rectangular prism. Which of the given points is
    located in the plane determined by the vertices G, H, and B ?

    (A) A (B) C (C) D (D) E (E) F

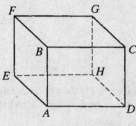

Figure 8

33. The sum of the two roots of a quadratic equation is 5 and their
    product is -6. Which of the following could be the equation?

    (A) $x^2 - 6x + 5 = 0$
    (B) $x^2 - 5x - 6 = 0$
    (C) $x^2 - 5x + 6 = 0$
    (D) $x^2 + 5x - 6 = 0$
    (E) $x^2 + 6x + 5 = 0$

34. In Figure 9, triangles ABC and DEC are similar and $w = 5$.
    What is the value of $\frac{x}{y}$?

    (A) $\frac{2}{5}$ (B) $\frac{3}{5}$ (C) $\frac{2}{3}$ (D) $\frac{3}{2}$ (E) $\frac{5}{2}$

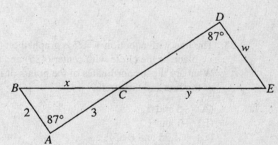

Note: Figure not drawn to scale.

Figure 9

35. $\left(\sin^2\theta + \cos^2\theta - 3\right)^4 =$

    (A) 256   (B) 81   (C) 64   (D) 32   (E) 16

GO ON TO THE NEXT PAGE

USE THIS SPACE FOR SCRATCH WORK.

36. In Figure 10, if △*ABC* is reflected across line ℓ, what will be the coordinates of the reflection of point *A* ?

    (A) (5, 1)   (B) (8, 1)   (C) (9, 1)   (D) (11, 1)   (E) (13, 1)

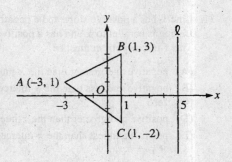

Figure 10

37. In Figure 11, the cube has edge of length 2. What is the distance from vertex *A* to the midpoint *C* of edge *BD* ?

    (A) $\sqrt{7}$
    (B) $2\sqrt{2}$
    (C) 3
    (D) 5
    (E) $\sqrt{29}$

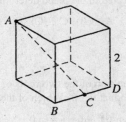

Figure 11

38. The line with equation $y = 7$ is graphed on the same xy-plane as the circle with center (4, 5) and radius 3. What are the x-coordinates of the points of intersection of the line and the circle?

    (A) −5 and 5
    (B) −1 and 1
    (C)   1.35 and 6.65
    (D)   1.76 and 6.24
    (E)   2 and 6

GO ON TO THE NEXT PAGE

MATHEMATICS LEVEL 1 TEST—*Continued*

39. In Figure 12, if $60 < q + s < 160$, which of the following describes all possible values of $t + r$?

(A) $0 < t + r < 60$
(B) $60 < t + r < 120$
(C) $120 < t + r < 200$
(D) $200 < t + r < 300$
(E) $420 < t + r < 520$

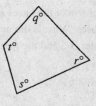

Figure 12

40. At the end of 1990, the population of a certain town was 6,250. If the population increases at the rate of 3.5 percent each year, what will the population of the town be at the end of 2005 ?

(A)   9,530
(B)   9,740
(C)   9,950
(D)   10,260
(E)   10,470

41. If points R, S, and T lie on a circle and if the center of the circle lies on segment RT, then $\triangle RST$ must be

(A)   acute
(B)   obtuse
(C)   right
(D)   isosceles
(E)   equilateral

42. The function f, where $f(x) = (1 + x)^2$, is defined for $-2 \leq x \leq 2$. What is the range of f ?

(A) $0 \leq f(x) \leq 4$
(B) $0 \leq f(x) \leq 9$
(C) $1 \leq f(x) \leq 4$
(D) $1 \leq f(x) \leq 5$
(E) $1 \leq f(x) \leq 9$

GO ON TO THE NEXT PAGE

MATHEMATICS LEVEL 1 TEST—*Continued*

USE THIS SPACE FOR SCRATCH WORK.

43. In the right circular cylinder shown in Figure 13, P and O are the centers of the bases and segment AB is a diameter of one of the bases. What is the perimeter of $\triangle ABO$ if the height of the cylinder is 5 and the radius of the base is 3 ?

(A) 11.83
(B) 14.66
(C) 16
(D) 16.66
(E) 17.66

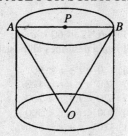

Figure 13

44. Sequential arrangements of squares are formed according to a pattern. Each arrangement after the first one is generated by adding a row of squares to the bottom of the previous arrangement, as shown in Figure 14. If this pattern continues, which of the following gives the number of squares in the nth arrangement?

(A) $2n^2$

(B) $2(2n-1)$

(C) $n(n-1)$

(D) $\frac{1}{2}n(n+1)$

(E) $n(n+1)$

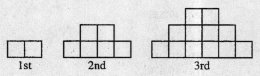

1st   2nd   3rd

Figure 14

45. If $f(x) = x^3 + 1$ and if f^{-1} is the inverse function of f, what is $f^{-1}(4)$?

(A) 0.02   (B) 1.44   (C) 1.71   (D) 27   (E) 65

GO ON TO THE NEXT PAGE

MATHEMATICS LEVEL 1 TEST—*Continued*

USE THIS SPACE FOR SCRATCH WORK.

46. Two positive integers j and k satisfy the relation $j\mathbf{R}k$ if and only if $j = k^2 + 1$. If m, n, and p satisfy the relations $m\mathbf{R}n$ and $n\mathbf{R}p$, what is the value of m in terms of p ?

    (A) $p^2 + 1$

    (B) $p^2 + 2$

    (C) $\left(p^2 + 1\right)^2$

    (D) $\left(p^2 + 1\right)^2 + 1$

    (E) $\left(p^2 + 2\right)^2$

47. The area of parallelogram *ABCD* in Figure 15 is

    (A) 12   (B) $6\sqrt{3}$ (C) 20   (D) $12\sqrt{3}$ (E) 24

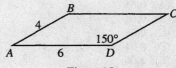

Figure 15

48. In Figure 16, the area of the shaded region bounded by the graph of the parabola $y = f(x)$ and the *x*-axis is 3. What is the area of the region bounded by the graph of $y = f(x - 2)$ and the *x*-axis?

    (A) 1   (B) $\dfrac{3}{2}$ (C) 2   (D) 3   (E) 6

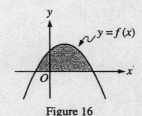

Figure 16

GO ON TO THE NEXT PAGE

MATHEMATICS LEVEL 1 TEST—Continued

USE THIS SPACE FOR SCRATCH WORK.

49. Marigolds are to be planted inside a circular flower garden so that there are 4 marigolds per square foot. The circumference of the garden is 20 feet. If marigolds are available only in packs of 6, how many packs of 6 flowers are needed?

(A) 6   (B) 13   (C) 14   (D) 20   (E) 22

50. A solution is made by mixing concentrate with water. How many liters of concentrate should be mixed with 2 liters of water so that 32 percent of the solution is concentrate?

(A) 0.63
(B) 0.64
(C) 0.68
(D) 0.94
(E) 1.06

STOP
IF YOU FINISH BEFORE TIME IS CALLED, YOU MAY CHECK YOUR WORK ON THIS TEST ONLY.
DO NOT TURN TO ANY OTHER TEST IN THIS BOOK.

How to Score the SAT Subject Test in Mathematics Level 1

When you take an actual SAT Subject Test in Mathematics Level 1, your answer sheet will be "read" by a scanning machine that will record your responses to each question. Then a computer will compare your answers with the correct answers and produce your raw score. You get one point for each correct answer. For each wrong answer, you lose one-quarter of a point. Questions you omit (and any for which you mark more than one answer) are not counted. This raw score is converted to a scaled score that is reported to you and to the colleges you specify.

Worksheet 1. Finding Your Raw Test Score

Step 1: Table A on the following page lists the correct answers for all the questions on the SAT Subject Test in Mathematics Level 1 that is reproduced in this book. It also serves as a worksheet for you to calculate your raw score.

- Compare your answers with those given in the table.
- Put a check in the column marked "Right" if your answer is correct.
- Put a check in the column marked "Wrong" if your answer is incorrect.
- Leave both columns blank if you omitted the question.

Step 2: Count the number of right answers.

Enter the total here:_____

Step 3: Count the number of wrong answers.

Enter the total here:_____

Step 4: Multiply the number of wrong answers by .250.

Enter the product here: _____

Step 5: Subtract the result obtained in Step 4 from the total you obtained in Step 2.

Enter the result here:_____

Step 6: Round the number obtained in Step 5 to the nearest whole number.

Enter the result here:_____

The number you obtained in Step 6 is your raw score.

TABLE A

Answers to the Subject Test in Mathematics Level 1 – Practice Test 2 and Percentage of Students Answering Each Question Correctly

Question Number	Correct Answer	Right	Wrong	Percentage of Students Answering the Question Correctly*	Question Number	Correct Answer	Right	Wrong	Percentage of Students Answering the Question Correctly*
1	E			92	26	C			68
2	A			76	27	D			72
3	A			93	28	C			52
4	E			91	29	E			57
5	C			65	30	D			53
6	D			77	31	B			58
7	E			86	32	A			51
8	B			77	33	B			24
9	A			88	34	A			51
10	D			80	35	E			49
11	D			78	36	E			38
12	A			75	37	C			34
13	A			80	38	D			25
14	B			75	39	D			37
15	B			86	40	E			25
16	A			71	41	C			25
17	E			71	42	B			14
18	E			65	43	E			51
19	B			80	44	E			42
20	A			72	45	B			28
21	B			68	46	D			32
22	E			66	47	A			19
23	C			60	48	D			19
24	C			72	49	E			22
25	B			63	50	D			27

* These percentages are based on an analysis of the answer sheets of a representative sample of 9,999 students who took the original administration of this test and whose mean score was 564. They may be used as an indication of the relative difficulty of a particular question.

Finding Your Scaled Score

When you take SAT Subject Tests, the scores sent to the colleges you specify are reported on the College Board scale, which ranges from 200 to 800. You can convert your practice test raw score to a scaled score by using Table B. To find your scaled score, locate your raw score in the left-hand column of Table B; the corresponding score in the right-hand column is your scaled score. For example, a raw score of 30 on this particular edition of the SAT Subject Test in Mathematics Level 1 corresponds to a scaled score of 620.

Raw scores are converted to scaled scores to ensure that a score earned on any one edition of a particular Subject Test is comparable to the same scaled score earned on any other edition of the same Subject Test. Because some editions of tests may be slightly easier or more difficult than others, scaled scores are adjusted so that they indicate the same level of performance regardless of the edition of the test taken and the ability of the group that takes it. Thus, for example, a score of 400 on one edition of a test taken at a particular administration indicates the same level of achievement as a score of 400 on a different edition of the test taken at a different administration.

When you take the SAT Subject Tests during a national administration, your scores are likely to differ somewhat from the scores you obtain on the tests in this book. People perform at different levels at different times for reasons unrelated to the tests themselves. The precision of any test is also limited because it represents only a sample of all the possible questions that could be asked.

Table B

Scaled Score Conversion Table					
Subject Test in Mathematics Level 1 – Practice Test 2					
Raw Score	Scaled Score	Raw Score	Scaled Score	Raw Score	Scaled Score
50	800	28	590	6	390
49	790	27	580	5	380
48	780	26	570	4	380
47	780	25	560	3	370
46	770	24	550	2	360
45	750	23	540	1	350
44	740	22	530	0	340
43	740	21	520	-1	340
42	730	20	510	-2	330
41	720	19	500	-3	320
40	710	18	490	-4	310
39	710	17	480	-5	300
38	700	16	470	-6	300
37	690	15	460	-7	280
36	680	14	460	-8	270
35	670	13	450	-9	260
34	660	12	440	-10	260
33	650	11	430	-11	250
32	640	10	420	-12	240
31	630	9	420		
30	620	8	410		
29	600	7	400		

How Did You Do on the Subject Test in Mathematics Level 1?

After you score your test and analyze your performance, think about the following questions:

Did you run out of time before reaching the end of the test?

If so, you may need to pace yourself better. For example, maybe you spent too much time on one or two hard questions. A better approach might be to skip the ones you can't answer right away and try answering all the remaining questions on the test. Then if there's time, go back to the questions you skipped.

Did you take a long time reading the directions?

You will save time when you take the test by learning the directions to the Subject Test in Mathematics Level 1 ahead of time. Each minute you spend reading directions during the test is a minute that you could use to answer questions.

How did you handle questions you were unsure of?

If you were able to eliminate one or more of the answer choices as wrong and guess from the remaining ones, your approach probably worked to your advantage. On the other hand, making haphazard guesses or omitting questions without trying to eliminate choices could cost you valuable points.

How difficult were the questions for you compared with other students who took the test?

Table A shows you how difficult the multiple-choice questions were for the group of students who took this test during its national administration. The right-hand column gives the percentage of students that answered each question correctly.

A question answered correctly by almost everyone in the group is obviously an easier question. For example, 91 percent of the students answered question 4 correctly. However, only 19 percent answered question 47 correctly.

Keep in mind that these percentages are based on just one group of students. They would probably be different with another group of students taking the test.

If you missed several easier questions, go back and try to find out why: Did the questions cover material you haven't reviewed yet? Did you misunderstand the directions?

Answer Explanations for Mathematics Level 1 – Practice Test 2

The solutions presented here provide one method for solving each of the problems on this test. Other mathematically correct approaches are possible.

1. Choice (E) is the correct answer. When like terms are combined, the equation simplifies to $5t = 10t - 10$. Solving for t gives $-5t = -10$ and $t = 2$.

2. Choice (A) is the correct answer. If $x \neq 0$, then $\dfrac{1}{\left(\dfrac{2}{x^2}\right)} = \dfrac{x^2}{2}$.

3. Choice (A) is the correct answer. Substituting $x = 1$ yields $(1 - 5)(1 + 2) = -4 \cdot 3 = -12$.

4. Choice (E) is the correct answer. From the figure you can see that points A and D have the same y-coordinate. Thus, $m = 2$ and $m + 3 = 5$. The y-coordinate of vertex C is 5. The x-coordinates of C and D are equal. Thus, the coordinates of C are $(7, 5)$.

5. Choice (C) is the correct answer. $(a + b + 2)(a + b + 2) = [(a + b) + 2]^2 = (a + b)^2 + 2 \cdot (a + b) \cdot 2 + 2^2 = (a + b)^2 + 4(a + b) + 4$.

6. Choice (D) is the correct answer. The point of intersection of the graph of $2x + 3y = 12$ and the y-axis is simply the point at which $x = 0$, since $x = 0$ for all points on the y-axis. If $x = 0$, then $2x + 3y = 12$ simplifies to $3y = 12$ or $y = 4$. The graph of $2x + 3y = 12$ intersects the y-axis at $(0, 4)$.

7. Choice (E) is the correct answer. Since $12x^2 = 7$, then $7(12x^2)^2 = 7(7)^2 = 7^3 = 343$.

8.

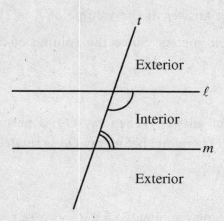

Choice (B) is the correct answer. It is helpful to draw a figure to solve the problem. Since $\ell \parallel m$, the sum of the interior angles on the same side of line t is 180°.

9. Choice (A) is the correct answer. One way to solve for x is to set up the system of equations $\begin{cases} x+y=5 \\ x-y=3 \end{cases}$. Adding the two equations gives $2x=8$ or $x=4$. Choice (C) is incorrect. If you add the left hand sides of the equations but subtract the right hand sides, you get $2x=2$ or $x=1$.

10. Choice (D) is the correct answer. The statement translates to the equation $\sqrt[3]{\sqrt{x}} = 2$. If you cube each side of the equation, you get $\sqrt{x}=2^3=8$. Now if you square each side, you get $x=8^2=64$. Choice (B) is incorrect. It results from thinking that $\sqrt[3]{\sqrt{x}} = 2$ is equal to $\sqrt[5]{x}=2$, thereby getting $x=32$.

11. Choice (D) is the correct answer. One face of the cube has the center square shaded, which implies its opposite face has 8 shaded squares, for a total of 9 shaded squares. Another face has 3 squares shaded, which implies its opposite face has 6 shaded squares, for a total of 9 shaded squares. The last face has 5 squares shaded, which implies its opposite face has 4 shaded squares, for a total of 9 shaded squares. Thus, the number of shaded squares on the six faces of the cube is $3(9)=27$. Choice (C) is incorrect. It results from counting the number of shaded squares shown and doubling that number.

12. Choice (A) is the correct answer. If the volume of A is 210 cubic meters, then the volume of B is 420 cubic meters. Since the volume of B is $\frac{2}{3}$ the volume of C, $420 = \frac{2}{3}C$ and $C = 630$.

13. Choice (A) is the correct answer. When ray OA is perpendicular to ray OB, the measure of $\angle AOB$ is 90°. Therefore, before ray OA is rotated 7 degrees clockwise, the measure of $\angle AOB$ is 97°.

14. Choice (B) is the correct answer. Since $3x = y$, $x - y = x - 3x = -2x$.

15. Choice (B) is the correct answer. $f(1.5)$ is equal to $\frac{1}{1.5} = 0.667$ or $\frac{2}{3}$. Alternatively, $f(1.5)$ can be expressed as $\frac{1}{\frac{3}{2}} = \frac{2}{3}$.

16. Choice (A) is the correct answer. Since $3^4 \cdot 5^4 = 15^4$, $m = 4$. Choice (C) is incorrect. If you think $3^4 \cdot 5^4 = (3 \cdot 5)^{(4 \cdot 4)}$, you will get $15^m = 15^{16}$.

17. Choice (E) is the correct answer. If $|x - 2| < 3$, then $-3 < x - 2 < 3$. This is equivalent to $-1 < x < 5$.

18. Choice (E) is the correct answer. You need to add the number of trials in which there were 3 heads, 4 heads, 5 heads, and 6 heads. This is equal to $30 + 23 + 10 + 3 = 66$. Since there were 100 trials, $\frac{66}{100} = 66\%$. Choice (B) is incorrect. This is the percent of trials for which there were more than 3 heads. Choice (C) is incorrect. This results from assuming that since the bar in the middle represents 3 heads, half of the trials had 3 or more heads.

19. Choice (B) is the correct answer. In the figure, $JG = JH = 6$, since chords $\overline{JG}$ and $\overline{JH}$ are radii of the circle. Thus, $\triangle GHJ$ is an isosceles right triangle, and it follows from the Pythagorean theorem that $GH = 6\sqrt{2} \approx 8.49$. Choice (C) is incorrect. $10.39 \approx 6\sqrt{3}$ instead of $6\sqrt{2}$.

20. Choice (A) is the correct answer. The graph represents a situation in which Janet starts out 6 miles from home. She departs there at about 11:00 a.m. and goes some

place farther from home. She stays there for a while and then returns to a location 6 miles from home. Choices (B), (C), (D), and (E) are incorrect. In each of these situations, Janet is at home during some part of the time period. For Janet to be at home, Janet's distance from home would have to be 0.

21. Choice (B) is the correct answer. There are 8 possible digits for the first digit, x, of the area code, 2 possible digits for y, and 10 possible digits for z. Therefore, the number of possible area codes would be $8 \cdot 2 \cdot 10 = 160$. Choice (E) is incorrect. It results from adding $8 + 2 + 10$.

22. Choice (E) is the correct answer. Since $\overline{EF} \| \overline{DG} \| \overline{AC}$, triangles EBF and DBG are equilateral. Thus, $EF = DE = 2$ and $DG = 4$. The perimeter of the shaded region is $2 + 2 + 2 + 4 = 10$.

23. Choice (C) is the correct answer. Since the circles are congruent, in order for $\tan x°$ to equal $\tan y°$, the distances from the vertex of each angle to the point where the circle touches the number line must be equal. Thus, the circle at 10 must be moved 3 units to the right.

24. Choice (C) is the correct answer. Since the beam of light can be seen every 9 seconds, it takes 9 seconds for the beacon to completely rotate once. In 1 second, the beacon makes $\frac{1}{9}$ of a rotation. Since a full rotation is 360°, then $\frac{1}{9}$ of a rotation is 40°.

25. Choice (B) is the correct answer. Since $i^2 = -1$, $(i^2)^3 = -1$. In order for $(-1)^k$ to equal 1, k must be even. Thus, the least positive integer value of k is 2.

26. Choice (C) is the correct answer. In the figure, $\tan \theta = \frac{c}{10}$. Thus, $\tan 44° = \frac{c}{10}$ and $c = 10 \tan 44° \approx 9.66$. Choice (A) is incorrect. If you use $\sin 44° = \frac{c}{10}$ instead of $\tan 44° = \frac{c}{10}$, you will get $c \approx 6.94$. Choice (B) is incorrect. If you use $\cos 44° = \frac{c}{10}$ instead of $\tan 44° = \frac{c}{10}$, you will get $c \approx 7.19$. Choice (D) is incorrect. This is equal to $\frac{10}{\tan 44°}$ instead of $10 \tan 44°$. Choice (E) is incorrect. This is equal to $\frac{10}{\cos 44°}$ instead of $10 \tan 44°$.

27. Choice (D) is the correct answer. The thickness, in inches, of the concrete at a depth of 10 feet is equal to $t(10) = \frac{1}{12}(10^2 - 2 \cdot 10 + 6) = \frac{86}{12} \approx 7.167$. This is closest to 7.2.

28. Choice (C) is the correct answer. By applying the rules for exponents, each choice can be written as a power of 10. Choice (A) is incorrect, 10^{100}, is already written as a power of 10. Choice (B) is incorrect, 100^{10}, is equal to $(10^2)^{10} = 10^{20}$. Choice (C) is equal to $(10^{11})^{10} = 10^{110}$. Choice (D) is equal to $(10^2 \cdot 10)^{10} = (10^3)^{10} = 10^{30}$. Choice (E), 10,000,000,000 is equal to 10^{10}. Thus, the greatest value is $(10 \cdot 10^{10})^{10} = 10^{110}$.

29.

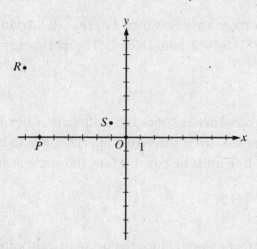

Choice (E) is the correct answer. It is helpful to draw a figure. From the figure, it is clear that $\overline{OS}$ is shorter than the other segments, so the answer cannot be choice (B) or choice (D).

$$OP = 6$$
$$OR = \sqrt{(-7)^2 + 5^2} = \sqrt{74}$$
$$RS = \sqrt{(-6)^2 + 4^2} = \sqrt{52}$$
$$PS = \sqrt{(-5)^2 + 1^2} = \sqrt{26}$$
$$PR = \sqrt{(-1)^2 + 5^2} = \sqrt{26}$$

$\overline{PS}$ and $\overline{PR}$ are the same length.

30. Choice (D) is the correct answer. Since the mean score for the 9 students was 86, the total of the scores of the 9 students was $9 \cdot 86 = 774$. The total of the scores for 4 of the students was $4 \cdot 81 = 324$. The total of the scores for the remaining 5 students was $774 - 324 = 450$. Thus, the average score for the remaining 5 students was $\frac{450}{5} = 90$.

31.

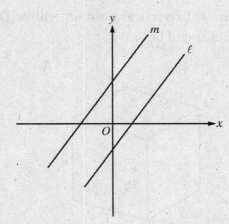

Choice (B) is the correct answer. It is helpful to draw a figure. The x-intercept of m must be negative and to the left of the x-intercept of ℓ.

32. Choice (A) is the correct answer. Since the figure is a rectangular solid, each of the faces is a rectangle. Thus, $\overline{AB}$ is parallel to $\overline{EF}$, and $\overline{EF}$ is parallel to $\overline{GH}$. It follows that $\overline{AB}$ is parallel to $\overline{GH}$, and so $\overline{AB}$ and $\overline{GH}$ lie in the same plane, which is the plane determined by points G, H, and B. Therefore, A is in the same plane as G, H, and B.

33. Choice (B) is the correct answer. One way to do this problem is to think about the properties of roots. Suppose the two roots of a quadratic equation are a and b. Then the quadratic equation can be written in factored form as $(x-a)(x-b)=0$. The sum of the roots is $a+b$, and the product is ab. Note that $(x-a)(x-b)=x^2-(a+b)x+ab$. In this question the sum of the roots is 5 and the product is -6. Therefore, $(a+b)=5$ and $ab=-6$. The equation could be $x^2-5x-6=0$. Note that the roots of this equation are 6 and -1. Their sum is 5 and their product is -6.

34. Choice (A) is the correct answer. Since $\triangle ABC$ is similar to $\triangle DEC$, $\dfrac{AB}{DE}=\dfrac{BC}{EC}$. Thus, $\dfrac{2}{w}=\dfrac{x}{y}$. Since $w=5$, $\dfrac{x}{y}=\dfrac{2}{5}$.

35. Choice (E) is the correct answer. By the Pythagorean identity, $\sin^2\theta+\cos^2\theta=1$. Therefore, $(\sin^2\theta+\cos^2\theta-3)^4=(1-3)^4=(-2)^4=16$.

36. Choice (E) is the correct answer. Point A is located 8 units to the left of line ℓ. Thus, when $\triangle ABC$ is reflected across line ℓ, the image of A will have a horizontal position

8 units to the right of line ℓ. Its vertical position will be the same as A. Thus, the coordinates of the image of A will be (13, 1).

37.

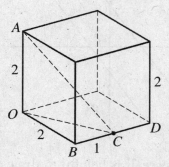

Choice (C) is the correct answer. In the figure, since the cube has edge of length 2, $AO = OB = 2$. Since C is the midpoint of edge BD, $BC = 1$. Using the Pythagorean theorem,

$$(OB)^2 + (BC)^2 = (OC)^2$$
$$4 + 1 = (OC)^2 \text{ and } OC = \sqrt{5}.$$

Using the Pythagorean theorem again,

$$(AO)^2 + (OC)^2 = (AC)^2$$
$$4 + 5 = (AC)^2 \text{ and } AC = \sqrt{9} = 3.$$

The distance from A to C is 3.

38.

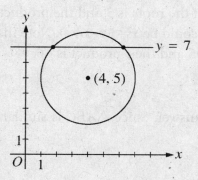

Choice (D) is the correct answer. It is helpful to draw a figure. The line $y = 7$ intersects the circle in 2 points. These 2 points and the center of the circle form a triangle with two sides of length 3, since the radius of the circle is 3. The triangle has height 2, since the distance between the point (4, 5) and the line $y = 7$ is the distance between (4, 5) and (4, 7).

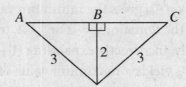

Using the Pythagorean theorem, you can find that $AB = \sqrt{5}$. The x-coordinate of point B is 4. Therefore, the x-coordinates of the points of intersection are $4 - \sqrt{5}$ and $4 + \sqrt{5}$ or 1.76 and 6.24. You could also solve the problem algebraically. The equation for a circle with center (4, 5) and radius 3 is $(x - 4)^2 + (y - 5)^2 = 9$. Substitute $y = 7$ into the equation, and it simplifies to $(x - 4)^2 = 5$. Solving for x produces the two x-coordinates of the points of intersection of the circle and the line.

39. Choice (D) is the correct answer. The sum of the degree measures of the angles of a quadrilateral is 360°. Since the sum of q and s is between 60 and 160, the sum of t and r must be between $(360 - 60)$ and $(360 - 160)$. Thus, $200 < t + r < 300$.

40. Choice (E) is the correct answer. Let P_0 represent the population of the town at the end of 1990. $P_0 = 6,250$. The population grows exponentially at the rate of 3.5% each year. The population of the town at the end of 15 years is given by $P_0(1.035)^{15} = 6,250(1.035)^{15} = 10,470.9 \approx 10,470$.

41.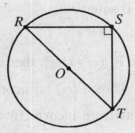

Choice (C) is the correct answer. Let O be the center of the circle. If O lies on $\overline{RT}$, then $\overline{RT}$ must be a diameter of the circle. Since $\angle RST$ is inscribed in the semicircle, $\triangle RST$ must be right.

42. Choice (B) is the correct answer. Since $(1 + x)^2$ is a perfect square, the minimum value of the function is 0, which occurs when $x = -1$. The maximum value of f occurs when $x = 2$ and $f(2) = 9$. Thus, the range is $0 \le f(x) \le 9$. You can also graph the function and see what values the function takes on for the given domain. The graph is a parabola that opens upward and has a vertex at $(-1, 0)$. Choices (A), (C), (D), and (E) are incorrect and arise from several errors. Making the assumption that the left

endpoint of the domain, $x = -2$, gives the minimum value for the range, yields $f(x) = 1$. Squaring an endpoint of the domain, $x = -2$ or $x = 2$, to give a maximum value for the range yields $f(x) = 4$. Lastly, incorrectly expanding $(1 + x)^2$ and getting $1 + x^2$, and then substituting $x = -2$ or $x = 2$ yields a maximum value of 5 for the range of f.

43. Choice (E) is the correct answer. Since the radius of the base is 3, $AP = PB = 3$ and $AB = 6$. Since the height of the cylinder is 5, $OP = 5$. Using the Pythagorean theorem, $(OP)^2 + (PB)^2 = (OB)^2$. $25 + 9 = (OB)^2$ and $OB = \sqrt{34} \approx 5.831$. Since $OA = OB$, the perimeter of the triangle is $OA + OB + AB = 2\sqrt{34} + 6 \approx 17.66$.

44. Choice (E) is the correct answer. The first arrangement has 2 squares. The second arrangement has 6 squares. The third arrangement has 12 squares. The fourth arrangement would add a row of 8 squares, giving a total of $12 + 8 = 20$ squares. Notice the pattern.

n	Number of Squares
1	$1 \cdot 2 = 2$
2	$2 \cdot 3 = 6$
3	$3 \cdot 4 = 12$
4	$4 \cdot 5 = 20$

The nth arrangement has $n(n + 1)$ squares.

45. Choice (B) is the correct answer. If $f(x) = x^3 + 1$, then $x = \left(f^{-1}(x)\right)^3 + 1$ and $f^{-1}(x) = \sqrt[3]{x - 1}$. Thus, $f^{-1}(4) = \sqrt[3]{4 - 1} = \sqrt[3]{3} \approx 1.44$. Choice (A) is incorrect. $f^{-1}(x)$ is not equal to $\frac{1}{f(x)}$. Choice (C) is incorrect. It results from incorrectly taking the sum of 4 and 1 first and then evaluating the cube root of this sum: $\sqrt[3]{4 + 1} \approx 1.71$. Choice (D) is incorrect. It results from taking the cube of the difference of 4 and 1 instead of the cube root: $(4 - 1)^3 = 27$. Choice (E) is incorrect. It results from $f(4) = 4^3 + 1 = 65$.

46. Choice (D) is the correct answer. Since mRn, then $m = n^2 + 1$. Since nRp, then $n = p^2 + 1$. Thus, $m = n^2 + 1 = (p^2 + 1)^2 + 1$.

47. Choice (A) is the correct answer. Since the measure of $\angle D$ is 150° and $ABCD$ is a parallelogram, the measure of $\angle A$ is 30°. The area of the parallelogram can be found

by $ab \sin A$, where A is the angle included between sides of length a and b. Thus, the area is equal to $(4)(6) \sin 30° = 24 \cdot \dfrac{1}{2} = 12$. Choice (D) is incorrect. It is equal to $ab \cos A$ instead of $ab \sin A$: $4 \cdot 6 \cdot \cos 30° = 24 \cdot \dfrac{\sqrt{3}}{2} = 12\sqrt{3}$. Choice (E) is incorrect. It results from simply multiplying 4 by 6 to get 24, but 4 is not the height of the parallelogram.

48. Choice (D) is the correct answer. Since the graph of $y = f(x-2)$ can be obtained from the graph of $y = f(x)$ by shifting the graph of $y = f(x)$ 2 units to the right, the shaded region will only be moved 2 units to the right. Therefore, there is no change in the shape or size of the shaded region. Thus, the area remains equal to 3.

49. Choice (E) is the correct answer. The first step is to determine the area of the garden. Since the circumference is 20 feet, the radius is $\dfrac{20}{2\pi} = \dfrac{10}{\pi}$ and the area is πr^2 or $\pi\left(\dfrac{10}{\pi}\right)^2 = \dfrac{100}{\pi}$ square feet. If there are 4 marigolds per square foot, $4 \cdot \dfrac{100}{\pi}$ marigolds are needed. To find out how many packs of 6 flowers are needed, divide $\dfrac{400}{\pi}$ by 6. The result is 21.22; thus, 22 packs would be needed. Choice (C) is incorrect. It results from using the circumference, 20, instead of the area, to determine the number of marigolds needed and getting $4 \cdot 20 = 80$. Since $80 \div 6 \approx 13.33$, 14 packs would be needed.

50. Choice (D) is the correct answer. Let x be the number of liters of concentrate added to the water. You can set up the proportion $\dfrac{x}{2+x} = \dfrac{32}{100}$.

$$100x = 64 + 32x$$
$$68x = 64$$
$$x = \frac{64}{68}$$
$$\approx 0.941$$

Mathematics Level 2

Sample Questions

All questions in the Mathematics Level 2 Test are multiple-choice questions in which you are asked to choose the BEST response from the five choices offered. The directions that follow are the same as those in the Mathematics Level 2 test.

Directions: For each of the following problems, decide which is the BEST of the choices given. If the exact numerical value is not one of the choices, select the choice that best approximates this value. Then fill in the corresponding circle on the answer sheet.

Notes: (1) A scientific or graphing calculator will be necessary for answering some (but not all) of the questions in this test. For each question you will have to decide whether or not you should use a calculator.

(2) For some questions on this test you may have to decide whether your calculator should be in the radian mode or in the degree mode.

(3) Figures that accompany problems in this test are intended to provide information useful in solving the problems. They are drawn as accurately as possible EXCEPT when it is stated in a specific problem that its figure is not drawn to scale. All figures lie in a plane unless otherwise indicated.

(4) Unless otherwise specified, the domain of any function f is assumed to be the set of all real numbers x for which $f(x)$ is a real number. The range of f is assumed to be the set of all real numbers $f(x)$, where x is in the domain of f.

(5) Reference information that may be useful in answering the questions in this test can be found on the following page.

Reference Information: The following information is for your reference in answering some of the questions in this test.

Volume of a right circular cone with radius r and height h: $V = \frac{1}{3}\pi r^2 h$

Volume of a sphere with radius r: $V = \frac{4}{3}\pi r^3$

Volume of a pyramid with base area B and height h: $V = \frac{1}{3}Bh$

Surface Area of a sphere with radius r: $S = 4\pi r^2$

Number and Operations

1. From a group of 6 juniors and 8 seniors on the student council, 2 juniors and 4 seniors will be chosen to make up a 6-person committee. How many different 6-person committees are possible?

   (A) 84
   (B) 85
   (C) 1,050
   (D) 1,710
   (E) 1,890

   Choice (C) is the correct answer. The 2 juniors on the committee can be chosen from the 6 juniors in $\binom{6}{2} = 15$ ways. The 4 seniors on the committee can be chosen from the 8 seniors in $\binom{8}{4} = 70$ ways. Therefore, there are $(15)(70) = 1,050$ possibilities for the 6-person committee.

Algebra and Functions

$$\text{If } x^4 < |x^3|, \text{ then } 0 < x < 1.$$

2. Which of the following values for x is a counterexample to the statement above?

(A) $-\dfrac{4}{3}$

(B) $-\dfrac{1}{2}$

(C) 0

(D) $\dfrac{1}{2}$

(E) 1

Choice (B) is the correct answer. A counterexample to the given statement would be a number x such that the hypothesis $x^4 < |x^3|$ is true, but the conclusion $0 < x < 1$ does not hold. Choice (B), $-\dfrac{1}{2}$, is a counterexample. It is true that $\left(-\dfrac{1}{2}\right)^4 < \left|\left(-\dfrac{1}{2}\right)^3\right|$, since $\dfrac{1}{16} < \dfrac{1}{8}$; but it is not true that $-\dfrac{1}{2}$ lies between 0 and 1. Choice (D) is incorrect. It is true that $\left(\dfrac{1}{2}\right)^4 < \left|\left(\dfrac{1}{2}\right)^3\right|$, but the conclusion $0 < \dfrac{1}{2} < 1$ is also true, so $x = \dfrac{1}{2}$ is not a counterexample. Choices (A), (C), and (E) are incorrect. None of these values of x satisfies the hypothesis $x^4 < |x^3|$.

3. If $\ln(x) = 1.25$, then $\ln(3x) =$

(A) 1.10

(B) 1.37

(C) 1.73

(D) 2.35

(E) 3.75

Choice (D) is the correct answer. By the properties of logarithms, $\ln(3x) = \ln(3) + \ln(x) \approx 1.10 + 1.25 = 2.35$.

4. During a thunderstorm, the distance between a person and the storm varies directly as the time interval between the person seeing a flash of lightning and hearing the sound of thunder. When a storm is 4,000 feet away, the time interval between the person seeing the lightning flash and hearing the sound of the thunder is 3.7 seconds. How far away from the person is the storm when this time interval is 5 seconds?

(A)   2,960 ft

(B)   4,650 ft

(C)   5,405 ft

(D)   6,284 ft

(E)   7,304 ft

Choice (C) is the correct answer. Since the person's distance from the storm varies directly with the time interval between the flash of lightning and the sound of thunder, the distance can be written as $d = kt$, where d is the distance in feet, t is the time in seconds, and k is a constant. This distance is 4,000 feet when the time interval is 3.7 seconds; therefore, $4,000 = k(3.7)$, and $k = \frac{4,000}{3.7}$. Thus, when the interval between the lightning flash and the sound of the thunder is 5 seconds, the storm is $\frac{4,000}{3.7}(5) \approx 5,405$ feet away.

5. If $x = \frac{3}{2}$ is a solution to the equation $5(4x - k)(x - 1) = 0$, what is the value of k ?

(A) $\frac{2}{3}$

(B)   1

(C)   4

(D)   5

(E)   6

Choice (E) is the correct answer. The expression $5(4x - k)(x - 1)$ is equal to 0 if and only if $x = 1$ or $4x = k$. If $x = \frac{3}{2}$, it cannot be true that $x = 1$. Thus, if $x = \frac{3}{2}$ is a solution to the equation, it must be true that $4x = k$. It follows that $(4)\left(\frac{3}{2}\right) = 6 = k$.

6.
$$p(t) = 110 + 20\sin(160\pi t)$$

A certain person's blood pressure $p(t)$, in millimeters of mercury, is modeled above as a function of time, t, in minutes. According to the model, how many times in the interval $0 \le t \le 1$ does the person's blood pressure reach its maximum of 130?

(A)   60

(B)   80

(C)   100

(D)   110

(E)   130

Choice (B) is the correct answer. The maximum of 130 millimeters is achieved exactly when $\sin(160\pi t) = 1$. The sine function has a value of 1 exactly for arguments $\frac{\pi}{2} + 2n\pi$, where n is any integer. Over the interval $0 \le t \le 1$, the argument of $\sin(160\pi t)$ ranges from 0 to 160π. Thus, over the interval in question, $\sin(160\pi t) = 1$, and $p(t) = 110 + 20\sin(160\pi) = 130$, for $160\pi t = \frac{\pi}{2}, \frac{5\pi}{2}, \frac{9\pi}{2}, \cdots, \frac{317\pi}{2}$. Thus, the maximum blood pressure is reached exactly 80 times in the interval. You can also use the period of p to answer the question. The period of p is $\frac{2\pi}{|160\pi|} = \frac{1}{80}$. This means that the graph of p has one complete cycle every $\frac{1}{80}$. On the interval $0 \le t \le 1$, p has 80 complete cycles.

7.

x	$f(x)$
−3	87
0	−15
1	15
3	171
5	455

The table above gives selected values for the function f. Which of the following could be the definition of f?

(A) $f(x) = 30x - 15$

(B) $f(x) = 30x + 15$

(C) $f(x) = 30x^2 + 15$

(D) $f(x) = 16x^2 - 14x + 15$

(E) $f(x) = 16x^2 + 14x - 15$

Choice (E) is the correct answer. The function in choice (A) takes on the correct values at $x = 0$ and $x = 1$, but the value at $x = 3$ is 75, not 171, so choice (A) cannot be correct. The function in choice (B) does not take on the correct value at $x = 1$, so choice (B) cannot be correct. (Another way to eliminate choices (A) and (B) is to note that $f(x)$ decreases and then increases, so that f cannot be linear.) The function in choice (C) takes on only positive values, so choice (C) cannot be correct. The function in choice (D) does not take on the correct value at $x = 0$, so choice (D) cannot be correct. The values of the function in choice (E) do agree with all the values in the table, so this could be the definition of the function. You can also find a quadratic regression for the values using the graphing calculator, which is $y = 16x^2 + 14x - 15$.

8. If $f(x) = \dfrac{1}{x-5}$ and $g(x) = \sqrt{x+4}$, what is the domain of $f - g$?

    (A)   All x such that $x \neq 5$ and $x \leq 4$

    (B)   All x such that $x \neq -5$ and $x \leq 4$

    (C)   All x such that $x \neq 5$ and $x \geq -4$

    (D)   All x such that $x \neq -4$ and $x \geq -5$

    (E)   All real numbers x

Choice (C) is the correct answer. The function $f - g$ will be defined at exactly those points where f and g are both defined. In other words, the domain of $f - g$ is the intersection of the domain of f and the domain of g. Since $f(x) = \dfrac{1}{x-5}$ is defined for all $x \neq 5$ and $g(x) = \sqrt{x+4}$ is defined for all $x \geq -4$, the domain of $f - g$ is all x such that $x \neq 5$ and $x \geq -4$. You can also examine the graph of $f - g$. The graph is defined for all real numbers $x \geq -4$ except for $x = 5$, where the graph has a vertical asymptote.

9. A sum of $10,000 is invested at a rate of 10 percent, with interest compounded semiannually. The value, in dollars, of this investment after t years is given by $V(t) = 10{,}000(1.05)^{2t}$. Approximately how much greater is the value of this investment at the end of 2 years than the same amount invested at the rate of 10 percent compounded annually?

    (A) $55

    (B) $200

    (C) $500

    (D) $1,075

    (E) $1,155

Choice (A) is the correct answer. Applying the given function with $t=2$ shows that the value of the investment compounded semiannually after 2 years would be approximately \$12,155. If \$10,000 were invested at 10 percent interest compounded annually, then at the end of 2 years the value of this investment would be $\$10,000(1.10)^2 = \$12,100$. Thus, difference in the amounts of the investments is approximately $\$12,155 - \$12,100 = \$55$.

10. For which of the following functions does $f(x,y) = -f(-x,-y)$ for all values of x and y ?
    (A) $f(x,y) = x + y^2$
    (B) $f(x,y) = x - y^2$
    (C) $f(x,y) = x^2 - y$
    (D) $f(x,y) = x + y^3$
    (E) $f(x,y) = x - y^4$

Choice (D) is the correct answer. If $f(x,y)$ is a polynomial in x and y, then $f(x,y) = -f(-x,-y)$ if and only if every nonzero term of f is of odd degree. Of the given choices, this is true only for $f(x,y) = x + y^3$. In this case, $f(-x,-y) = (-x) + (-y)^3 = -x - y^3 = -(x + y^3) = -f(x,y)$. So, $f(x,y) = -f(-x,-y)$.

Geometry and Measurement: Coordinate Geometry

11. Which of the following describes the set of points (a,b) for which $|a| + |b| = 5$ in the xy-plane?
    (A) A circle with radius 5
    (B) A circle with radius $5\sqrt{2}$
    (C) A square with sides of length $5\sqrt{2}$
    (D) A square with sides of length 10
    (E) A regular hexagon with sides of length 5

If $|a| + |b| = 5$, consider the four cases:

$a>0$, $b>0$: $a+b=5$ so $b=5-a$ is a line with slope –1 and y-intercept 5

$a>0$, $b<0$: $a-b=5$ so $b=-5+a$ is a line with slope 1 and y-intercept –5

$a<0$, $b>0$: $-a+b=5$ so $b=5+a$ is a line with slope 1 and y-intercept 5

$a<0$, $b<0$: $-a-b=5$ so $b=-5-a$ is a line with slope –1 and y-intercept –5

Sketch the graphs of the 4 lines. The 4 lines intersect to form a square with vertices on the coordinate axes located 5 units from the origin.

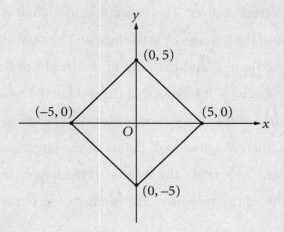

Choice (C) is the correct answer. As shown in the figure above, the set of points (a, b) for which $|a| + |b| = 5$ is the square with vertices $(0, 5)$, $(5, 0)$, $(0, -5)$, and $(-5, 0)$. By the Pythagorean theorem, the sides of this square are of length $5\sqrt{2}$.

Geometry and Measurement: Three-Dimensional Geometry

12.

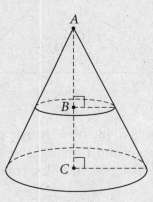

In the figure above, points B and C are the centers of the bases of two right circular cones, each with vertex A. If $AB = 1$ and $AC = 2$, what is the ratio of the volume of the smaller cone to the volume of the larger cone?

(A) $\dfrac{1}{8}$

(B) $\dfrac{1}{4}$

(C) $\dfrac{3}{8}$

(D) $\dfrac{1}{2}$

(E) It cannot be determined from the information given.

Choice (A) is the correct answer. The volume V of a cone is given by $V = \frac{1}{3}\pi r^2 h$, where r is the radius of the base and h is the height. The smaller cone and larger cone are similar geometric figures, and the ratio of the height of the smaller cone to the height of the larger cone is $\frac{1}{2}$. It follows that the ratio of the base radius of the smaller cone to the base radius of the larger cone is also $\frac{1}{2}$. Therefore, if r is the base radius of the smaller cone, then $2r$ is the base radius of the larger cone. Thus, the volume of the smaller cone is $V = \frac{1}{3}\pi r^2 (1)$, the volume of the larger cone is $V = \frac{1}{3}\pi (2r)^2 (2) = \frac{8}{3}\pi r^2$. Thus, the ratio of the volume of the smaller cone to the volume of the larger cone is $\dfrac{\frac{1}{3}}{\frac{8}{3}} = \frac{1}{8}$.

Geometry and Measurement: Trigonometry

13.

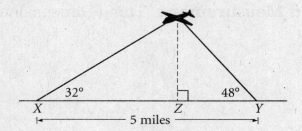

The airplane in the figure above is flying directly over point Z on a straight, level road. The angles of elevation for points X and Y are 32° and 48°, respectively. If points X and Y are 5 miles apart, what is the distance, in miles, from the airplane to point X?

(A) 1.60

(B) 2.40

(C) 2.69

(D) 3.77

(E) 7.01

Choice (D) is the correct answer. Label the location of the airplane as point W. Then in $\triangle XYW$, the measure of $\angle X$ is 32°, the measure of $\angle Y$ is 48°, and the measure of $\angle W$ is 100°. Let x, y, and w denote the lengths, in miles, of the sides of $\triangle XYW$ opposite $\angle X$, $\angle Y$, and $\angle W$, respectively. Then by the law of sines, $\dfrac{x}{\sin X} = \dfrac{y}{\sin Y} = \dfrac{w}{\sin W}$. Since $w = 5$ and the distance from the plane to point X is y, it follows that $\dfrac{5}{\sin 100°} = \dfrac{y}{\sin 48°}$. This gives $y \approx 3.77$ for the distance, in miles, from the plane to point X.

14. If $\cos\theta = \dfrac{x}{3}$, where $0 < \theta < \dfrac{\pi}{2}$ and $0 < x < 3$, then $\sin\theta =$

(A) $\dfrac{\sqrt{9-x^2}}{3}$

(B) $\dfrac{\sqrt{x^2-9}}{x}$

(C) $\dfrac{\sqrt{9-x^2}}{x}$

(D) $\dfrac{\sqrt{3-x^2}}{3}$

(E) $\dfrac{\sqrt{3-x^2}}{x}$

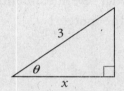

Choice (A) is the correct answer. Since $\cos\theta = \dfrac{x}{3}$, $0 < \theta < \dfrac{\pi}{2}$, and $0 < x < 3$, the figure above can be drawn. By the Pythagorean theorem, the other leg of the right triangle is $\sqrt{9-x^2}$. Thus, $\sin\theta = \dfrac{\sqrt{9-x^2}}{3}$. Alternatively, since $\sin^2\theta + \cos^2\theta = 1$,

$$\sin^2\theta = 1 - \cos^2\theta$$
$$= 1 - \left(\dfrac{x}{3}\right)^2$$
$$= \dfrac{9-x^2}{9}$$
$$\sin\theta = \dfrac{\sqrt{9-x^2}}{3}$$

since $0 < \theta < \dfrac{\pi}{2}$ and $0 < x < 3$.

Data Analysis, Statistics, and Probability

15.

Revenue for Company X	
Years after merger	Revenue (in billions of dollars)
0	$3
2	$4
4	$11
7	$25

Two companies merged to form Company X, whose revenues are shown in the table above for selected years after the merger. If a least-squares exponential regression is used to model the data above, what revenue, in billions of dollars, would be predicted for the company 13 years after the merger?

(A) $31

(B) $43

(C) $109

(D) $172

(E) $208

Choice (D) is the correct answer. A graphing calculator can be used to find the least-squares exponential regression for the data $(0, 3)$, $(2, 4)$, $(4, 11)$, and $(7, 25)$. This gives a function of the form $y = ab^x$, where $a \approx 2.678$ and $b \approx 1.377$. The exponential regression is $y = (2.678)(1.377)^x$. Evaluating this function at $t = 13$, without rounding the values of a and b, gives approximately 172. Thus, the revenue predicted is $172 billion.

Mathematics Level 2 – Practice Test 1

Practice Helps

The test that follows is an actual, previously administered SAT Subject Test in Mathematics Level 2. To get an idea of what it's like to take this test, practice under conditions that are much like those of an actual test administration.

- Set aside an hour when you can take the test uninterrupted.

- Sit at a desk or table with no other books or papers. Dictionaries, other books, or notes are not allowed in the test room.

- Remember to have a scientific or graphing calculator with you.

- Tear out an answer sheet from the back of this book and fill it in just as you would on the day of the test. One answer sheet can be used for up to three Subject Tests.

- Read the instructions that precede the practice test. During the actual administration you will be asked to read them before answering test questions.

- Use a clock or kitchen timer to time yourself.

- After you finish the practice test, read the sections "How to Score the SAT Subject Test in Mathematics Level 2" and "How Did You Do on the Subject Test in Mathematics Level 2?"

- The appearance of the answer sheet in this book may differ from the answer sheet you see on test day.

- The Reference Information at the start of the practice test is slightly different from what appeared on the original test. It has been modified to reflect the language included on tests administered at the time of this book's printing. These changes are minor and will not affect how you answer the questions.

MATHEMATICS LEVEL 2 TEST

The top portion of the page of the answer sheet that you will use to take the Mathematics Level 2 Test must be filled in exactly as illustrated below. When your supervisor tells you to fill in the circle next to the name of the test you are about to take, mark your answer sheet as shown.

○ Literature	○ Mathematics Level 1	○ German	○ Chinese Listening	○ Japanese Listening
○ Biology E	● Mathematics Level 2	○ Italian	○ French Listening	○ Korean Listening
○ Biology M	○ U.S. History	○ Latin	○ German Listening	○ Spanish Listening
○ Chemistry	○ World History	○ Modern Hebrew		
○ Physics	○ French	○ Spanish	**Background Questions:** ① ② ③ ④ ⑤ ⑥ ⑦ ⑧ ⑨	

After filling in the circle next to the name of the test you are taking, locate the Background Questions section, which also appears at the top of your answer sheet (as shown above). This is where you will answer the following Background Questions on your answer sheet.

BACKGROUND QUESTIONS

Please answer Part I and Part II below by filling in the appropriate circle in the Background Questions box on your answer sheet. <u>The information you provide is for statistical purposes only and will not affect your test score.</u>

<u>Part I.</u>   Which of the following describes a mathematics course you have taken or are currently taking? (FILL IN **ALL** CIRCLES THAT APPLY.)

- Algebra I or Elementary Algebra **OR** Course I of a college preparatory mathematics sequence   —Fill in circle 1.

- Geometry **OR** Course II of a college preparatory mathematics sequence   —Fill in circle 2.

- Algebra II or Intermediate Algebra **OR** Course III of a college preparatory mathematics sequence   —Fill in circle 3.

- Elementary Functions (Precalculus) and/or Trigonometry **OR** beyond Course III of a college
  preparatory mathematics sequence   —Fill in circle 4.

- Advanced Placement Mathematics (Calculus AB or Calculus BC)   —Fill in circle 5.

<u>Part II.</u>   What type of calculator did you bring to use for this test? (FILL IN THE **ONE** CIRCLE THAT APPLIES. If you did not bring a scientific or graphing calculator, do not fill in any of circles 6-9.)

- Scientific   —Fill in circle 6.

- Graphing (Fill in the circle corresponding to the model you used.)

    Casio 9700, Casio 9750, Casio 9800, Casio 9850, Casio 9860, Casio FX 1.0, Casio CG-10, Sharp 9200,
    Sharp 9300, Sharp 9600, Sharp 9900, TI-82, TI-83, TI-83 Plus, TI-83 Plus Silver, TI-84 Plus,
    TI-84 Plus Silver, TI-85, TI-86, or TI-Nspire   —Fill in circle 7.

    Casio 9970, Casio Algebra FX 2.0, HP 38G, HP 39 series, HP 40 series, HP 48 series, HP 49 series,
    HP 50 series, TI-89, TI-89 Titanium, or TI-Nspire CAS   —Fill in circle 8.

    Some other graphing calculator   —Fill in circle 9.

When the supervisor gives the signal, turn the page and begin the Mathematics Level 2 Test. There are 100 numbered circles on the answer sheet and 50 questions in the Mathematics Level 2 Test. Therefore, use only circles 1 to 50 for recording your answers.

MATHEMATICS LEVEL 2 TEST

REFERENCE INFORMATION

THE FOLLOWING INFORMATION IS FOR YOUR REFERENCE IN ANSWERING SOME OF THE QUESTIONS IN THIS TEST.

Volume of a right circular cone with radius r and height h: $V = \dfrac{1}{3}\pi r^2 h$

Volume of a sphere with radius r: $V = \dfrac{4}{3}\pi r^3$

Volume of a pyramid with base area B and height h: $V = \dfrac{1}{3}Bh$

Surface Area of a sphere with radius r: $S = 4\pi r^2$

DO NOT DETACH FROM BOOK.

GO ON TO THE NEXT PAGE

MATHEMATICS LEVEL 2 TEST

For each of the following problems, decide which is the BEST of the choices given. If the exact numerical value is not one of the choices, select the choice that best approximates this value. Then fill in the corresponding circle on the answer sheet.

<u>Notes:</u> (1) A scientific or graphing calculator will be necessary for answering some (but not all) of the questions in this test. For each question you will have to decide whether or not you should use a calculator.

(2) For some questions in this test you may have to decide whether your calculator should be in the radian mode or the degree mode.

(3) Figures that accompany problems in this test are intended to provide information useful in solving the problems. They are drawn as accurately as possible EXCEPT when it is stated in a specific problem that its figure is not drawn to scale. All figures lie in a plane unless otherwise indicated.

(4) Unless otherwise specified, the domain of any function f is assumed to be the set of all real numbers x for which $f(x)$ is a real number. The range of f is assumed to be the set of all real numbers $f(x)$, where x is in the domain of f.

(5) Reference information that may be useful in answering the questions in this test can be found on the page preceding Question 1.

USE THIS SPACE FOR SCRATCHWORK.

1. If $3x + 6 = \dfrac{k}{4}(x + 2)$ for all x, then $k =$

(A) $\dfrac{1}{4}$ (B) 3   (C) 4   (D) 12   (E) 24

GO ON TO THE NEXT PAGE

MATHEMATICS LEVEL 2 TEST—*Continued*

USE THIS SPACE FOR SCRATCHWORK.

2. The relationship between a reading C on the Celsius temperature scale and a reading F on the Fahrenheit temperature scale is $C = \dfrac{5}{9}(F - 32)$, and the relationship between a reading on the Celsius temperature scale and a reading K on the Kelvin temperature scale is $K = C + 273$. Which of the following expresses the relationship between readings on the Kelvin and Fahrenheit temperature scales?

(A) $K = \dfrac{5}{9}(F - 241)$

(B) $K = \dfrac{5}{9}(F + 305)$

(C) $K = \dfrac{5}{9}(F - 32) + 273$

(D) $K = \dfrac{5}{9}(F - 32) - 273$

(E) $K = \dfrac{5}{9}(F + 32) + 273$

3. What is the slope of the line containing the points $(3, 11)$ and $(-2, 5)$?

(A) 0.17
(B) 0.83
(C) 1.14
(D) 1.20
(E) 6

4. If $x + y = 2$, $y + z = 5$, and $x + y + z = 10$, then $y =$

(A) -3

(B) $\dfrac{3}{17}$

(C) 1

(D) 3

(E) $\dfrac{17}{3}$

GO ON TO THE NEXT PAGE

MATHEMATICS LEVEL 2 TEST—*Continued*

USE THIS SPACE FOR SCRATCHWORK.

5. If $f(x) = 3\ln(x) - 1$ and $g(x) = e^x$,
    then $f(g(5)) =$

    (A)   6.83
    (B)   12
    (C)   14
    (D)   45.98
    (E)   568.17

6. The intersection of a cube with a plane could
    be which of the following?

    I. A square
    II. A parallelogram
    III. A triangle

    (A) I only
    (B) II only
    (C) III only
    (D) I and III only
    (E) I, II, and III

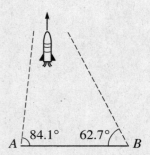

7. The figure above shows a rocket taking off
    vertically. When the rocket reaches a height of
    12 kilometers, the angles of elevation from points
    A and B on level ground are 84.1° and 62.7°,
    respectively. What is the distance between
    points A and B ?

    (A)   0.97 km
    (B)   6.36 km
    (C)   7.43 km
    (D)   22.60 km
    (E)   139.37 km

GO ON TO THE NEXT PAGE

MATHEMATICS LEVEL 2 TEST—*Continued*

8. What is the value of x^2 if $x = \sqrt{15^2 - 12^2}$?

   (A) $\sqrt{3}$ (B) 3   (C) 9   (D) 81   (E) 81^2

9. The points in the rectangular coordinate plane are transformed in such a way that each point $P(x, y)$ is moved to the point $P'(2x, 2y)$. If the distance between a point P and the origin is d, then the distance between the point P' and the origin is

   (A) $\dfrac{1}{d}$

   (B) $\dfrac{d}{2}$

   (C) d

   (D) $2d$

   (E) d^2

10. If $f\big(g(x)\big) = \dfrac{2\sqrt{x^2 + 1} - 1}{\sqrt{x^2 + 1} + 1}$ and $f(x) = \dfrac{2x - 1}{x + 1}$,

   then $g(x) =$

   (A) $\sqrt{x}$

   (B) $\sqrt{x^2 + 1}$

   (C) x

   (D) x^2

   (E) $x^2 + 1$

GO ON TO THE NEXT PAGE

MATHEMATICS LEVEL 2 TEST—*Continued*

USE THIS SPACE FOR SCRATCHWORK.

11. If A is the degree measure of an acute angle and $\sin A = 0.8$, then $\cos(90° - A) =$

(A) 0.2
(B) 0.4
(C) 0.5
(D) 0.6
(E) 0.8

12. The set of points (x, y, z) such that $x^2 + y^2 + z^2 = 1$ is

(A) empty
(B) a point
(C) a sphere
(D) a circle
(E) a plane

13. The graph of the rational function f, where $f(x) = \dfrac{5}{x^2 - 8x + 16}$, has a vertical asymptote at $x =$

(A) 0 only
(B) 4 only
(C) 5 only
(D) 0 and 4 only
(E) 0, 4, and 5

GO ON TO THE NEXT PAGE

MATHEMATICS LEVEL 2 TEST—*Continued*

USE THIS SPACE FOR SCRATCHWORK.

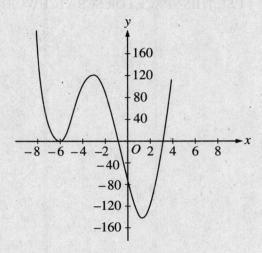

14. The graph of $y = x^4 + 10x^3 + 10x^2 - 96x + c$
is shown above. Which of the following could be
the value of c ?

(A)   3,240
(B)   1,080
(C)   72
(D)   −72
(E) −3,240

15. If $\cos x = 0.4697$, then $\sec x =$

(A) 2.1290
(B) 2.0452
(C) 1.0818
(D) 0.9243
(E) 0.4890

GO ON TO THE NEXT PAGE

MATHEMATICS LEVEL 2 TEST—*Continued*

USE THIS SPACE FOR SCRATCHWORK.

16. A club is planning a trip to a museum that has an admission price of $7 per person. The club members going on the trip must share the $200 cost of a bus and the admission price for 2 chaperones who will accompany them on the trip. Which of the following correctly expresses the cost, in dollars, for each club member as a function of n, the number of club members going on the trip?

(A) $c(n) = \dfrac{200 + 7n}{n}$

(B) $c(n) = \dfrac{214 + 7n}{n}$

(C) $c(n) = \dfrac{200 + 7n}{n + 2}$

(D) $c(n) = \dfrac{200 + 7n}{n - 2}$

(E) $c(n) = \dfrac{214 + 7n}{n - 2}$

17. Which of the following is an equation whose graph is the set of points equidistant from the points $(0, 0)$ and $(0, 4)$?

(A) $x = 2$
(B) $y = 2$
(C) $x = 2y$
(D) $y = 2x$
(E) $y = x + 2$

18. What is the sum of the infinite geometric series

$\dfrac{1}{4} + \dfrac{1}{8} + \dfrac{1}{16} + \dfrac{1}{32} + \ldots$?

(A) $\dfrac{1}{2}$ (B) 1   (C) $\dfrac{3}{2}$ (D) 2   (E) $\dfrac{5}{2}$

GO ON TO THE NEXT PAGE

MATHEMATICS LEVEL 2 TEST—*Continued*

USE THIS SPACE FOR SCRATCHWORK.

19. Which of the following is equivalent to
$p + s > p - s$?

(A) $p > s$
(B) $p > 0$
(C) $s > p$
(D) $s > 0$
(E) $s < 0$

20. If a and b are in the domain of a function f and $f(a) < f(b)$, which of the following must be true?

(A) $a = 0$ or $b = 0$
(B) $a < b$
(C) $a > b$
(D) $a \neq b$
(E) $a = b$

21. In a recent survey, it was reported that 75 percent of the population of a certain state lived within ten miles of its largest city and that 40 percent of those who lived within ten miles of the largest city lived in single-family houses. If a resident of this state is selected at random, what is the probability that the person lives in a single-family house within ten miles of the largest city?

(A) 0.10
(B) 0.15
(C) 0.30
(D) 0.35
(E) 0.53

22. To the nearest degree, what is the measure of the smallest angle in a right triangle with sides of lengths 3, 4, and 5 ?

(A) 27°
(B) 30°
(C) 37°
(D) 45°
(E) 53°

GO ON TO THE NEXT PAGE

MATHEMATICS LEVEL 2 TEST—*Continued*

23. Which of the following is an equation of a line perpendicular to $y = -2x + 3$?

    (A) $y = 3x - 2$

    (B) $y = 2x - 3$

    (C) $y = \frac{1}{2}x + 4$

    (D) $y = -\frac{1}{2}x + 3$

    (E) $y = \dfrac{1}{-2x + 3}$

24. What is the range of the function f, where $f(x) = -4 + 3\sin(2x + 5\pi)$?

    (A) $-7 \le f(x) \le 3$
    (B) $-7 \le f(x) \le -1$
    (C) $-3 \le f(x) \le 3$
    (D) $-3 \le f(x) \le -1$
    (E) $-1 \le f(x) \le 1$

25. Of the following lists of numbers, which has the smallest standard deviation?

    (A) 1, 5, 9
    (B) 3, 5, 8
    (C) 4, 5, 8
    (D) 7, 8, 9
    (E) 8, 8, 8

GO ON TO THE NEXT PAGE

MATHEMATICS LEVEL 2 TEST—*Continued*

USE THIS SPACE FOR SCRATCHWORK.

26. The formula $A = Pe^{0.08t}$ gives the amount A that a savings account will be worth after an initial investment P is compounded continuously at an annual rate of 8 percent for t years. Under these conditions, how many years will it take an initial investment of $1,000 to be worth approximately $5,000 ?

(A) 4.1
(B) 5.0
(C) 8.7
(D) 20.1
(E) 23.0

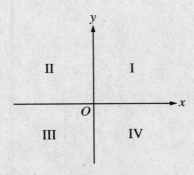

27. If $\sin \theta > 0$ and $\sin \theta \cos \theta < 0$, then θ must be in which quadrant in the figure above?

(A) I
(B) II
(C) III
(D) IV
(E) There is no quadrant in which both conditions are true.

GO ON TO THE NEXT PAGE

MATHEMATICS LEVEL 2 TEST—*Continued*

USE THIS SPACE FOR SCRATCHWORK.

28. If $f(-x) = f(x)$ for all real numbers x and if $(3, 8)$ is a point on the graph of f, which of the following points must also be on the graph of f ?

    (A) $(-8, -3)$
    (B) $(-3, -8)$
    (C) $(-3, 8)$
    (D) $(3, -8)$
    (E) $(8, 3)$

$$\text{If } x = y, \text{ then } x^2 = y^2.$$

29. If x and y are real numbers, which of the following CANNOT be inferred from the statement above?

    (A) In order for x^2 to be equal to y^2, it is sufficient that x be equal to y.
    (B) A necessary condition for x to be equal to y is that x^2 be equal to y^2.
    (C) x is equal to y implies that x^2 is equal to y^2.
    (D) If x^2 is not equal to y^2, then x is not equal to y.
    (E) If x^2 is equal to y^2, then x is equal to y.

30. In how many different orders can 9 students arrange themselves in a straight line?

    (A) 9
    (B) 81
    (C) 181,440
    (D) 362,880
    (E) 387,420,489

GO ON TO THE NEXT PAGE

USE THIS SPACE FOR SCRATCHWORK.

31. What value does $\dfrac{\ln x}{x - 1}$ approach as x approaches 1 ?

    (A) 0
    (B) 0.43
    (C) 1
    (D) 2
    (E) It does not approach a unique value.

32. If $f(x) = |5 - 3x|$, then $f(2) =$

    (A) $f(-2)$

    (B) $f(-1)$

    (C) $f(1)$

    (D) $f\left(\dfrac{4}{3}\right)$

    (E) $f\left(\dfrac{7}{3}\right)$

33. What is the period of the graph of
    $y = 2 \tan(3\pi x + 4)$?

    (A) $\dfrac{2\pi}{3}$

    (B) $\dfrac{2}{3}$

    (C) 2

    (D) $\dfrac{1}{3}$

    (E) $\dfrac{\pi}{3}$

GO ON TO THE NEXT PAGE

USE THIS SPACE FOR SCRATCHWORK.

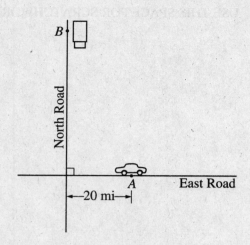

34. The figure above shows a car that has broken
down on East Road. A tow truck leaves a garage
on North Road at point *B*. The straight-line distance
between points *A* and *B* is 50 miles. If the tow
truck travels at an average speed of 45 miles per
hour along North and East Roads, how long will
it take the tow truck to get to the car?

(A) 27 minutes
(B) 1 hour and 7 minutes
(C) 1 hour and 28 minutes
(D) 1 hour and 33 minutes
(E) 1 hour and 46 minutes

GO ON TO THE NEXT PAGE

MATHEMATICS LEVEL 2 TEST—*Continued*

x	$f(x)$
-1	0
0	1
1	-1
2	0

35. If f is a polynomial of degree 3, four of whose values are shown in the table above, then $f(x)$ could equal

(A) $\left(x + \dfrac{1}{2}\right)(x + 1)(x + 2)$

(B) $(x + 1)(x - 2)\left(x - \dfrac{1}{2}\right)$

(C) $(x + 1)(x - 2)(x - 1)$

(D) $(x + 2)\left(x - \dfrac{1}{2}\right)(x - 1)$

(E) $(x + 2)(x + 1)(x - 2)$

36. The only prime factors of a number n are 2, 5, 7, and 17. Which of the following could NOT be a factor of n ?

(A) 10   (B) 20   (C) 25   (D) 30   (E) 34

37. If $0 \le x \le \dfrac{\pi}{2}$ and $\sin x = 3 \cos x$, what is the value of x ?

(A) 0.322
(B) 0.333
(C) 0.340
(D) 1.231
(E) 1.249

GO ON TO THE NEXT PAGE

MATHEMATICS LEVEL 2 TEST—*Continued*

USE THIS SPACE FOR SCRATCHWORK.

38. If $f(x) = 5\sqrt{2x}$, what is the value of $f^{-1}(10)$?

(A) 0.04
(B) 0.89
(C) 2.00
(D) 2.23
(E) 22.36

39. The Fibonacci sequence can be defined recursively as

$$a_1 = 1$$

$$a_2 = 1$$

$$a_n = a_{n-1} + a_{n-2} \text{ for } n \geq 3.$$

What is the 10th term of this sequence?

(A) 21
(B) 34
(C) 55
(D) 89
(E) 144

40. If $f(x) = x^3 - 4x^2 - 3x + 2$, which of the following statements are true?

I. The function f is increasing for $x \geq 3$.
II. The equation $f(x) = 0$ has two nonreal solutions.
III. $f(x) \geq -16$ for all $x \geq 0$.

(A) I only
(B) II only
(C) I and II
(D) I and III
(E) II and III

GO ON TO THE NEXT PAGE

MATHEMATICS LEVEL 2 TEST—*Continued*

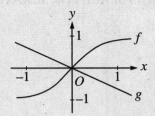

41. Portions of the graphs of f and g are shown above. Which of the following could be a portion of the graph of fg ?

(A)
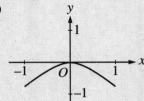

(B)
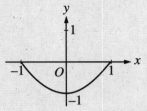

(C)
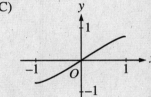

(D)
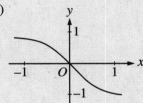

(E)
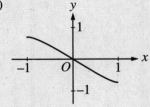

GO ON TO THE NEXT PAGE

MATHEMATICS LEVEL 2 TEST—*Continued*

USE THIS SPACE FOR SCRATCHWORK.

42. The set of all real numbers x such that
$\sqrt{x^2} = -x$ consists of

(A) zero only
(B) nonpositive real numbers only
(C) positive real numbers only
(D) all real numbers
(E) no real numbers

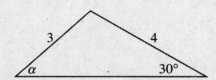

43. In the triangle shown above, $\sin \alpha =$

(A) $\dfrac{3}{8}$

(B) $\dfrac{1}{2}$

(C) $\dfrac{2}{3}$

(D) $\dfrac{3}{4}$

(E) $\dfrac{4}{5}$

44. The length, width, and height of a rectangular solid are 8, 4, and 1, respectively. What is the length of the longest line segment whose end points are two vertices of this solid?

(A) $4\sqrt{5}$
(B) 9
(C) $3\sqrt{10}$
(D) 10
(E) 12

GO ON TO THE NEXT PAGE ⇒

MATHEMATICS LEVEL 2 TEST—*Continued*

45. If $\log_a 3 = x$ and $\log_a 5 = y$, then $\log_a 45 =$

   (A) $2x + y$
   (B) $x^2 + y$
   (C) $x^2 y$
   (D) $x + y$
   (E) $9x + y$

46. If $\sin \theta = t$, then, for all θ in the interval $0 < \theta < \dfrac{\pi}{2}$, $\tan \theta =$

   (A) $\dfrac{1}{\sqrt{1 - t^2}}$

   (B) $\dfrac{t}{\sqrt{1 - t^2}}$

   (C) $\dfrac{1}{1 - t^2}$

   (D) $\dfrac{t}{1 - t^2}$

   (E) 1

47. Which of the following shifts of the graph of $y = x^2$ would result in the graph of $y = x^2 - 2x + k$, where k is a constant greater than 2 ?

   (A) Left 2 units and up k units
   (B) Left 1 unit and up $k + 1$ units
   (C) Right 1 unit and up $k + 1$ units
   (D) Left 1 unit and up $k - 1$ units
   (E) Right 1 unit and up $k - 1$ units

GO ON TO THE NEXT PAGE

MATHEMATICS LEVEL 2 TEST—*Continued*

48. If the height of a right circular cone is decreased by 8 percent, by what percent must the radius of the base be decreased so that the volume of the cone is decreased by 15 percent?

    (A) 4%
    (B) 7%
    (C) 8%
    (D) 30%
    (E) 45%

49. If matrix A has dimensions $m \times n$ and matrix B has dimensions $n \times p$, where m, n, and p are distinct positive integers, which of the following statements must be true?

    I. The product BA does not exist.
    II. The product AB exists and has dimensions $m \times p$.
    III. The product AB exists and has dimensions $n \times n$.

    (A) I only
    (B) II only
    (C) III only
    (D) I and II
    (E) I and III

GO ON TO THE NEXT PAGE

MATHEMATICS LEVEL 2 TEST—*Continued*

USE THIS SPACE FOR SCRATCHWORK.

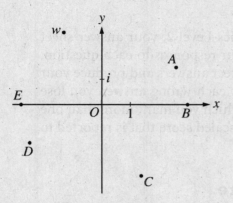

50. If w is the complex number shown in the figure
above, which of the following points could be
$-iw$?

(A) A (B) B (C) C (D) D (E) E

S T O P

**IF YOU FINISH BEFORE TIME IS CALLED, YOU MAY CHECK YOUR WORK ON THIS TEST ONLY.
DO NOT TURN TO ANY OTHER TEST IN THIS BOOK.**

How to Score the SAT Subject Test in Mathematics Level 2

When you take an actual SAT Subject Test in Mathematics Level 2, your answer sheet will be "read" by a scanning machine that will record your responses to each question. Then a computer will compare your answers with the correct answers and produce your raw score. You get one point for each correct answer. For each wrong answer, you lose one-quarter of a point. Questions you omit (and any for which you mark more than one answer) are not counted. This raw score is converted to a scaled score that is reported to you and to the colleges you specify.

Worksheet 1. Finding Your Raw Test Score

STEP 1: Table A on the following page lists the correct answers for all the questions on the Subject Test in Mathematics Level 2 that is reproduced in this book. It also serves as a worksheet for you to calculate your raw score.

- Compare your answers with those given in the table.
- Put a check in the column marked "Right" if your answer is correct.
- Put a check in the column marked "Wrong" if your answer is incorrect.
- Leave both columns blank if you omitted the question.

STEP 2: Count the number of right answers.

Enter the total here: _____

STEP 3: Count the number of wrong answers.

Enter the total here: _____

STEP 4: Multiply the number of wrong answers by .250.

Enter the product here: _____

STEP 5: Subtract the result obtained in Step 4 from the total you obtained in Step 2.

Enter the result here: _____

STEP 6: Round the number obtained in Step 5 to the nearest whole number.

Enter the result here: _____

The number you obtained in Step 6 is your raw score.

TABLE A

Answers to the Subject Test in Mathematics Level 2 – Practice Test 1 and Percentage of Students Answering Each Question Correctly

Question Number	Correct Answer	Right	Wrong	Percentage of Students Answering the Question Correctly*	Question Number	Correct Answer	Right	Wrong	Percentage of Students Answering the Question Correctly*
1	D			88	26	D			85
2	C			91	27	B			70
3	D			90	28	C			65
4	A			87	29	E			47
5	C			90	30	D			73
6	E			54	31	C			54
7	C			62	32	D			72
8	D			93	33	D			23
9	D			85	34	C			62
10	B			89	35	B			57
11	E			84	36	D			51
12	C			54	37	E			63
13	B			87	38	C			52
14	D			75	39	C			52
15	A			88	40	D			48
16	B			67	41	A			42
17	B			62	42	B			33
18	A			70	43	C			63
19	D			76	44	B			54
20	D			72	45	A			46
21	C			82	46	B			46
22	C			67	47	E			44
23	C			70	48	A			35
24	B			66	49	D			25
25	E			60	50	A			26

* These percentages are based on an analysis of the answer sheets of a representative sample of 15,855 students who took the original administration of this test and whose mean score was 652. They may be used as an indication of the relative difficulty of a particular question.

Finding Your Scaled Score

When you take SAT Subject Tests, the scores sent to the colleges you specify are reported on the College Board scale, which ranges from 200 to 800. You can convert your practice test raw score to a scaled score by using Table B. To find your scaled score, locate your raw score in the left-hand column of Table B; the corresponding score in the right-hand column is your scaled score. For example, a raw score of 26 on this particular edition of the Subject Test in Mathematics Level 2 corresponds to a scaled score of 620.

Raw scores are converted to scaled scores to ensure that a score earned on any one edition of a particular Subject Test is comparable to the same scaled score earned on any other edition of the same Subject Test. Because some editions of the tests may be slightly easier or more difficult than others, College Board scaled scores are adjusted so that they indicate the same level of performance regardless of the edition of the test taken and the ability of the group that takes it. Thus, for example, a score of 400 on one edition of a test taken at a particular administration indicates the same level of achievement as a score of 400 on a different edition of the test taken at a different administration.

When you take the SAT Subject Tests during a national administration, your scores are likely to differ somewhat from the scores you obtain on the tests in this book. People perform at different levels at different times for reasons unrelated to the tests themselves. The precision of any test is also limited because it represents only a sample of all the possible questions that could be asked.

Table B

| Scaled Score Conversion Table ||||||
| Subject Test in Mathematics Level 2 – Practice Test 1 ||||||
Raw Score	Scaled Score	Raw Score	Scaled Score	Raw Score	Scaled Score
50	800	28	630	6	470
49	800	27	630	5	460
48	800	26	620	4	450
47	800	25	610	3	440
46	800	24	600	2	430
45	800	23	600	1	420
44	800	22	590	0	410
43	790	21	580	-1	400
42	780	20	580	-2	390
41	770	19	570	-3	370
40	760	18	560	-4	360
39	750	17	560	-5	350
38	740	16	550	-6	340
37	730	15	540	-7	340
36	710	14	530	-8	330
35	700	13	530	-9	330
34	690	12	520	-10	320
33	680	11	510	-11	310
32	670	10	500	-12	300
31	660	9	490		
30	650	8	480		
29	640	7	480		

How Did You Do on the Subject Test in Mathematics Level 2?

After you score your test and analyze your performance, think about the following questions:

Did you run out of time before reaching the end of the test?

If so, you may need to pace yourself better. For example, maybe you spent too much time on one or two hard questions. A better approach might be to skip the ones you can't answer right away and try answering all the remaining questions on the test. Then if there's time, go back to the questions you skipped.

Did you take a long time reading the directions?

You will save time when you take the test by learning the directions to the Subject Test in Mathematics Level 2 ahead of time. Each minute you spend reading directions during the test is a minute that you could use to answer questions.

How did you handle questions you were unsure of?

If you were able to eliminate one or more of the answer choices as wrong and guess from the remaining ones, your approach probably worked to your advantage. On the other hand, making haphazard guesses or omitting questions without trying to eliminate choices could cost you valuable points.

How difficult were the questions for you compared with other students who took the test?

Table A shows you how difficult the multiple-choice questions were for the group of students who took this test during its national administration. The right-hand column gives the percentage of students that answered each question correctly.

A question answered correctly by almost everyone in the group is obviously an easier question. For example, 93 percent of the students answered question 8 correctly. However, only 23 percent answered question 33 correctly.

Keep in mind that these percentages are based on just one group of students. They would probably be different with another group of students taking the test.

If you missed several easier questions, go back and try to find out why: Did the questions cover material you haven't yet reviewed? Did you misunderstand the directions?

Answer Explanations for Mathematics Level 2 – Practice Test 1

The solutions presented here provide one method for solving each of the problems on this test. Other mathematically correct approaches are possible.

1. Choice (D) is the correct answer. You need to solve the equation $3x + 6 = \frac{k}{4}(x+2)$ for k.

$$3x + 6 = \frac{k}{4}(x+2)$$
$$4(3x + 6) = k(x+2)$$
$$12x + 24 = k(x+2)$$
$$12(x+2) = k(x+2)$$
$$12 = k$$

2. Choice (C) is the correct answer. Since $C = \frac{5}{9}(F - 32)$, you can substitute for C in the equation $K = C + 273$. Thus, $K = \frac{5}{9}(F - 32) + 273$.

3. Choice (D) is the correct answer. The slope of the line is $\frac{11-5}{3-(-2)} = \frac{6}{5} = 1.2$.

4. Choice (A) is the correct answer. One way to find the value of y is to notice that if $x + y = 2$ and $y + z = 5$, then $x + y + y + z = 2 + 5 = 7$. Since $x + y + z = 10$, you can conclude that $y = 7 - 10 = -3$.

5. Choice (C) is the correct answer. $g(5) = e^5$, and $f(e^5) = 3\ell n(e^5) - 1 = 3 \cdot 5 - 1 = 14$. Thus, $f(g(5)) = 14$.

6. Choice (E) is the correct answer. If a plane intersects a cube such that the plane is parallel to a face of the cube, the intersection will be a square, so I is possible. Since a square is a type of parallelogram, II is possible. If a plane intersects a cube so that

it slices through three adjacent faces at a corner of the cube, the intersection will be a triangle, so III is possible. Since I, II, and III are all possible.

7.

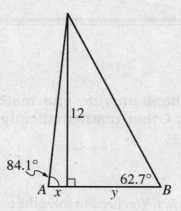

Choice (C) is the correct answer. It is helpful to draw a figure with the information given in the problem. The distance between A and B is $x + y$, so you need to find x and y. Since $\tan 84.1° = \dfrac{12}{x}$, $x = \dfrac{12}{\tan 84.1°}$, which is approximately 1.24. Since $\tan 62.7° = \dfrac{12}{y}$, $y = \dfrac{12}{\tan 62.7°}$, which is approximately 6.19. Thus, $AB = x + y \approx 1.24 + 6.19 = 7.43\,\text{km}$.

Choice (A) is incorrect. $0.97 \approx \dfrac{\tan 84.1°}{12} + \dfrac{\tan 62.7°}{12}$. Choice (D) is incorrect. This results from using incorrect ratios.

$$\sin 84.1° = \frac{x}{12} \qquad\qquad \sin 62.7° = \frac{y}{12}$$
$$x = 12 \sin 84.1° \qquad\qquad y = 12 \sin 62.7°$$
$$AB = x + y$$
$$= 12 \sin 84.1° + 12 \sin 62.7°$$
$$\approx 22.60$$

Choice (E) is incorrect. This results from using incorrect ratios.

$$\tan 84.1° = \frac{x}{12} \qquad\qquad \tan 62.7° = \frac{y}{12}$$
$$x = 12 \tan 84.1° \qquad\qquad y = 12 \tan 62.7°$$
$$AB = x + y$$
$$= 12 \tan 84.1° + 12 \tan 62.7°$$
$$\approx 139.37$$

8. Choice (D) is the correct answer. If $x = \sqrt{15^2 - 12^2}$, then $x^2 = 15^2 - 12^2$, which is equal to $225 - 144 = 81$.

9. Choice (D) is the correct answer. The distance d from the origin to point $P(x, y)$ is equal to $\sqrt{x^2+y^2}$. The distance from the origin to point $P'(2x, 2y)$ is equal to $\sqrt{4x^2+4y^2} = \sqrt{4(x^2+y^2)} = 2\sqrt{x^2+y^2}$, which is $2d$.

10. Choice (B) is the correct answer. You are looking for the input value that gives an output value of $\dfrac{2\sqrt{x^2+1}-1}{\sqrt{x^2+1}+1}$. In this case, $f\left(\sqrt{x^2+1}\right) = \dfrac{2\sqrt{x^2+1}-1}{\sqrt{x^2+1}+1}$. Thus, $g(x) = \sqrt{x^2+1}$.

11. Choice (E) is the correct answer. Since $\sin A = \cos(90° - A)$, it follows that if $\sin A = 0.8$, then $\cos(90° - A)$ is also equal to 0.8.

12. Choice (C) is the correct answer. $x^2 + y^2 + z^2 = r^2$ is the standard form for the equation of a sphere with center $(0, 0, 0)$ and radius r. Thus, $x^2 + y^2 + z^2 = 1$ is a sphere with center $(0, 0, 0)$ and radius 1.

13. Choice (B) is the correct answer. The graph of f has vertical asymptotes at x values for which $f(x)$ is undefined. This occurs when the denominator equals 0. Since $x^2 - 8x + 16 = (x - 4)^2 = 0$ when $x = 4$, the graph has a vertical asymptote at $x = 4$ only. Choice (A) is incorrect. Since $f(0)$ is defined, $x = 0$ is not a vertical asymptote. The graph of f has a horizontal asymptote at $y = 0$. Choice (C) is incorrect. The numerator does not give information about vertical asymptotes. Since $f(5)$ is defined, $x = 5$ is not a vertical asymptote.

14. Choice (D) is the correct answer. To answer this question, it is helpful to realize that finding c in the equation is equivalent to finding the y-intercept of the graph, since $y = c$ when $x = 0$. From the figure shown, the graph appears to intersect the y-axis near –80. Only –72 is near –80. Since $(-6, 0)$ is a point on the graph, you can verify that –72 is correct by substituting –6 for x in the equation $(-6)^4 + 10(-6)^3 + 10(-6)^2 - 96(-6) - 72 = 0$.

15. Choice (A) is the correct answer. Since the secant of an angle is the reciprocal of the cosine, $\sec x = \dfrac{1}{\cos x} = \dfrac{1}{0.4697} \approx 2.1290$.

16. Choice (B) is the correct answer. The question asks for the cost for each club member to go on the trip. Each club member must pay the admission price of $7. The n club members must share the $200 cost of the bus, so each member must pay $\dfrac{200}{n}$ dollars. In addition, the n club members must share the $14 for admission for the 2 chaperones. So each member must pay a total of $7 + \dfrac{200}{n} + \dfrac{14}{n}$ dollars. This is equal to $7 + \dfrac{214}{n}$ or $\dfrac{7n+214}{n}$ dollars. Choice (A) is incorrect. This answer does not include the $14 for admission for the 2 chaperones. Each member must pay $\dfrac{14}{n}$ dollars of that amount.

17. Choice (B) is the correct answer. For any point (x, y) on the graph, the distance between (x, y) and $(0, 0)$ should equal the distance between (x, y) and $(0, 4)$. That is, $\sqrt{x^2 + y^2} = \sqrt{x^2 + (y-4)^2}$. Solving the equation gives $y = 2$. Both of the given points lie on the y-axis. The set of points equidistant from these points is a horizontal line that goes through $(0, 2)$. The equation of this line is $y = 2$.

18. Choice (A) is the correct answer. The sum S of an infinite geometric series is given by $S = \dfrac{a}{1-r}$, where a is the first term and r is the common ratio. In this series, $a = \dfrac{1}{4}$ and $r = \dfrac{1}{2}$. Thus, the sum is $\dfrac{\frac{1}{4}}{1 - \frac{1}{2}} = \dfrac{\frac{1}{4}}{\frac{1}{2}} = \dfrac{1}{2}$. Choice (D) is incorrect. This results from $\dfrac{1}{1 - \frac{1}{2}} = 2$ (forgetting to include the first term) or from thinking that $S = \dfrac{1-r}{a} = \dfrac{\frac{1}{2}}{\frac{1}{4}} = 2$.

19. Choice (D) is the correct answer. The inequality $p + s > p - s$ is equivalent to $s > -s$, which is equivalent to $2s > 0$. So, $s > 0$.

20. Choice (D) is the correct answer. Since a and b are in the domain of the function f and $f(a) < f(b)$, it must be true that $f(a) \neq f(b)$. This implies that $a \neq b$. Note that a could be less than b if, for example, the function is increasing, and a could be greater than b if the function is decreasing.

21. Choice (C) is the correct answer. You need to recognize that the probability you seek corresponds to a compound event, since the person must live within 10 miles of the largest city *and* live in a single-family house. If P represents the entire state's population, then $0.75P$ residents live within 10 miles of the largest city. Of the $0.75P$ residents, 40% live in single-family houses. This is equal to $(0.40)(0.75P) = (0.30)P$. This tells you that 30% of the state's population live in single-family houses within 10 miles of the largest city. This means that the desired probability is 0.30. Choice (A) is incorrect. This results from taking 40% of the 25% of the population that do not live within ten miles of the largest city (0.40×0.25). Choice (B) is incorrect. This is equal to 0.60×0.25. Choice (D) is incorrect. This is equal to $0.75 - 0.40$.

22. Choice (C) is the correct answer. In the right triangle, the length of the hypotenuse is 5, and the length of the side opposite the smallest angle A in the triangle is 3. Thus, $\sin A = \dfrac{3}{5}$ and $\sin^{-1}\left(\dfrac{3}{5}\right) \approx 36.87°$. The measure of the smallest angle in the right triangle rounded to the nearest degree is 37°.

23. Choice (C) is the correct answer. The product of the slopes of two perpendicular lines is –1. Since the line $y = -2x + 3$ has a slope of –2, a line perpendicular to that line has a slope of $\dfrac{1}{2}$. Among the choices, only choice (C) gives the equation of a line that has a slope of $\dfrac{1}{2}$.

24. Choice (B) is the correct answer. The range of the function f depends on the range of $\sin(2x + 5\pi)$. Since $-1 \le \sin(2x + 5\pi) \le 1, -3 \le 3\sin(2x + 5\pi) \le 3$ and $-7 \le -4 + 3\sin(2x + 5\pi) \le -1$.

25. Choice (E) is the correct answer. The standard deviation of three numbers will be smallest for the numbers that are closest to each other. In choice (E), the three numbers all have the same value, so their standard deviation is 0. If all three numbers are not identical, then the standard deviation of the numbers, regardless of how small the numbers are, will always be greater than 0.

26. Choice (D) is the correct answer. According to the formula, $5{,}000 = 1{,}000e^{0.08t}$, which is equivalent to $5 = e^{0.08t}$. Taking the natural logarithm of both sides of the equation gives $\ln 5 = 0.08t$. Thus, $t = \dfrac{\ln 5}{0.08} \approx 20.1$.

27. Choice (B) is the correct answer. Since $\sin\theta > 0$, the product $\sin\theta\cos\theta$ will be negative only when $\cos\theta$ is negative. Since $\sin\theta$ is positive in the first and second quadrants, and $\cos\theta$ is negative in the second and third quadrants, θ must be in the second quadrant. Choice (A) is incorrect. In quadrant I, the second inequality fails. Choice (C) is incorrect. In quadrant III, $\sin\theta < 0$, so the first inequality fails.

28. Choice (C) is the correct answer. The graph of the function f is the set of points $(x, f(x))$. Since $(3, 8)$ is on the graph, $f(3) = 8$. Since $f(-x) = f(x)$, $f(-3) = f(3) = 8$. This means that the point $(-3, 8)$ is also on the graph of f.

29. Choice (E) is the correct answer. It is given that if $x = y$, then $x^2 = y^2$. You need to examine each choice to see if it can or cannot be inferred. Choice (A) can be inferred. If $x = y$, we know that x^2 must be equal to y^2 from the given statement. Choice (B) can be inferred. If $x^2 \neq y^2$, then it must be true that $x \neq y$. Choice (C) can be inferred. This is another way to state that if $x = y$, then $x^2 = y^2$. Choice (D) can be inferred. If $x^2 \neq y^2$, then it is not possible for x to equal y. Choice (E) cannot be inferred. If $x^2 = y^2$, then $x = y$ or $x = -y$.

30. Choice (D) is the correct answer. There are 9 choices for the first position, 8 choices for the second position, and so on. So, nine students can arrange themselves in a straight line in $9 \cdot 8 \cdot 7 \cdot 6 \cdot 5 \cdot 4 \cdot 3 \cdot 2 \cdot 1$ ways. The product is $9! = 362{,}880$.

31. Choice (C) is the correct answer. By using a graphing calculator, one can see that the value of the function $\dfrac{\ln x}{x - 1}$ approaches 1 as x approaches 1 from both sides. You can examine the graph of the function or a table of values for the function as x approaches 1 from both sides. Thus, $\lim\limits_{x \to 1} \dfrac{\ln x}{x - 1} = 1$.

32. Choice (D) is the correct answer. $f(2) = |5 - 3 \cdot 2| = |-1| = 1$. Since $|-1| = |1|$, $f(x) = |1|$ when $5 - 3x = 1$ or when $x = \dfrac{4}{3}$. Thus, $f(2) = f\!\left(\dfrac{4}{3}\right)$.

33. Choice (D) is the correct answer. The period of the graph of $y = 2\tan(3\pi x + 4)$ is the same as the period of the graph of $y = \tan(3\pi x)$. Since the period of the graph of $y = \tan x$ is π, the period of the graph of $y = \tan(3\pi x)$ is $\left(\dfrac{1}{3\pi}\right)\pi = \dfrac{1}{3}$.

34. Choice (C) is the correct answer. Let n represent the distance the truck travels along North Road. Then $n^2 + 20^2 = 50^2$, so $n = \sqrt{2{,}100}$ miles. Thus, the total distance traveled by the truck from point B to point A is $\sqrt{2{,}100} + 20$ miles. The time it takes the truck to get to the car is equal to $\dfrac{(\sqrt{2{,}100} + 20) \text{ miles}}{45 \text{ miles/hour}} \approx 1.46$ hours. The 0.46 hours is converted to minutes by multiplying 0.46 by 60, which gives 27.6 or 28 minutes. Choice (A) is incorrect. This is equal to the time it takes to travel from the intersection to A along East Road. Choice (B) is incorrect. This is equal to the time it takes to drive from B to A directly instead of along North and East Roads. Choice (D) is incorrect. This is obtained by adding the two given values, 50 miles and 20 miles, and computing the time to travel 70 miles. Choice (E) is incorrect. It takes the truck 1.46 hours to get to the car, and 0.46 hour is not the same as 46 minutes.

35. Choice (B) is the correct answer. Since $f(-1) = 0$, $(x + 1)$ is a factor of $f(x)$. Similarly, since $f(2) = 0$, $(x - 2)$ is a factor of $f(x)$. This means that $f(x)$ can be written as $f(x) = (x + 1)(x - 2)(x - a)$ for some real number a. Using $f(0) = 1$ gives $(0 + 1)(0 - 2)(0 - a) = 1$, which simplifies to $a = \dfrac{1}{2}$. Similarly, using $f(1) = -1$ gives $(1 + 1)(1 - 2)(1 - a) = -1$, which also simplifies to $a = \dfrac{1}{2}$. Thus, $f(x)$ could be equal to $f(x) = (x + 1)(x - 2)(x - \dfrac{1}{2})$.

36. Choice (D) is the correct answer. Since the only prime factors of the number n are 2, 5, 7, and 17, the only prime factors of any factor of n are 2, 5, 7, and 17. Hence the numbers $10 = 2 \times 5$, $20 = 2^2 \times 5$, $25 = 5^2$, and $34 = 2 \times 17$ are all possible factors of n, but $30 = 2 \times 3 \times 5$ could <u>not</u> be a factor of n, since 3 is not one of the prime factors of n.

37. Choice (E) is the correct answer. The equation $\sin x = 3\cos x$ can be rewritten as $\tan x = 3$, when $x \neq \dfrac{\pi}{2}$. Solving for x yields $x = \tan^{-1}(3) \approx 1.249$.

38. Choice (C) is the correct answer. To find $f^{-1}(10)$, you need to find the value of x for which $10 = 5\sqrt{2x}$. This equation simplifies to $2 = \sqrt{2x}$ and so $x = 2$.

39. Choice (C) is the correct answer. In the sequence, a_n is equal to the sum of the previous two terms for $n \geq 3$. Thus, the first ten terms of the sequence are 1, 1, 2, 3, 5, 8, 13, 21, 34, 55. Choice (A) is incorrect. This is a_8. Choice (B) is incorrect. This is a_9. Choice (D) is incorrect. This is $a_{11} = a_{10} + a_9 = 89$. Choice (E) is incorrect. This is $a_{12} = a_{11} + a_{10} = 144$.

40. Choice (D) is the correct answer. Use a graphing calculator to draw the graph of the function f. The graph shows that f has three x-intercepts; therefore, the equation $f(x) = 0$ has three real solutions. Thus, statement II is false. The graph also shows that f has just two turning points: a local maximum at the point $\left(-\dfrac{1}{3}, \dfrac{68}{27}\right)$ and a local minimum at the point $(3, -16)$. Thus, f is increasing for $x \geq 3$ and $f(x) \geq -16$ for all $x \geq 0$. Statements I and III are true.

41. Choice (A) is the correct answer. For $x > 0$, $f(x) > 0$ and $g(x) < 0$, so $(fg)(x) = f(x)g(x) < 0$. For $x < 0$, $f(x) < 0$ and $g(x) > 0$, so $(fg)(x) = f(x)g(x) < 0$. Thus, $(fg)(x) < 0$ for all nonzero x shown and $(fg)(0) = f(0)g(0) = 0 \cdot 0 = 0$. Moreover, since $|(fg)(x)|$ increases as $|x|$ increases, fg is increasing for $x < 0$ and decreasing for $x > 0$.

42. Choice (B) is the correct answer. Every positive number n has two square roots, one positive and the other negative, but $\sqrt{n}$ denotes the positive number whose square is n. The square root of 0 is 0. In this case, this means that $\sqrt{x^2} \geq 0$, therefore $-x$ must be nonnegative and x must be nonpositive. Hence, the set of all real numbers x such that $\sqrt{x^2} = -x$ consists of nonpositive real numbers only.

43. Choice (C) is the correct answer. Using the law of sines, $\dfrac{4}{\sin \alpha} = \dfrac{3}{\sin 30°}$. Since $\sin 30° = \dfrac{1}{2}$ this becomes $\dfrac{4}{\sin \alpha} = 6$. Hence, $\sin \alpha = \dfrac{4}{6} = \dfrac{2}{3}$.

44.

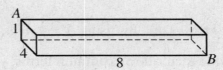

Choice (B) is the correct answer. To answer this question, it is helpful to draw a figure. The longest line segment shown in the figure is the segment between the points labeled A and B. $\overline{AB}$ is the hypotenuse of a right triangle in which one leg is the height of the rectangular solid and the second leg is the diagonal of the face with sides of length 4 and 8. By the Pythagorean theorem, the length of $\overline{AB}$ is $\sqrt{1^2 + \left(\sqrt{4^2 + 8^2}\right)^2} = \sqrt{1 + \left(\sqrt{80}\right)^2} = \sqrt{81} = 9$. Choice (A) is incorrect. This is the length of the longest diagonal of any face of the solid. However, a segment joining opposite vertices is longer than a diagonal of a face.

45. Choice (A) is the correct answer.
Since $\log_a 45 = \log_a(9 \cdot 5) = \log_a 9 + \log_a 5 = \log_a 3^2 + \log_a 5 = 2\log_a 3 + \log_a 5 = 2x + y$, thus, $\log_a 45 = 2x + y$.

46. Choice (B) is the correct answer. Since $\sin^2\theta + \cos^2\theta = 1$, $\cos^2\theta = 1 - \sin^2\theta$. Thus, $\cos^2\theta = 1 - t^2$, since $\sin\theta = t$; and $\cos\theta = \sqrt{1 - t^2}$, since $0 < \theta < \dfrac{\pi}{2}$. Hence, $\tan\theta = \dfrac{\sin\theta}{\cos\theta} = \dfrac{t}{\sqrt{1 - t^2}}$.

47. Choice (E) is the correct answer. Completing the square yields $y = (x^2 - 2x + 1) - 1 + k = (x - 1)^2 + (k - 1)$. Hence, shifting the graph of $y = x^2$ right 1 unit and up $k - 1$ units would result in the graph of $y = x^2 - 2x + k$.

48. Choice (A) is the correct answer. You can solve this problem by comparing the volumes of the original and new cones. If you use h and r for the height and radius, respectively, of the original cone, its volume is $V = \dfrac{1}{3}\pi r^2 h$. In the new cone, the height is $0.92h$ and the volume is $0.85V$. You need to determine the percent decrease in the radius, so you could represent the new radius length by kr, where $0 < k < 1$ and $(1 - k)(100)$ is the percent you are looking for. This gives you the volume of the

new cone as $0.85V = \frac{1}{3}\pi(kr)^2(0.92h)$. By using $V = \frac{1}{3}\pi r^2 h$, we have $0.85\left(\frac{1}{3}\pi r^2 h\right) = \frac{1}{3}\pi(kr)^2(0.92h)$. If you divide each side by common terms, you get $0.85 = k^2 \cdot (0.92)$ so that $k^2 \approx 0.9239$ or $k \approx 0.9612$. The percent decrease in the radius is $100(1-k)$, so the correct answer is 4%. Choice (C) is incorrect. If V is the volume of the original cone, the volume of the new cone is equal to $0.85V = \frac{1}{3}\pi(kr)^2(0.92h)$. If you use k instead of k^2, your answer will be 8%.

49. Choice (D) is the correct answer. For two matrices M and N, the product MN exists provided the number of columns of M equals the number of rows of N. The product MN has as many rows as M and as many columns as N. Since matrix B has p columns and matrix A has m rows, the product BA does not exist, so statement I is true. Since A has n columns and B has n rows, the product AB exists and has as many rows as A, which is m rows, and as many columns as B, which is p columns. Thus, statement II is true and statement III is false.

50. Choice (A) is the correct answer. The complex number w is equal to $a + bi$, where $a < 0$ and $b > 0$. Multiplying by $-i$ will give $-ai - bi^2 = b - ai$. Thus, $b > 0$ and $-a > 0$. So $-iw$ is in quadrant I. The x-coordinate of $-iw$ equals b, and the y-coordinate equals $-a$. Choice (C) is incorrect. It results from not recognizing that a was originally negative and thus $-a$ is positive, which will give a point in quadrant IV. Choice (D) is incorrect. This corresponds to omitting the minus sign, and concluding that the point iw is in quadrant III. Choices (B) and (E) are incorrect. They both result from ignoring the a term in $a + bi$. This would mean that $w = bi$, so multiplying by i would produce a complex number with only a real part.

Mathematics Level 2 – Practice Test 2

Practice Helps

The test that follows is an actual, previously administered SAT Subject Test in Mathematics Level 2. To get an idea of what it's like to take this test, practice under conditions that are much like those of an actual test administration.

- Set aside an hour when you can take the test uninterrupted.

- Sit at a desk or table with no other books or papers. Dictionaries, other books, or notes are not allowed in the test room.

- Remember to have a scientific or graphing calculator with you.

- Tear out an answer sheet from the back of this book and fill it in just as you would on the day of the test. One answer sheet can be used for up to three Subject Tests.

- Read the instructions that precede the practice test. During the actual administration you will be asked to read them before answering test questions.

- Use a clock or kitchen timer to time yourself.

- After you finish the practice test, read the sections "How to Score the SAT Subject Test in Mathematics Level 2" and "How Did You Do on the Subject Test in Mathematics Level 2?"

- The appearance of the answer sheet in this book may differ from the answer sheet you see on test day.

MATHEMATICS LEVEL 2 TEST

The top portion of the page of the answer sheet that you will use to take the Mathematics Level 2 Test must be filled in exactly as illustrated below. When your supervisor tells you to fill in the circle next to the name of the test you are about to take, mark your answer sheet as shown.

○ Literature	○ Mathematics Level 1	○ German	○ Chinese Listening	○ Japanese Listening
○ Biology E	● Mathematics Level 2	○ Italian	○ French Listening	○ Korean Listening
○ Biology M	○ U.S. History	○ Latin	○ German Listening	○ Spanish Listening
○ Chemistry	○ World History	○ Modern Hebrew		
○ Physics	○ French	○ Spanish	**Background Questions:** ①②③④⑤⑥⑦⑧⑨	

After filling in the circle next to the name of the test you are taking, locate the Background Questions section, which also appears at the top of your answer sheet (as shown above). This is where you will answer the following Background Questions on your answer sheet.

BACKGROUND QUESTIONS

Please answer Part I and Part II below by filling in the appropriate circle in the Background Questions box on your answer sheet. <u>The information you provide is for statistical purposes only and will not affect your test score.</u>

<u>Part I.</u>   Which of the following describes a mathematics course you have taken or are currently taking? (FILL IN **ALL** CIRCLES THAT APPLY.)

- Algebra I or Elementary Algebra **OR** Course I of a college preparatory mathematics sequence   —Fill in circle 1.

- Geometry **OR** Course II of a college preparatory mathematics sequence   —Fill in circle 2.

- Algebra II or Intermediate Algebra **OR** Course III of a college preparatory mathematics sequence   —Fill in circle 3.

- Elementary Functions (Precalculus) and/or Trigonometry **OR** beyond Course III of a college preparatory mathematics sequence   —Fill in circle 4.

- Advanced Placement Mathematics (Calculus AB or Calculus BC)   —Fill in circle 5.

<u>Part II.</u>   What type of calculator did you bring to use for this test? (FILL IN THE **ONE** CIRCLE THAT APPLIES. If you did not bring a scientific or graphing calculator, do not fill in any of circles 6-9.)

- Scientific   —Fill in circle 6.

- Graphing (Fill in the circle corresponding to the model you used.)

    Casio 9700, Casio 9750, Casio 9800, Casio 9850, Casio 9860, Casio FX 1.0, Casio CG-10, Sharp 9200, Sharp 9300, Sharp 9600, Sharp 9900, TI-82, TI-83, TI-83 Plus, TI-83 Plus Silver, TI-84 Plus, TI-84 Plus Silver, TI-85, TI-86, or TI-Nspire   —Fill in circle 7.

    Casio 9970, Casio Algebra FX 2.0, HP 38G, HP 39 series, HP 40 series, HP 48 series, HP 49 series, HP 50 series, TI-89, TI-89 Titanium, or TI-Nspire CAS   —Fill in circle 8.

    Some other graphing calculator   —Fill in circle 9.

When the supervisor gives the signal, turn the page and begin the Mathematics Level 2 Test. There are 100 numbered circles on the answer sheet and 50 questions in the Mathematics Level 2 Test. Therefore, use only circles 1 to 50 for recording your answers.

MATHEMATICS LEVEL 2 TEST

REFERENCE INFORMATION

THE FOLLOWING INFORMATION IS FOR YOUR REFERENCE IN ANSWERING SOME OF THE QUESTIONS IN THIS TEST.

Volume of a right circular cone with radius r and height h: $V = \frac{1}{3}\pi r^2 h$

Volume of a sphere with radius r: $V = \frac{4}{3}\pi r^3$

Volume of a pyramid with base area B and height h: $V = \frac{1}{3}Bh$

Surface Area of a sphere with radius r: $S = 4\pi r^2$

DO NOT DETACH FROM BOOK.

MATHEMATICS LEVEL 2 TEST

For each of the following problems, decide which is the BEST of the choices given. If the exact numerical value is not one of the choices, select the choice that best approximates this value. Then fill in the corresponding circle on the answer sheet.

Notes: (1) A scientific or graphing calculator will be necessary for answering some (but not all) of the questions in this test. For each question you will have to decide whether or not you should use a calculator.

(2) For some questions in this test you may have to decide whether your calculator should be in the radian mode or the degree mode.

(3) Figures that accompany problems in this test are intended to provide information useful in solving the problems. They are drawn as accurately as possible EXCEPT when it is stated in a specific problem that its figure is not drawn to scale. All figures lie in a plane unless otherwise indicated.

(4) Unless otherwise specified, the domain of any function f is assumed to be the set of all real numbers x for which $f(x)$ is a real number. The range of f is assumed to be the set of all real numbers $f(x)$, where x is in the domain of f.

(5) Reference information that may be useful in answering the questions in this test can be found on the page preceding Question 1.

USE THIS SPACE FOR SCRATCH WORK.

1. If $1 - \dfrac{1}{x} = 3 - \dfrac{3}{x}$, then $1 - \dfrac{1}{x} =$

   (A) $-\dfrac{1}{2}$ (B) 0 (C) $\dfrac{1}{2}$ (D) $\dfrac{2}{3}$ (E) 3

2. $a\left(\dfrac{1}{b} + \dfrac{1}{c}\right) =$

   (A) $\dfrac{a}{bc}$

   (B) $\dfrac{a}{b+c}$

   (C) $\dfrac{2a}{b+c}$

   (D) $\dfrac{ab+ac}{bc}$

   (E) $\dfrac{1}{ab+ac}$

GO ON TO THE NEXT PAGE

MATHEMATICS LEVEL 2 TEST—*Continued*

USE THIS SPACE FOR SCRATCH WORK.

3. Figure 1 shows one cycle of the graph of the function $y = \sin x$ for $0 \le x \le 2\pi$. If the minimum value of the function occurs at point P, then the coordinates of P are

(A) $\left(\dfrac{4\pi}{3}, -\pi\right)$

(B) $\left(\dfrac{4\pi}{3}, -1\right)$

(C) $\left(\dfrac{3\pi}{2}, -\pi\right)$

(D) $\left(\dfrac{3\pi}{2}, -1\right)$

(E) $\left(\dfrac{3\pi}{2}, 0\right)$

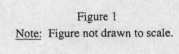

Figure 1
Note: Figure not drawn to scale.

4. If P and Q are different points in a plane, the set of all points in this plane that are closer to P than to Q is

(A) the region of the plane on one side of a line
(B) the interior of a square
(C) a wedge-shaped region of the plane
(D) the region of the plane bounded by a parabola
(E) the interior of a circle

5. If $\sqrt{6y} = 4.73$, then $y =$

(A) 0.62   (B) 1.93   (C) 3.73   (D) 5.33   (E) 11.59

$(4.73^2 =$

GO ON TO THE NEXT PAGE

MATHEMATICS LEVEL 2 TEST—*Continued*

USE THIS SPACE FOR SCRATCH WORK.

6. In Figure 2, $r \cos \theta =$

(A) x
(B) y
(C) r
(D) $x + y$
(E) $r + y$

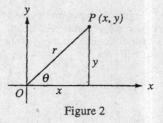

Figure 2

7. If $f(x) = \sqrt{0.3x^2 - x}$ and $g(x) = \dfrac{x + 1}{x - 1}$, then $g(f(10)) =$

(A) 0.2   (B) 1.2   (C) 1.6   (D) 4.5   (E) 5.5

8. If n, p, and t are nonzero real numbers and if $n^4 p^7 t^9 = \dfrac{4n^3 p^7}{t^{-9}}$, then $n =$

(A) $\dfrac{1}{4}$ (B) $\dfrac{1}{2}$ (C) 4   (D) $4p^2 t^2$ (E) $4p^{18} t^{18}$

9. In the triangle in Figure 3, if $OA = AB$, what is the slope of segment AB ?

(A) $\sqrt{2}$

(B) $\dfrac{\sqrt{2}}{2}$

(C) $-\dfrac{\sqrt{2}}{2}$

(D) $-\sqrt{2}$

(E) It cannot be determined from the information given.

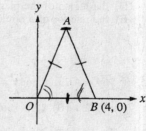

Figure 3

GO ON TO THE NEXT PAGE

MATHEMATICS LEVEL 2 TEST—*Continued*

USE THIS SPACE FOR SCRATCH WORK.

10. Where defined, $\csc(2\theta) \sin(2\theta) =$

   (A) 1
   (B) 0
   (C) −1
   (D) $2 \csc(4\theta)$
   (E) $2 \sec(4\theta)$

11. The graph of $y = f(x)$ is shown in Figure 4. Which of the following could be the graph of $y = |f(x)|$?

Figure 4

(A)

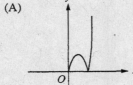

(B)

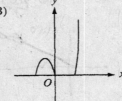

(C)

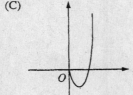

(D)

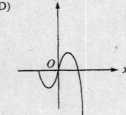

(E)

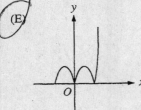

GO ON TO THE NEXT PAGE

MATHEMATICS LEVEL 2 TEST—Continued

USE THIS SPACE FOR SCRATCH WORK.

12. If 3 and −2 are both zeros of the polynomial $p(x)$, then a factor of $p(x)$ is

(A) $x^2 - 6$
(B) $x^2 - x - 6$
(C) $x^2 + 6$
(D) $x^2 + x - 6$
(E) $x^2 + x + 6$

$(x-3)(x+2)$

$x^2-x-6)$

13. A kite string is attached to a peg in the ground. If 100 meters of kite string are played out on the kite and the string makes an angle of 49° with the ground, what is the distance, in meters, from the kite to the ground? (Assume that the string is taut and the ground is level.)

(A) 133   (B) 115   (C) 75   (D) 66   (E) 52

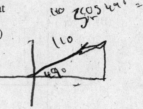

14. If $f(x) = 3x + 5$ and $f(g(1)) = 11$, which of the following could be $g(x)$?

(A) $7x - 5$
(B) $5x + 7$
(C) $5x - 7$
(D) $5x + 3$
(E) $-5x + 3$

$3x + 5 = 11$
$3(g(1)) + 5 = 11$
$3(g(1)) = 6$
$g(1) = 2$

GO ON TO THE NEXT PAGE

MATHEMATICS LEVEL 2 TEST—*Continued*

USE THIS SPACE FOR SCRATCH WORK.

15. Figure 5 shows a cube with edge of length 3 centimeters. If points *A* and *C* are midpoints of the edges of the cube, what is the perimeter of region *ABCD* ?

(A) 6.71 cm
(B) 11.25 cm
(C) 13.42 cm
(D) 22.50 cm
(E) 45.00 cm

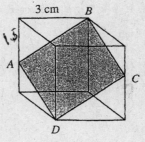

Figure 5

16. An equation of line ℓ in Figure 6 is

(A) $x = 2$
(B) $y = 2$
(C) $x = 0$
(D) $y = x + 2$
(E) $x + y = 2$

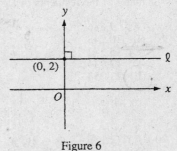

Figure 6

17. The mean weight of the 19 members of an algebra class was 112 pounds. When a new student enrolled, the mean decreased to 111 pounds. What was the weight, in pounds, of the new student?

(A) 91   (B) 92   (C) 93   (D) 101   (E) 110

GO ON TO THE NEXT PAGE

MATHEMATICS LEVEL 2 TEST—*Continued*

USE THIS SPACE FOR SCRATCH WORK.

18. If $0 < x < \pi$ and $\cos x = 0.875$, what is the value of

$\tan \left(\dfrac{x}{2} \right)$?

 (A) 0.008
 (B) 0.017
 (C) 0.258
 (D) 0.277
 (E) 0.553

19. Recently 30,744 residents of Lyon County and 20,496 residents of Saline County voted on a referendum. A total of 38,430 residents of the two counties voted yes. If the same percentage of the voters in each county voted yes, how many of the residents of Lyon County voted yes?

 (A) 7,686
 (B) 10,248
 (C) 15,372
 (D) 17,934
 (E) 23,058

20. If $f:(x, y) \rightarrow (x + 2y, y)$ for every pair (x, y) in the plane, for what points (x, y) is it true that $(x, y) \rightarrow (x, y)$?

 (A) The set of points (x, y) such that $x = 0$
 (B) The set of points (x, y) such that $y = 0$
 (C) The set of points (x, y) such that $y = 1$
 (D) $(0, 0)$ only
 (E) $(-1, 1)$ only

GO ON TO THE NEXT PAGE

MATHEMATICS LEVEL 2 TEST—*Continued*

USE THIS SPACE FOR SCRATCH WORK.

21. What number should be added to each of the three numbers 1, 7, and 19 so that the resulting three numbers form a geometric progression?

    (A) 2   (B) 3   (C) 4   (D) 5   (E) 6

22. If $f(x) = ax^2 + bx + c$ for all real numbers x and if $f(0) = 1$ and $f(1) = 2$, then $a + b =$

    (A) −2   (B) −1   (C) 0   (D) 1   (E) 2

23. What is the degree measure of the largest angle of a triangle that has sides of length 7, 6, and 6 ?

    (A) 31.00°
    (B) 54.31°
    (C) 71.37°
    (D) 125.69°
    (E) 144.31°

24. What is the domain of $f(x) = \sqrt[3]{-x^2 + 13}$?

    (A) $x > 0$
    (B) $x > 2.35$
    (C) $-2.35 < x < 2.35$
    (D) $-3.61 < x < 3.61$
    (E) All real numbers

GO ON TO THE NEXT PAGE

MATHEMATICS LEVEL 2 TEST—*Continued*

USE THIS SPACE FOR SCRATCH WORK.

25. If $\cos x = \tan x$, which of the following is a possible radian value of x ?

(A) -1.00
(B) -0.52
(C) 0.00
(D) 0.52
(E) 0.67

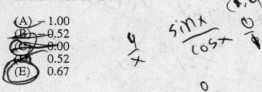

26. Figure 7 shows a portion of the graph of $y = 3^x$. What is the sum of the areas of the three inscribed rectangles shown?

(A) 4,698   (B) 1,638   (C) 819   (D) 182   (E) 91

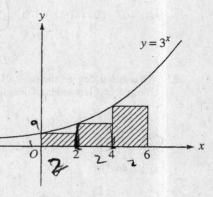

Figure 7

<u>Note:</u> Figure not drawn to scale.

GO ON TO THE NEXT PAGE

MATHEMATICS LEVEL 2 TEST—*Continued*

USE THIS SPACE FOR SCRATCH WORK.

27. When a certain radioactive element decays, the amount that exists at any time t can be calculated by the function $E(t) = ae^{\frac{-t}{1,000}}$, where a is the initial amount and t is the elapsed time in years. How many years would it take for an initial amount of 600 milligrams of this element to decay to 300 milligrams?

(A)   0.5
(B)   500
(C)   693
(D)   1,443
(E)   5,704

28. Which of the following lines are asymptotes of the graph of $y = \dfrac{1 + x}{x}$?

  I. $x = 0$
  II. $y = 0$
  III. $y = 1$

(A) I only
(B) II only
(C) I and II only
(D) I and III only
(E) I, II, and III

29. If $f(2x + 1) = 2x - 1$ for all real numbers x, then $f(x) =$

(A) $-x + 1$

(B) $x - 1$

(C) $x - 2$

(D) $2x - 1$

(E) $\dfrac{1}{2}x - 1$

GO ON TO THE NEXT PAGE

MATHEMATICS LEVEL 2 TEST—*Continued*

USE THIS SPACE FOR SCRATCH WORK.

30. Which of the following could be the coordinates of the center of a circle tangent to the x-axis and the y-axis?

    (A) $(-1, 0)$
    (B) $(-1, 2)$
    (C) $(0, 2)$
    (D) $(2, -2)$
    (E) $(2, 1)$

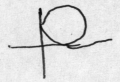

31. What is the range of the function defined by

$$f(x) = \begin{cases} x^{\frac{1}{3}}, & x > 2 \\ 2x - 1, & x \leq 2 \end{cases} ?$$

    (A) $y > 2^{\frac{1}{3}}$

    (B) $y \leq 3$

    (C) $2^{\frac{1}{3}} < y < 3$

    (D) $y \geq 3$

    (E) All real numbers

32. If $3x - 4y + 7 = 0$ and $2y - x^2 = 0$ for $x \geq 0$, then $x =$

    (A) 1.27
    (B) 2.07
    (C) 2.77
    (D) 4.15
    (E) 5.53

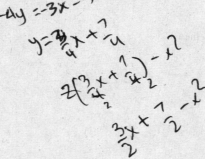

GO ON TO THE NEXT PAGE

MATHEMATICS LEVEL 2 TEST—*Continued*

USE THIS SPACE FOR SCRATCH WORK.

33. If $f(x) = \log_2 x$ for $x > 0$, then $f^{-1}(x) =$

(A) 2^x

(B) x^2

(C) $\dfrac{x}{2}$

(D) $\dfrac{2}{x}$

(E) $\log_x 2$

$y = \log_2 x$

$x = \log_2 y$

$2^x = y$

34. If $x_0 = 0$ and $x_{n+1} = \sqrt{6 + x_n}$, then $x_3 =$

(A) 2.449
(B) 2.907
(C) 2.984
(D) 2.997
(E) 3.162

$x_1 = \sqrt{6 + x_n}$　$x_2 = \sqrt{6 + x_1}$

$x_1 = \sqrt{6 + 0}$　$x_2 = \sqrt{6 + \sqrt{6}}$

$x_1 = \sqrt{6}$　$x_3 = \sqrt{6 + \sqrt{6 + \sqrt{6}}}$

35. Figure 8 shows a triangle inscribed in a semicircle. What is the area of the triangle in terms of θ?

(A) $\dfrac{\theta\pi}{2}$

(B) $\dfrac{\theta}{2}$

(C) $\tan\theta$

(D) $\sin\theta$

(E) $2\sin\theta\cos\theta$

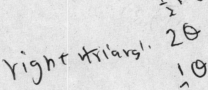

right triangl.

$\frac{1}{2}r^2\theta$

2θ

$\frac{1\theta}{2}$

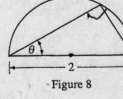

Figure 8

GO ON TO THE NEXT PAGE

USE THIS SPACE FOR SCRATCH WORK.

36. In a certain experiment, there is a 0.2 probability that any thermometer used is in error by more than 1°C. If 4 thermometers are used, what is the probability that all of them are in error by more than 1°C?

   (A) 0.0016
   (B) 0.0081
   (C) 0.16
   (D) 0.25
   (E) 0.80

37. If the magnitudes of vectors **a** and **b** are 5 and 12, respectively, then the magnitude of vector (**b** − **a**) could NOT be

   (A) 5
   (B) 7
   (C) 10
   (D) 12
   (E) 17

38. If $(6.31)^m = (3.02)^n$, what is the value of $\dfrac{m}{n}$?

   (A) −0.32   (B) 0.32   (C) 0.48   (D) 0.60   (E) 1.67

GO ON TO THE NEXT PAGE

MATHEMATICS LEVEL 2 TEST—*Continued*

USE THIS SPACE FOR SCRATCH WORK.

39. If $\arccos(\cos x) = 0$ and $0 \leq x \leq \frac{\pi}{2}$, then x could equal

(A) 0

(B) $\frac{\pi}{6}$

(C) $\frac{\pi}{4}$

(D) $\frac{\pi}{3}$

(E) $\frac{\pi}{2}$

40. If the 20th term of an arithmetic sequence is 100 and the 40th term of the sequence is 250, what is the first term of the sequence?

(A) −50

(B) −42.5

(C) 5

(D) 42.5

(E) 50

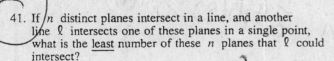

$a_{20} = 100$

$a_{40} = 250$

$a_n = a_1 + (n-1)d$

41. If n distinct planes intersect in a line, and another line ℓ intersects one of these planes in a single point, what is the <u>least</u> number of these n planes that ℓ could intersect?

(A) n (B) $n-1$ (C) $n-2$ (D) $\frac{n}{2}$ (E) $\frac{n-1}{2}$

GO ON TO THE NEXT PAGE

MATHEMATICS LEVEL 2 TEST—Continued

USE THIS SPACE FOR SCRATCH WORK.

42. For all θ, $\sin \theta + \sin(-\theta) + \cos \theta + \cos(-\theta) =$

(A) 0   (B) 2   (C) $2 \sin \theta$ (D) $2 \cos \theta$ (E) $2(\sin \theta + \cos \theta)$

$\sin\theta - \sin\theta$

43. $\dfrac{[(n-1)!]^2}{[n!]^2} =$

(A) $\dfrac{1}{n}$

(B) $\dfrac{1}{n^2}$

(C) $\dfrac{n-1}{n}$

(D) $\left(\dfrac{n-1}{n}\right)^2$

(E) $(n-1)^2$

44. The radius of the base of a right circular cone is 6 and the radius of a parallel cross section is 4. If the distance between the base and the cross section is 8, what is the height of the cone?

(A) 11

(B) $13\frac{1}{3}$

(C) 16

(D) 20

(E) 24

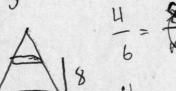

USE THIS SPACE FOR SCRATCH WORK.

45. An indirect proof of the statement "If $x = 2$, then $\sqrt{x}$ is not a rational number" could begin with the assumption that

(A) $x = \sqrt{2}$
(B) $x^2 = 2$
(C) $\sqrt{x}$ is rational
(D) $\sqrt{x}$ is not rational
(E) x is nonnegative

46. Suppose the graph of $f(x) = -x^2$ is translated 3 units left and 1 unit up. If the resulting graph represents $g(x)$, what is the value of $g(-1.6)$?

(A) 2.96
(B) −0.96
(C) −1.56
(D) −1.96
(E) −2.56

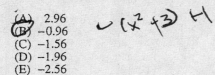

47. In how many ways can 10 people be divided into two groups, one with 7 people and the other with 3 people?

(A) 120   (B) 210   (C) 240   (D) 5,040   (E) 14,400

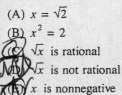

GO ON TO THE NEXT PAGE

MATHEMATICS LEVEL 2 TEST—*Continued*

USE THIS SPACE FOR SCRATCH WORK.

48. Which of the following has an element that is less than any other element in that set?

   I.   The set of positive rational numbers

   II. The set of positive rational numbers r such that $r^2 \geq 2$

   III. The set of positive rational numbers r such that $r^2 > 4$

(A) None
(B) I only
(C) II only
(D) III only
(E) I and III

49. What is the length of the major axis of the ellipse whose equation is $60x^2 + 30y^2 = 150$?

(A) 1.26
(B) 2.50
(C) 3.16
(D) 4.47
(E) 5.00

50. Under which of the following conditions is $\dfrac{a - b}{ab}$ positive?

(A) $0 < a < b$
(B) $a < b < 0$
(C) $b < a < 0$
(D) $b < 0 < a$
(E) None of the above

S T O P

IF YOU FINISH BEFORE TIME IS CALLED, YOU MAY CHECK YOUR WORK ON THIS TEST ONLY.
DO NOT TURN TO ANY OTHER TEST IN THIS BOOK.

GO ON TO THE NEXT PAGE

How to Score the SAT Subject Test in Mathematics Level 2

When you take the actual SAT Subject Test in Mathematics Level 2, your answer sheet will be "read" by a scanning machine that will record your responses to each question. Then a computer will compare your answers with the correct answers and produce your raw score. You get one point for each correct answer. For each wrong answer, you lose one-quarter of a point. Questions you omit (and any for which you mark more than one answer) are not counted. This raw score is converted to a scaled score that is reported to you and to the colleges you specify.

Worksheet 1. Finding Your Raw Test Score

Step 1: Table A on the following page lists the correct answers for all the questions on the SAT Subject Test in Mathematics Level 2 that is reproduced in this book. It also serves as a worksheet for you to calculate your raw score.

- Compare your answers with those given in the table.
- Put a check in the column marked "Right" if your answer is correct.
- Put a check in the column marked "Wrong" if your answer is incorrect.
- Leave both columns blank if you omitted the question.

Step 2: Count the number of right answers.

Enter the total here:_____

Step 3: Count the number of wrong answers.

Enter the total here:_____

Step 4: Multiply the number of wrong answers by .250.

Enter the product here: _____

Step 5: Subtract the result obtained in Step 4 from the total you obtained in Step 2.

Enter the result here:_____

Step 6: Round the number obtained in Step 5 to the nearest whole number.

Enter the result here:_____

The number you obtained in Step 6 is your raw score.

TABLE A

Answers to the Subject Test in Mathematics Level 2 – Practice Test 2 and Percentage of Students Answering Each Question Correctly

Question Number	Correct Answer	Right	Wrong	Percentage of Students Answering the Question Correctly*	Question Number	Correct Answer	Right	Wrong	Percentage of Students Answering the Question Correctly*
1	B			79	26	D			66
2	D			81	27	C			57
3	D			89	28	D			56
4	A			52	29	C			54
5	C			94	30	D			84
6	A			84	31	E			48
7	C			89	32	C			52
8	C			80	33	A			52
9	E			82	34	C			42
10	A			84	35	E			34
11	E			74	36	A			60
12	B			84	37	A			24
13	C			85	38	D			45
14	A			89	39	A			56
15	C			71	40	B			28
16	B			96	41	B			22
17	B			80	42	D			56
18	C			85	43	B			51
19	E			65	44	E			32
20	B			59	45	C			28
21	D			64	46	B			33
22	D			79	47	A			26
23	C			67	48	A			14
24	E			61	49	D			24
25	E			68	50	C			45

* These percentages are based on an analysis of the answer sheets of a representative sample of 9,983 students who took the original administration of this test and whose mean score was 649. They may be used as an indication of the relative difficulty of a particular question.

Finding Your Scaled Score

When you take SAT Subject Tests, the scores sent to the colleges you specify are reported on the College Board scale, which ranges from 200 to 800. You can convert your practice test raw score to a scaled score by using Table B. To find your scaled score, locate your raw score in the left-hand column of Table B; the corresponding score in the right-hand column is your scaled score. For example, a raw score of 30 on this particular edition of the SAT Subject Test in Mathematics Level 2 corresponds to a scaled score of 670.

Raw scores are converted to scaled scores to ensure that a score earned on any one edition of a particular Subject Test is comparable to the same scaled score earned on any other edition of the same Subject Test. Because some editions of tests may be slightly easier or more difficult than others, scaled scores are adjusted so that they indicate the same level of performance regardless of the edition of the test taken and the ability of the group that takes it. Thus, for example, a score of 400 on one edition of a test taken at a particular administration indicates the same level of achievement as a score of 400 on a different edition of the test taken at a different administration.

When you take the SAT Subject Tests during a national administration, your scores are likely to differ somewhat from the scores you obtain on the tests in this book. People perform at different levels at different times for reasons unrelated to the tests themselves. The precision of any test is also limited because it represents only a sample of all the possible questions that could be asked.

Table B

Scaled Score Conversion Table					
Subject Test in Mathematics Level 2 – Practice Test 2					
Raw Score	Scaled Score	Raw Score	Scaled Score	Raw Score	Scaled Score
50	800	28	650	6	480
49	800	27	640	5	470
48	800	26	630	4	460
47	800	25	630	3	450
46	800	24	620	2	440
45	800	23	610	1	430
44	800	22	600	0	410
43	800	21	590	-1	390
42	790	20	580	-2	370
41	780	19	570	-3	360
40	770	18	560	-4	340
39	760	17	560	-5	340
38	750	16	550	-6	330
37	740	15	540	-7	320
36	730	14	530	-8	320
35	720	13	530	-9	320
34	710	12	520	-10	320
33	700	11	510	-11	310
32	690	10	500	-12	310
31	680	9	500		
30	670	8	490		
29	660	7	480		

How Did You Do on the Subject Test in Mathematics Level 2?

After you score your test and analyze your performance, think about the following questions:

Did you run out of time before reaching the end of the test?

If so, you may need to pace yourself better. For example, maybe you spent too much time on one or two hard questions. A better approach might be to skip the ones you can't answer right away and try answering all the remaining questions on the test. Then if there's time, go back to the questions you skipped.

Did you take a long time reading the directions?

You will save time when you take the test by learning the directions to the Subject Test in Mathematics Level 2 ahead of time. Each minute you spend reading directions during the test is a minute that you could use to answer questions. Also be familiar with what formulas are given at the front of the test so that you know when to refer to them during the test.

How did you handle questions you were unsure of?

If you were able to eliminate one or more of the answer choices as wrong and guess from the remaining ones, your approach probably worked to your advantage. On the other hand, making haphazard guesses or omitting questions without trying to eliminate choices could cost you valuable points.

How difficult were the questions for you compared with other students who took the test?

Table A shows you how difficult the multiple-choice questions were for the group of students who took this test during its national administration. The right-hand column gives the percentage of students that answered each question correctly.

A question answered correctly by almost everyone in the group is obviously an easier question. For example, 96 percent of the students answered question 16 correctly. However, only 24 percent answered question 49 correctly.

Keep in mind that these percentages are based on just one group of students. They would probably be different with another group of students taking the test.

If you missed several easier questions, go back and try to find out why: Did the questions cover material you haven't reviewed yet? Did you misunderstand the directions?

Answer Explanations for Mathematics Level 2 – Practice Test 2

The solutions presented here provide one method for solving each of the problems on this test. Other mathematically correct approaches are possible.

1. Choice (B) is the correct answer. Since $1 - \dfrac{1}{x} = 3 - \dfrac{3}{x}$, then $\dfrac{2}{x} = 2$. Solving for x gives $x = 1$. The value of $1 - \dfrac{1}{x}$ when $x = 1$ is equal to $1 - \dfrac{1}{1} = 0$.

2. Choice (D) is the correct answer. Using the distributive property, $a\left(\dfrac{1}{b} + \dfrac{1}{c}\right) = \dfrac{a}{b} + \dfrac{a}{c}$. To add these fractions, you need to find the least common denominator, which is bc. Thus, $\dfrac{a}{b} + \dfrac{a}{c} = \dfrac{ac}{bc} + \dfrac{ab}{bc}$, which is equivalent to choice (D).

3. Choice (D) is the correct answer. On the closed interval $[0, 2\pi]$, the minimum value of $y = \sin x$ occurs when $x = \dfrac{3\pi}{2}$. $\sin\left(\dfrac{3\pi}{2}\right)$ is -1. Thus, the coordinates of P are $\left(\dfrac{3\pi}{2}, -1\right)$. Using a graphing calculator to see the graph of $y = \sin x$ may be helpful in solving this problem.

4. Choice (A) is the correct answer. The set of all points in the plane the same distance from P and Q is the line that is perpendicular to $\overline{PQ}$ and bisects $\overline{PQ}$. Thus, the set of all points closer to P than Q is the region in the plane on the side of the line where P lies. The other choices do not include ALL such points that are closer to P than Q.

5. Choice (C) is the correct answer. If $\sqrt{6y} = 4.73$, then $6y = 4.73^2 = 22.3729$ and $y \approx 3.729 \approx 3.73$.

6. Choice (A) is the correct answer. The cosine of an angle is equal to $\dfrac{\text{length of adjacent side}}{\text{length of hypotenuse}}$. Thus, $\cos\theta = \dfrac{x}{r}$, and $r\cos\theta = r\left(\dfrac{x}{r}\right) = x$.

7. Choice (C) is the correct answer. $f(10) = \sqrt{0.3(10)^2 - 10} = \sqrt{20} \approx 4.472$ and
$g\left(\sqrt{20}\right) = \dfrac{\sqrt{20} + 1}{\sqrt{20} - 1} \approx 1.576 \approx 1.6$.

8. Choice (C) is the correct answer. The equation given is equivalent to $n^4 p^7 t^9 = 4n^3 p^7 t^9$. This simplifies to $n^4 = 4n^3$. Dividing both sides by n^3, you get $n = 4$.

9. Choice (E) is the correct answer because there is not enough information given. If $OA = AB$, then $\triangle OAB$ is an isosceles triangle. The slope of $\overline{AB}$ can be found if the measure of $\angle ABO$ is known or if the coordinates of A can be determined. In this problem, point A is not fixed vertically.

10. Choice (A) is the correct answer. Since $\csc(2\theta) = \dfrac{1}{\sin(2\theta)}$, $\csc(2\theta)\sin(2\theta) = 1$.

11. Choice (E) is the correct answer. Since $|f(x)| \geq 0$, the graph of $y = |f(x)|$ consists of points (x, y), where $y \geq 0$. This eliminates choices (C) and (D). The graphs of $y = f(x)$ and $y = |f(x)|$ are identical where $f(x) \geq 0$. This eliminates choice (A). The portion of the graph of $y = f(x)$ where $f(x) < 0$ must be reflected about the x-axis to produce the graph of $y = |f(x)|$. This eliminates choice (B) because it does not include the reflection of $y = f(x)$ where $f(x) < 0$. Choice (E) is the complete graph of $y = |f(x)|$.

12. Choice (B) is the correct answer. If 3 and -2 are zeros of $p(x)$, then $(x - 3)$ and $(x + 2)$ are factors of $p(x)$. $(x - 3)(x + 2) = x^2 - x - 6$, which is also a factor of $p(x)$. Choices (A), (C), (D), and (E) are incorrect. These choices result from sign errors in determining the factors that give the zeros of $p(x)$ or sign errors in the multiplication of those factors.

13.

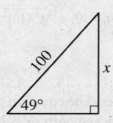

Choice (C) is the correct answer. It is helpful to draw a figure to solve this problem. x represents the distance from the kite to the ground, and $\sin 49° = \dfrac{x}{100}$. Solving for x gives $x \approx 75.471$, which is closest to choice (C). Choice (A) is incorrect. It results from using the incorrect equation $\sin 49° = \dfrac{100}{x}$. Choice (B) is incorrect. It results from using $\tan 49°$ instead of $\sin 49°$. Choice (D) is incorrect. It results from using $\cos 49°$ instead of $\sin 49°$. Choice (E) is incorrect. It results from using the incorrect equation $\cos 49° = \dfrac{100}{x}$ and then subtracting 100 from the solution to the equation.

14. Choice (A) is the correct answer. One way to solve this problem is to first find the value of x for which $f(x) = 11$. Since $3x + 5 = 11$, then $x = 2$. This implies that $g(1) = 2$, and we must determine which of the choices is equal to 2 when $x = 1$. Only choice (A) meets this condition. $7x - 5 = 2$ when $x = 1$.

15. Choice (C) is the correct answer. You can use the Pythagorean theorem to find the length of $\overline{AB}$. $(3)^2 + (1.5)^2 = x^2$ and $x = \sqrt{11.25} \approx 3.35\,\text{cm}$. All sides of $ABCD$ have the same length, so its perimeter is $4x \approx 13.416 \approx 13.42$ cm. Choice (B) is incorrect. It is the area, in square centimeters, of $ABCD$. Choice (E) is incorrect. It is the perimeter if 11.25 cm is used as the length of a side.

16. Choice (B) is the correct answer. Since line ℓ is perpendicular to the y-axis and intersects the y-axis at $(0, 2)$, each point on line ℓ has the y-coordinate 2, and therefore, the equation of ℓ is $y = 2$.

17. Choice (B) is the correct answer. You can set up an equation to solve this problem. Let x be the weight of the new student, in pounds. The total weight of the 20 students is equal to $19(112) + x$. Since the mean weight is 111, it follows that $\dfrac{19(112) + x}{20} = 111$. Solving for x gives 92 as the weight of the new student.

18. Choice (C) is the correct answer. For $0 < x < \pi$, you can set your calculator in radian mode to find the value of x, which is equal to $\cos^{-1}(0.875) \approx 0.5054$. Keep this value in your calculator to evaluate $\tan\left(\dfrac{x}{2}\right)$. $\tan\left(\dfrac{x}{2}\right) \approx \tan\left(\dfrac{0.5054}{2}\right) \approx 0.2582$. Choice (D) is incorrect. It is equal to $\dfrac{\tan(28.955°)}{2}$, where $28.955° \approx \cos^{-1}(0.875)$ with the calculator set in degree mode. Choice (E) is incorrect. It is equal to $\tan(28.955°)$, where $28.955° \approx \cos^{-1}(0.875)$ with the calculator set in degree mode.

19. Choice (E) is the correct answer. You can set up an equation to solve this problem. Let $\dfrac{x}{100}$ represent the percent of residents that voted "yes." $30,744\left(\dfrac{x}{100}\right) + 20,496\left(\dfrac{x}{100}\right) = 38,430$. This simplifies to $307.44x + 204.96x = 38,430$. Solving for x gives 75. Thus, 75% of the residents voted "yes," and 75% of 30,744 is 23,058. Choice (A) is incorrect. It is 25% of those who voted from Lyon County. Choice (C) is incorrect. It is 75% of those who voted from Saline County.

20. Choice (B) is the correct answer. In this problem, the function f maps a point (x, y) in the plane to the point $(x + 2y, y)$. You are looking for all points at which the image has the same x-coordinate as the original point. If $x = x + 2y$, then y must equal 0. Thus, you want all points (x, y) such that $y = 0$.

21. Choice (D) is the correct answer. Let x be the number to be added so that $1 + x$, $7 + x$, and $19 + x$ form a geometric progression. Then, $\dfrac{19 + x}{7 + x} = \dfrac{7 + x}{1 + x}$. This equation simplifies to $6x = 30$. Therefore, $x = 5$.

22. Choice (D) is the correct answer. Since $f(0) = 1$, $1 = a(0) + b(0) + c$ and $c = 1$. Since $f(1) = 2$, $2 = a(1) + b(1) + 1 = a + b + 1$. Thus, $a + b = 1$.

23.

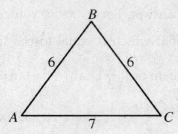

Choice (C) is the correct answer. It is helpful to draw a figure to solve this problem. The largest angle is $\angle B$, since it is opposite the longest side. The measure of $\angle B$ can be found using the law of cosines.

$$(AC)^2 = (AB)^2 + (BC)^2 - 2(AB)(BC)\cos\angle B$$

$$\cos\angle B = \frac{(AC)^2 - (AB)^2 - (BC)^2}{-2(AB)(BC)}$$

$$= \frac{49 - 36 - 36}{-2(6)(6)}$$

Since $\cos\angle B = \frac{23}{72}$, the measure of $\angle B$ is $\cos^{-1}\left(\frac{23}{72}\right) \approx 71.37°$. Choice (B) is incorrect. It is the measure of $\angle A$ and $\angle C$.

24. Choice (E) is the correct answer. The cube root of any real number is a real number. Thus, the domain of f is all real numbers. Choices (B) and (C) are incorrect. They both incorrectly use $\sqrt[3]{13} \approx 2.35$. Choice (D) is incorrect. It incorrectly assumes that $-x^2 + 13 \geq 0$.

25. Choice (E) is the correct answer. Since $\tan x = \frac{\sin x}{\cos x}$, the equation can be rewritten as $\cos x = \frac{\sin x}{\cos x}$, and $\cos^2 x - \sin x = 0$. Using the identity $\sin^2 x + \cos^2 x = 1$, the equation becomes $1 - \sin^2 x - \sin x = 0$. This is a quadratic equation in $\sin x$. Let $y = \sin x$ and use the quadratic formula to solve $y^2 + y - 1 = 0$.

$$y = \frac{-1 \pm \sqrt{1 - 4(1)(-1)}}{2}$$

$$= \frac{-1 \pm \sqrt{5}}{2} \approx 0.6180, -1.6180$$

$\sin x = -1.6180$ has no solution. Solving $\sin x = 0.6180$ gives $x = \sin^{-1}(0.6180) \approx 0.67$. Alternatively, you can use a graphing calculator to graph $y = \cos x$ and $y = \tan x$ on the interval $\left[0, \frac{\pi}{2}\right]$ and find the x-coordinate of the point of intersection.

26. Choice (D) is the correct answer. The width of each rectangle is 2. The heights of the rectangles are 3^0, 3^2, and 3^4, respectively. The sum of the areas is $3^0(2) + 3^2(2) + 3^4(2) = 2 + 18 + 162 = 182$. Choice (B) is incorrect. It results from using the right endpoint instead of the left one for the heights of the rectangles (3^2, 3^4, and 3^6). Choice (C) is incorrect. It results from using the right endpoint for the heights of the rectangles and forgetting to multiply by 2. Choice (E) is incorrect. It results from forgetting to multiply by 2.

27. Choice (C) is the correct answer. For the function given, let $a = 600$ and $E(t) = 300$. Thus, $300 = 600e^{-t/1000}$, which simplifies to $\frac{1}{2} = e^{-t/1000}$. Taking the natural logarithm of both sides of the equation gives $\ln\left(\frac{1}{2}\right) = \frac{-t}{1,000}$. Solving for t yields $t \approx 693.147 \approx 693$. Alternatively, you can use a graphing calculator to graph $y = 300$ and $y = 600e^{-t/1000}$ and find the x-coordinate of the point of intersection.

28. Choice (D) is the correct answer. The lines $x = 0$ and $y = 1$ are asymptotes of the graph of $y = \frac{1+x}{x}$. The correct answer is I and III only. The line $y = 1$ is a horizontal asymptote, because as the value of x increases without bound, the value of y approaches 1. The line $x = 0$ is a vertical asymptote, because the value of y is undefined when $x = 0$.

29. Choice (C) is the correct answer. To find an expression for $f(x)$, you must understand what $f(2x + 1)$ means. If f is evaluated at $2x + 1$, the value is $2x - 1$, which is equal to $(2x + 1) - 2$. So, the "input" value for f has 2 subtracted from it to produce the "output" value of the function. Thus, if the original "input" value is x, the "output" value is $x - 2$. Therefore, $f(x) = x - 2$.

30. Choice (D) is the correct answer. In order for the circle to be tangent to both the x-axis and y-axis, the center of the circle must be the same distance from both axes. Choices (A) and (C) are incorrect. They can be eliminated because they are each on a coordinate axis. Choices (B) and (E) are incorrect. They can be eliminated because each of these points is closer to one of the coordinate axes than the other. $(2, -2)$ is the answer because it is 2 units from both coordinate axes.

31. Choice (E) is the correct answer. To find the range of this piecewise-defined function, you must consider both parts. For $x > 2$, $f(x) = x^{\frac{1}{3}}$. The range of the function is $y > 2^{\frac{1}{3}}$, since the function is increasing for all $x > 2$. For $x \le 2$, $f(x) = 2x - 1$. The range of this function is $y \le 3$, since the function is decreasing as x is decreasing for $x \le 2$. Combining $y > 2^{\frac{1}{3}}$ and $y \le 3$ gives all real numbers for the range. Choices (A) and (B) are incorrect. They result from considering only one part of the function. Choice (C) is incorrect. It results from incorrectly looking at the interval between the endpoints of the ranges of the respective parts.

32. Choice (C) is the correct answer. Since $2y - x^2 = 0$, $y = \frac{x^2}{2}$ for $x \ge 0$. Substituting that into the first equation yields $3x - 4\left(\frac{x^2}{2}\right) + 7 = 0$. This simplifies to $3x - 2x^2 + 7 = 0$ or $2x^2 - 3x - 7 = 0$. Using the quadratic formula,

$$x = \frac{3 \pm \sqrt{9 - 4(2)(-7)}}{4}$$

$$= \frac{3 \pm \sqrt{65}}{4}$$

$$\approx 2.77, -1.27.$$

Since $x \ge 0$, the answer is 2.77. Choice (A) is incorrect. It results from a sign error in solving for x.

33. Choice (A) is the correct answer. The inverse of a logarithmic function with base a ($f(x) = \log_a x$, where $x > 0$) is an exponential function with base a ($f^{-1}(x) = a^x$). In this case, the inverse of $f(x) = \log_2 x$ for $x > 0$ is $f^{-1}(x) = 2^x$.

34. Choice (C) is the correct answer. Since $x_0 = 0$, $x_1 = \sqrt{6 + x_0} = \sqrt{6} \approx 2.449$, which is choice (A). Choice (A) is incorrect. $x_2 = \sqrt{6 + x_1} = \sqrt{6 + \sqrt{6}} \approx 2.907$, which is choice (B). Choice (B) is incorrect. $x_3 = \sqrt{6 + x_2} = \sqrt{6 + \sqrt{6 + \sqrt{6}}} \approx 2.984$. Choice (D) is incorrect. It is x_4.

35.

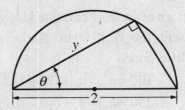

Choice (E) is the correct answer. Since the triangle is inscribed in a semicircle, it is a right triangle. The area of the triangle is equal to $\frac{1}{2}ab\sin\theta$, where a and b represent adjacent sides and θ is the included angle. In the figure, $\cos\theta=\frac{y}{2}$ and $y=2\cos\theta$. Thus, the area of the triangle is equal to $\frac{1}{2}(2)(2\cos\theta)\sin\theta=2\cos\theta\sin\theta$ which is equivalent to choice (E).

36. Choice (A) is the correct answer. Since the use of each thermometer is an independent event, the probability is equal to $(0.2)^4=0.0016$.

37.

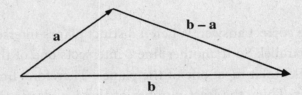

Choice (A) is the correct answer. Vectors **a**, **b**, and **b – a** can be represented as shown in the figure. Using the triangle inequality, $7\le$ magnitude of **b – a** ≤ 17. Thus, the magnitude of **b – a** cannot be 5. The other choices are all possible magnitudes.

38. Choice (D) is the correct answer. Since $(6.31)^m=(3.02)^n$, $\log(6.31)^m=\log(3.02)^n$ and $m\log 6.31=n\log 3.02$. $\frac{m}{n}=\frac{\log 3.02}{\log 6.31}\approx 0.60$. Choice (A) is incorrect. It is equal to $\log\left(\frac{3.02}{6.31}\right)$. Choice (C) is incorrect. It is equal to $\frac{3.02}{6.31}$. Choice (E) is incorrect. It is equal to $\frac{\log 6.31}{\log 3.02}$.

39. Choice (A) is the correct answer. $\cos x$ and $\arccos x$ are inverses of each other on the interval $0\le x\le\frac{\pi}{2}$. If $\arccos(\cos x)=0$, x could equal 0.

40. Choice (B) is the correct answer. You can use the given information to set up two equations. Let a_1 represent the first term of the arithmetic sequence, and let d represent the common difference.

$$100 = a_{20} = a_1 + (20 - 1)d$$
$$250 = a_{40} = a_1 + (40 - 1)d$$

$a_1 + (n-1)d$

Solving both of these for a_1 yields $a_1 = 100 - 19d$ and $a_1 = 250 - 39d$.

$$100 - 19d = 250 - 39d$$

$$d = \frac{15}{2} = 7.5$$

$$a_1 = 100 - 19(7.5) = -42.5$$

Choice (A) is incorrect. It results from using $a_{20} = a_1 + 20d$ and $a_{40} = a_1 + 40d$. Choice (C) is incorrect. It results from thinking that the first term is $\frac{100}{20}$. Choice (D) is incorrect. It results from a sign error.

41. Choice (B) is the correct answer. When n distinct planes intersect in a line, no two of the planes are parallel. So if another line ℓ intersects one of these planes in a single point, it is parallel to at most one of the planes. Therefore, line ℓ would intersect at least $n - 1$ planes. Thus, the least number of these n planes that line ℓ intersects is $n - 1$.

42. Choice (D) is the correct answer. Since $\sin \theta$ is odd, $\sin(-\theta) = -\sin(\theta)$. Since $\cos \theta$ is even, $\cos(-\theta) = \cos(\theta)$. Thus, $\sin \theta + \sin(-\theta) + \cos \theta + \cos(-\theta) = \sin \theta - \sin(\theta) + \cos \theta + \cos \theta = 2 \cos \theta$.

43. Choice (B) is the correct answer. Since $n! = (n-1)!n$, then $\frac{((n-1)!)^2}{(n!)^2} = \frac{(n-1)!(n-1)!}{(n-1)!n(n-1)!n} = \frac{1}{n^2}$.

44.

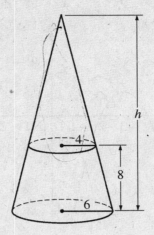

Choice (E) is the correct answer. It is helpful to draw a figure. This problem can be solved using similar triangles. Setting up the proportion $\frac{4}{6} = \frac{h-8}{h}$ results in

$$4h = 6(h - 8)$$
$$4h = 6h - 48$$
$$48 = 2h$$
$$h = 24$$

Choice (C) is incorrect. It is the height of the smaller cone whose base is the parallel cross section.

45. Choice (C) is the correct answer. An indirect proof begins with assuming the negative of the conclusion. The conclusion is "$\sqrt{x}$ is NOT a rational number." The negative of this statement is "$\sqrt{x}$ is a rational number."

46.

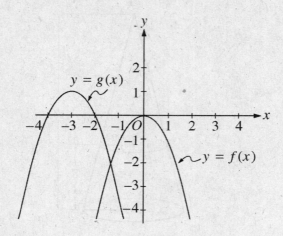

It may be helpful to draw a graph of f and g.

Choice (B) is the correct answer. The function g is given by $g(x) = -(x+3)^2 + 1$. Therefore, $g(-1.6) = -(-1.6+3)^2 + 1 = -0.96$. Choice (A) is incorrect. It results from using $g(x) = (x+3)^2 + 1$. Choice (C) is incorrect. It is $f(-1.6) + 1$. Choice (D) is incorrect. It results from using $g(x) = -(x+3)^2$. Choice (E) is incorrect. It is $f(-1.6)$.

47. Choice (A) is the correct answer. To determine the number of ways that 10 people can be divided into the two groups, find either $\binom{10}{7}$ or $\binom{10}{3}$, which are equivalent. Once the number of ways to form one of the groups is determined, there is only one way to form the other group. So, $\binom{10}{7} = \frac{10!}{3!7!} = \frac{10 \cdot 9 \cdot 8 \cdot 7!}{3 \cdot 2 \cdot 7!} = 120$.

48. Choice (A) is the correct answer. You need to examine each set separately. Consider I. There is no least positive rational number, so "the set of positive rational numbers" does not satisfy the desired condition. Consider II. $\sqrt{2}$ is the smallest positive real number that satisfies $r^2 \geq 2$, but $\sqrt{2}$ is irrational. Thus, there is no smallest positive rational number that satisfies the desired condition. Consider III. $r > 2$, but there is no smallest rational number that satisfies this condition. None of the three sets has an element that is less than any other element in the set.

49. Choice (D) is the correct answer. The standard form for the equation of an ellipse centered at the origin is $\frac{x^2}{a^2} + \frac{y^2}{b^2} = 1$. $60x^2 + 30y^2 = 150$ can be rewritten as $\frac{60x^2}{150} + \frac{30y^2}{150} = \frac{150}{150}$, which is equivalent to $\frac{x^2}{2.5} + \frac{y^2}{5} = 1$. Because the denominator of the y^2 term is larger than the denominator of the x^2 term, the major axis of this ellipse is vertical. Since $b^2 = 5$, the vertices are $(0, \sqrt{5})$ and $(0, -\sqrt{5})$. The length of the major axis is $2b = 2\sqrt{5} \approx 4.47$. Choice (B) is incorrect. It is a^2. Choice (C) is incorrect. It is $2a = 2\sqrt{2.5} \approx 3.16$, which is the length of the minor axis of this ellipse. Choice (E) is incorrect. It is b^2.

50. Choice (C) is the correct answer. You need to determine for which of the conditions $\frac{a-b}{ab} > 0$. It is helpful to examine each of the answer choices. Choice (A) is incorrect. $0 < a < b$. In this case, $a - b < 0$ and $ab > 0$, so the expression is NEGATIVE. Choice (B) is incorrect. $a < b < 0$. In this case, $a - b < 0$ and $ab > 0$, so the expression is NEGATIVE. In choice (C), $a - b > 0$ and $ab > 0$, so the expression is POSITIVE. You are looking for a positive result. Choice (D) is incorrect. $b < 0 < a$. In this case, $a - b > 0$ and $ab < 0$, so the expression is NEGATIVE.

CollegeBoard SAT

2010-11 SAT Subject Tests™

MARKS MUST BE COMPLETE

COMPLETE MARK ● EXAMPLES OF INCOMPLETE MARKS ⊛ ⊗ ⊜ ⊙ ◖ ⊘ ⦸ ⊜ ⊛

You must use a No. 2 pencil. Do not use a mechanical pencil. *It is very important that you fill in the entire circle darkly and completely. If you change your response, erase as completely as possible. Incomplete marks or erasures may affect your score. It is very important that you follow these instructions when filling out your answer sheet.*

1 Your Name:
(Print)

Last ___ First ___ M.I. ___

I agree to the conditions on the front and back of the SAT Subject Tests™ book. I also agree to use only a No. 2 pencil to complete my answer sheet.

Signature: ___ Date: ___ / ___ / ___
MM DD YY

Home Address: ___
(Print) Number and Street ___ City ___ State ___ Zip Code

Home Phone: (___) ___ Test Center: ___
(Print) City ___ State/Country

2 YOUR NAME
Last Name (First 6 Letters) | First Name (First 4 Letters) | Mid. Init.

3 DATE OF BIRTH
MONTH | DAY | YEAR
Jan, Feb, Mar, Apr, May, Jun, Jul, Aug, Sep, Oct, Nov, Dec

5 SEX
○ Female ○ Male

6 REGISTRATION NUMBER
(Copy from Admission Ticket.)

○ I turned in my registration form today.

Important: Fill in items 8 and 9 exactly as shown on the back of test book.

9 BOOK ID
(Copy from back of test book.)

8 BOOK CODE
(Copy and grid as on back of test book.)

10 TEST BOOK SERIAL NUMBER
(Copy from front of test book.)

4 ZIP CODE

7 TEST CENTER
(Supplied by Test Center Supervisor.)

FOR OFFICIAL USE ONLY
0 1 2 3 4 5 6
0 1 2 3 4 5 6
0 1 2 3 4 5 6

83161-77191 • NS60C1285 • Printed in U.S.A.
755275

184596-001:321 Printed in the USA by Pearson ISD0479

PLEASE DO NOT WRITE IN THIS AREA
○○○○○○○○○○○○○○○○○○○○○○○○○○○○○○ **SERIAL #**

COMPLETE MARK ● **EXAMPLES OF INCOMPLETE MARKS** ⊘ ⊗ ⊖ ⊙ ◐ ∅ ⊛ ⊜

You must use a No. 2 pencil and marks must be complete. Do not use a mechanical pencil. It is very important that you fill in the entire circle darkly and completely. If you change your response, erase as completely as possible. Incomplete marks or erasures may affect your score.

○ Literature
○ Biology E
○ Biology M
○ Chemistry
○ Physics

○ Mathematics Level 1
○ Mathematics Level 2
○ U.S. History
○ World History
○ French

○ German
○ Italian
○ Latin
○ Modern Hebrew
○ Spanish

○ Chinese Listening
○ French Listening
○ German Listening

○ Japanese Listening
○ Korean Listening
○ Spanish Listening

Background Questions: ① ② ③ ④ ⑤ ⑥ ⑦ ⑧ ⑨

1 Ⓐ Ⓑ Ⓒ Ⓓ Ⓔ	26 Ⓐ Ⓑ Ⓒ Ⓓ Ⓔ	51 Ⓐ Ⓑ Ⓒ Ⓓ Ⓔ	76 Ⓐ Ⓑ Ⓒ Ⓓ Ⓔ
2 Ⓐ Ⓑ Ⓒ Ⓓ Ⓔ	27 Ⓐ Ⓑ Ⓒ Ⓓ Ⓔ	52 Ⓐ Ⓑ Ⓒ Ⓓ Ⓔ	77 Ⓐ Ⓑ Ⓒ Ⓓ Ⓔ
3 Ⓐ Ⓑ Ⓒ Ⓓ Ⓔ	28 Ⓐ Ⓑ Ⓒ Ⓓ Ⓔ	53 Ⓐ Ⓑ Ⓒ Ⓓ Ⓔ	78 Ⓐ Ⓑ Ⓒ Ⓓ Ⓔ
4 Ⓐ Ⓑ Ⓒ Ⓓ Ⓔ	29 Ⓐ Ⓑ Ⓒ Ⓓ Ⓔ	54 Ⓐ Ⓑ Ⓒ Ⓓ Ⓔ	79 Ⓐ Ⓑ Ⓒ Ⓓ Ⓔ
5 Ⓐ Ⓑ Ⓒ Ⓓ Ⓔ	30 Ⓐ Ⓑ Ⓒ Ⓓ Ⓔ	55 Ⓐ Ⓑ Ⓒ Ⓓ Ⓔ	80 Ⓐ Ⓑ Ⓒ Ⓓ Ⓔ
6 Ⓐ Ⓑ Ⓒ Ⓓ Ⓔ	31 Ⓐ Ⓑ Ⓒ Ⓓ Ⓔ	56 Ⓐ Ⓑ Ⓒ Ⓓ Ⓔ	81 Ⓐ Ⓑ Ⓒ Ⓓ Ⓔ
7 Ⓐ Ⓑ Ⓒ Ⓓ Ⓔ	32 Ⓐ Ⓑ Ⓒ Ⓓ Ⓔ	57 Ⓐ Ⓑ Ⓒ Ⓓ Ⓔ	82 Ⓐ Ⓑ Ⓒ Ⓓ Ⓔ
8 Ⓐ Ⓑ Ⓒ Ⓓ Ⓔ	33 Ⓐ Ⓑ Ⓒ Ⓓ Ⓔ	58 Ⓐ Ⓑ Ⓒ Ⓓ Ⓔ	83 Ⓐ Ⓑ Ⓒ Ⓓ Ⓔ
9 Ⓐ Ⓑ Ⓒ Ⓓ Ⓔ	34 Ⓐ Ⓑ Ⓒ Ⓓ Ⓔ	59 Ⓐ Ⓑ Ⓒ Ⓓ Ⓔ	84 Ⓐ Ⓑ Ⓒ Ⓓ Ⓔ
10 Ⓐ Ⓑ Ⓒ Ⓓ Ⓔ	35 Ⓐ Ⓑ Ⓒ Ⓓ Ⓔ	60 Ⓐ Ⓑ Ⓒ Ⓓ Ⓔ	85 Ⓐ Ⓑ Ⓒ Ⓓ Ⓔ
11 Ⓐ Ⓑ Ⓒ Ⓓ Ⓔ	36 Ⓐ Ⓑ Ⓒ Ⓓ Ⓔ	61 Ⓐ Ⓑ Ⓒ Ⓓ Ⓔ	86 Ⓐ Ⓑ Ⓒ Ⓓ Ⓔ
12 Ⓐ Ⓑ Ⓒ Ⓓ Ⓔ	37 Ⓐ Ⓑ Ⓒ Ⓓ Ⓔ	62 Ⓐ Ⓑ Ⓒ Ⓓ Ⓔ	87 Ⓐ Ⓑ Ⓒ Ⓓ Ⓔ
13 Ⓐ Ⓑ Ⓒ Ⓓ Ⓔ	38 Ⓐ Ⓑ Ⓒ Ⓓ Ⓔ	63 Ⓐ Ⓑ Ⓒ Ⓓ Ⓔ	88 Ⓐ Ⓑ Ⓒ Ⓓ Ⓔ
14 Ⓐ Ⓑ Ⓒ Ⓓ Ⓔ	39 Ⓐ Ⓑ Ⓒ Ⓓ Ⓔ	64 Ⓐ Ⓑ Ⓒ Ⓓ Ⓔ	89 Ⓐ Ⓑ Ⓒ Ⓓ Ⓔ
15 Ⓐ Ⓑ Ⓒ Ⓓ Ⓔ	40 Ⓐ Ⓑ Ⓒ Ⓓ Ⓔ	65 Ⓐ Ⓑ Ⓒ Ⓓ Ⓔ	90 Ⓐ Ⓑ Ⓒ Ⓓ Ⓔ
16 Ⓐ Ⓑ Ⓒ Ⓓ Ⓔ	41 Ⓐ Ⓑ Ⓒ Ⓓ Ⓔ	66 Ⓐ Ⓑ Ⓒ Ⓓ Ⓔ	91 Ⓐ Ⓑ Ⓒ Ⓓ Ⓔ
17 Ⓐ Ⓑ Ⓒ Ⓓ Ⓔ	42 Ⓐ Ⓑ Ⓒ Ⓓ Ⓔ	67 Ⓐ Ⓑ Ⓒ Ⓓ Ⓔ	92 Ⓐ Ⓑ Ⓒ Ⓓ Ⓔ
18 Ⓐ Ⓑ Ⓒ Ⓓ Ⓔ	43 Ⓐ Ⓑ Ⓒ Ⓓ Ⓔ	68 Ⓐ Ⓑ Ⓒ Ⓓ Ⓔ	93 Ⓐ Ⓑ Ⓒ Ⓓ Ⓔ
19 Ⓐ Ⓑ Ⓒ Ⓓ Ⓔ	44 Ⓐ Ⓑ Ⓒ Ⓓ Ⓔ	69 Ⓐ Ⓑ Ⓒ Ⓓ Ⓔ	94 Ⓐ Ⓑ Ⓒ Ⓓ Ⓔ
20 Ⓐ Ⓑ Ⓒ Ⓓ Ⓔ	45 Ⓐ Ⓑ Ⓒ Ⓓ Ⓔ	70 Ⓐ Ⓑ Ⓒ Ⓓ Ⓔ	95 Ⓐ Ⓑ Ⓒ Ⓓ Ⓔ
21 Ⓐ Ⓑ Ⓒ Ⓓ Ⓔ	46 Ⓐ Ⓑ Ⓒ Ⓓ Ⓔ	71 Ⓐ Ⓑ Ⓒ Ⓓ Ⓔ	96 Ⓐ Ⓑ Ⓒ Ⓓ Ⓔ
22 Ⓐ Ⓑ Ⓒ Ⓓ Ⓔ	47 Ⓐ Ⓑ Ⓒ Ⓓ Ⓔ	72 Ⓐ Ⓑ Ⓒ Ⓓ Ⓔ	97 Ⓐ Ⓑ Ⓒ Ⓓ Ⓔ
23 Ⓐ Ⓑ Ⓒ Ⓓ Ⓔ	48 Ⓐ Ⓑ Ⓒ Ⓓ Ⓔ	73 Ⓐ Ⓑ Ⓒ Ⓓ Ⓔ	98 Ⓐ Ⓑ Ⓒ Ⓓ Ⓔ
24 Ⓐ Ⓑ Ⓒ Ⓓ Ⓔ	49 Ⓐ Ⓑ Ⓒ Ⓓ Ⓔ	74 Ⓐ Ⓑ Ⓒ Ⓓ Ⓔ	99 Ⓐ Ⓑ Ⓒ Ⓓ Ⓔ
25 Ⓐ Ⓑ Ⓒ Ⓓ Ⓔ	50 Ⓐ Ⓑ Ⓒ Ⓓ Ⓔ	75 Ⓐ Ⓑ Ⓒ Ⓓ Ⓔ	100 Ⓐ Ⓑ Ⓒ Ⓓ Ⓔ

Important: Fill in items 8 and 9 exactly as shown on the back of test book.

8 BOOK CODE (Copy and grid as on back of test book.)

9 BOOK ID (Copy from back of test book.)

10 TEST BOOK SERIAL NUMBER (Copy from front of test book.)

Quality Assurance Mark

Chemistry *Fill in circle CE only if II is correct explanation of I.

	I	II	CE*		I	II	CE*
101	Ⓣ Ⓕ	Ⓣ Ⓕ	○	109	Ⓣ Ⓕ	Ⓣ Ⓕ	○
102	Ⓣ Ⓕ	Ⓣ Ⓕ	○	110	Ⓣ Ⓕ	Ⓣ Ⓕ	○
103	Ⓣ Ⓕ	Ⓣ Ⓕ	○	111	Ⓣ Ⓕ	Ⓣ Ⓕ	○
104	Ⓣ Ⓕ	Ⓣ Ⓕ	○	112	Ⓣ Ⓕ	Ⓣ Ⓕ	○
105	Ⓣ Ⓕ	Ⓣ Ⓕ	○	113	Ⓣ Ⓕ	Ⓣ Ⓕ	○
106	Ⓣ Ⓕ	Ⓣ Ⓕ	○	114	Ⓣ Ⓕ	Ⓣ Ⓕ	○
107	Ⓣ Ⓕ	Ⓣ Ⓕ	○	115	Ⓣ Ⓕ	Ⓣ Ⓕ	○
108	Ⓣ Ⓕ	Ⓣ Ⓕ	○				

FOR OFFICIAL USE ONLY				
R/C	W/S1	FS/S2	CS/S3	WS

CERTIFICATION STATEMENT
Copy the statement below (do not print) and sign your name as you would an official document.

I hereby agree to the conditions set forth online at sat.collegeboard.com and in any paper registration materials given to me and certify that I am the person whose name and address appear on this answer sheet.

_____

_____

_____

_____

Signature _____   Date _____

By registering, you agreed not to share any specific test question with anyone by any form of communication, including, but not limited to: email, text messages, or use of the Internet. Doing so can result in score cancellation and other possible sanctions.

○ Literature
○ Biology E
○ Biology M
○ Chemistry
○ Physics

○ Mathematics Level 1
○ Mathematics Level 2
○ U.S. History
○ World History
○ French

○ German
○ Italian
○ Latin
○ Modern Hebrew
○ Spanish

Background Questions: ① ② ③ ④ ⑤ ⑥ ⑦ ⑧ ⑨

1 Ⓐ Ⓑ Ⓒ Ⓓ Ⓔ
2 Ⓐ Ⓑ Ⓒ Ⓓ Ⓔ
3 Ⓐ Ⓑ Ⓒ Ⓓ Ⓔ
4 Ⓐ Ⓑ Ⓒ Ⓓ Ⓔ
5 Ⓐ Ⓑ Ⓒ Ⓓ Ⓔ
6 Ⓐ Ⓑ Ⓒ Ⓓ Ⓔ
7 Ⓐ Ⓑ Ⓒ Ⓓ Ⓔ
8 Ⓐ Ⓑ Ⓒ Ⓓ Ⓔ
9 Ⓐ Ⓑ Ⓒ Ⓓ Ⓔ
10 Ⓐ Ⓑ Ⓒ Ⓓ Ⓔ
11 Ⓐ Ⓑ Ⓒ Ⓓ Ⓔ
12 Ⓐ Ⓑ Ⓒ Ⓓ Ⓔ
13 Ⓐ Ⓑ Ⓒ Ⓓ Ⓔ
14 Ⓐ Ⓑ Ⓒ Ⓓ Ⓔ
15 Ⓐ Ⓑ Ⓒ Ⓓ Ⓔ
16 Ⓐ Ⓑ Ⓒ Ⓓ Ⓔ
17 Ⓐ Ⓑ Ⓒ Ⓓ Ⓔ
18 Ⓐ Ⓑ Ⓒ Ⓓ Ⓔ
19 Ⓐ Ⓑ Ⓒ Ⓓ Ⓔ
20 Ⓐ Ⓑ Ⓒ Ⓓ Ⓔ
21 Ⓐ Ⓑ Ⓒ Ⓓ Ⓔ
22 Ⓐ Ⓑ Ⓒ Ⓓ Ⓔ
23 Ⓐ Ⓑ Ⓒ Ⓓ Ⓔ
24 Ⓐ Ⓑ Ⓒ Ⓓ Ⓔ
25 Ⓐ Ⓑ Ⓒ Ⓓ Ⓔ

26 Ⓐ Ⓑ Ⓒ Ⓓ Ⓔ
27 Ⓐ Ⓑ Ⓒ Ⓓ Ⓔ
28 Ⓐ Ⓑ Ⓒ Ⓓ Ⓔ
29 Ⓐ Ⓑ Ⓒ Ⓓ Ⓔ
30 Ⓐ Ⓑ Ⓒ Ⓓ Ⓔ
31 Ⓐ Ⓑ Ⓒ Ⓓ Ⓔ
32 Ⓐ Ⓑ Ⓒ Ⓓ Ⓔ
33 Ⓐ Ⓑ Ⓒ Ⓓ Ⓔ
34 Ⓐ Ⓑ Ⓒ Ⓓ Ⓔ
35 Ⓐ Ⓑ Ⓒ Ⓓ Ⓔ
36 Ⓐ Ⓑ Ⓒ Ⓓ Ⓔ
37 Ⓐ Ⓑ Ⓒ Ⓓ Ⓔ
38 Ⓐ Ⓑ Ⓒ Ⓓ Ⓔ
39 Ⓐ Ⓑ Ⓒ Ⓓ Ⓔ
40 Ⓐ Ⓑ Ⓒ Ⓓ Ⓔ
41 Ⓐ Ⓑ Ⓒ Ⓓ Ⓔ
42 Ⓐ Ⓑ Ⓒ Ⓓ Ⓔ
43 Ⓐ Ⓑ Ⓒ Ⓓ Ⓔ
44 Ⓐ Ⓑ Ⓒ Ⓓ Ⓔ
45 Ⓐ Ⓑ Ⓒ Ⓓ Ⓔ
46 Ⓐ Ⓑ Ⓒ Ⓓ Ⓔ
47 Ⓐ Ⓑ Ⓒ Ⓓ Ⓔ
48 Ⓐ Ⓑ Ⓒ Ⓓ Ⓔ
49 Ⓐ Ⓑ Ⓒ Ⓓ Ⓔ
50 Ⓐ Ⓑ Ⓒ Ⓓ Ⓔ

51 Ⓐ Ⓑ Ⓒ Ⓓ Ⓔ
52 Ⓐ Ⓑ Ⓒ Ⓓ Ⓔ
53 Ⓐ Ⓑ Ⓒ Ⓓ Ⓔ
54 Ⓐ Ⓑ Ⓒ Ⓓ Ⓔ
55 Ⓐ Ⓑ Ⓒ Ⓓ Ⓔ
56 Ⓐ Ⓑ Ⓒ Ⓓ Ⓔ
57 Ⓐ Ⓑ Ⓒ Ⓓ Ⓔ
58 Ⓐ Ⓑ Ⓒ Ⓓ Ⓔ
59 Ⓐ Ⓑ Ⓒ Ⓓ Ⓔ
60 Ⓐ Ⓑ Ⓒ Ⓓ Ⓔ
61 Ⓐ Ⓑ Ⓒ Ⓓ Ⓔ
62 Ⓐ Ⓑ Ⓒ Ⓓ Ⓔ
63 Ⓐ Ⓑ Ⓒ Ⓓ Ⓔ
64 Ⓐ Ⓑ Ⓒ Ⓓ Ⓔ
65 Ⓐ Ⓑ Ⓒ Ⓓ Ⓔ
66 Ⓐ Ⓑ Ⓒ Ⓓ Ⓔ
67 Ⓐ Ⓑ Ⓒ Ⓓ Ⓔ
68 Ⓐ Ⓑ Ⓒ Ⓓ Ⓔ
69 Ⓐ Ⓑ Ⓒ Ⓓ Ⓔ
70 Ⓐ Ⓑ Ⓒ Ⓓ Ⓔ
71 Ⓐ Ⓑ Ⓒ Ⓓ Ⓔ
72 Ⓐ Ⓑ Ⓒ Ⓓ Ⓔ
73 Ⓐ Ⓑ Ⓒ Ⓓ Ⓔ
74 Ⓐ Ⓑ Ⓒ Ⓓ Ⓔ
75 Ⓐ Ⓑ Ⓒ Ⓓ Ⓔ

76 Ⓐ Ⓑ Ⓒ Ⓓ Ⓔ
77 Ⓐ Ⓑ Ⓒ Ⓓ Ⓔ
78 Ⓐ Ⓑ Ⓒ Ⓓ Ⓔ
79 Ⓐ Ⓑ Ⓒ Ⓓ Ⓔ
80 Ⓐ Ⓑ Ⓒ Ⓓ Ⓔ
81 Ⓐ Ⓑ Ⓒ Ⓓ Ⓔ
82 Ⓐ Ⓑ Ⓒ Ⓓ Ⓔ
83 Ⓐ Ⓑ Ⓒ Ⓓ Ⓔ
84 Ⓐ Ⓑ Ⓒ Ⓓ Ⓔ
85 Ⓐ Ⓑ Ⓒ Ⓓ Ⓔ
86 Ⓐ Ⓑ Ⓒ Ⓓ Ⓔ
87 Ⓐ Ⓑ Ⓒ Ⓓ Ⓔ
88 Ⓐ Ⓑ Ⓒ Ⓓ Ⓔ
89 Ⓐ Ⓑ Ⓒ Ⓓ Ⓔ
90 Ⓐ Ⓑ Ⓒ Ⓓ Ⓔ
91 Ⓐ Ⓑ Ⓒ Ⓓ Ⓔ
92 Ⓐ Ⓑ Ⓒ Ⓓ Ⓔ
93 Ⓐ Ⓑ Ⓒ Ⓓ Ⓔ
94 Ⓐ Ⓑ Ⓒ Ⓓ Ⓔ
95 Ⓐ Ⓑ Ⓒ Ⓓ Ⓔ
96 Ⓐ Ⓑ Ⓒ Ⓓ Ⓔ
97 Ⓐ Ⓑ Ⓒ Ⓓ Ⓔ
98 Ⓐ Ⓑ Ⓒ Ⓓ Ⓔ
99 Ⓐ Ⓑ Ⓒ Ⓓ Ⓔ
100 Ⓐ Ⓑ Ⓒ Ⓓ Ⓔ

Quality Assurance Mark ●

Important: Fill in items 8 and 9 exactly as shown on the back of test book.

8 BOOK CODE (Copy and grid as on back of test book.)

9 BOOK ID (Copy from back of test book.)

10 TEST BOOK SERIAL NUMBER (Copy from front of test book.)

Chemistry *Fill in circle CE only if II is correct explanation of I.

	I	II	CE*		I	II	CE*
101	Ⓣ Ⓕ	Ⓣ Ⓕ	○	109	Ⓣ Ⓕ	Ⓣ Ⓕ	○
102	Ⓣ Ⓕ	Ⓣ Ⓕ	○	110	Ⓣ Ⓕ	Ⓣ Ⓕ	○
103	Ⓣ Ⓕ	Ⓣ Ⓕ	○	111	Ⓣ Ⓕ	Ⓣ Ⓕ	○
104	Ⓣ Ⓕ	Ⓣ Ⓕ	○	112	Ⓣ Ⓕ	Ⓣ Ⓕ	○
105	Ⓣ Ⓕ	Ⓣ Ⓕ	○	113	Ⓣ Ⓕ	Ⓣ Ⓕ	○
106	Ⓣ Ⓕ	Ⓣ Ⓕ	○	114	Ⓣ Ⓕ	Ⓣ Ⓕ	○
107	Ⓣ Ⓕ	Ⓣ Ⓕ	○	115	Ⓣ Ⓕ	Ⓣ Ⓕ	○
108	Ⓣ Ⓕ	Ⓣ Ⓕ	○				

FOR OFFICIAL USE ONLY				
R/C	W/S1	FS/S2	CS/S3	WS

| COMPLETE MARK ● | EXAMPLES OF INCOMPLETE MARKS | You must use a No. 2 pencil and marks must be complete. Do not use a mechanical pencil. It is very important that you fill in the entire circle darkly and completely. If you change your response, erase as completely as possible. Incomplete marks or erasures may affect your score. |

○ Literature
○ Biology E
○ Biology M
○ Chemistry
○ Physics

○ Mathematics Level 1
○ Mathematics Level 2
○ U.S. History
○ World History
○ French

○ German
○ Italian
○ Latin
○ Modern Hebrew
○ Spanish

Background Questions: ① ② ③ ④ ⑤ ⑥ ⑦ ⑧ ⑨

1 Ⓐ Ⓑ Ⓒ Ⓓ Ⓔ
2 Ⓐ Ⓑ Ⓒ Ⓓ Ⓔ
3 Ⓐ Ⓑ Ⓒ Ⓓ Ⓔ
4 Ⓐ Ⓑ Ⓒ Ⓓ Ⓔ
5 Ⓐ Ⓑ Ⓒ Ⓓ Ⓔ
6 Ⓐ Ⓑ Ⓒ Ⓓ Ⓔ
7 Ⓐ Ⓑ Ⓒ Ⓓ Ⓔ
8 Ⓐ Ⓑ Ⓒ Ⓓ Ⓔ
9 Ⓐ Ⓑ Ⓒ Ⓓ Ⓔ
10 Ⓐ Ⓑ Ⓒ Ⓓ Ⓔ
11 Ⓐ Ⓑ Ⓒ Ⓓ Ⓔ
12 Ⓐ Ⓑ Ⓒ Ⓓ Ⓔ
13 Ⓐ Ⓑ Ⓒ Ⓓ Ⓔ
14 Ⓐ Ⓑ Ⓒ Ⓓ Ⓔ
15 Ⓐ Ⓑ Ⓒ Ⓓ Ⓔ
16 Ⓐ Ⓑ Ⓒ Ⓓ Ⓔ
17 Ⓐ Ⓑ Ⓒ Ⓓ Ⓔ
18 Ⓐ Ⓑ Ⓒ Ⓓ Ⓔ
19 Ⓐ Ⓑ Ⓒ Ⓓ Ⓔ
20 Ⓐ Ⓑ Ⓒ Ⓓ Ⓔ
21 Ⓐ Ⓑ Ⓒ Ⓓ Ⓔ
22 Ⓐ Ⓑ Ⓒ Ⓓ Ⓔ
23 Ⓐ Ⓑ Ⓒ Ⓓ Ⓔ
24 Ⓐ Ⓑ Ⓒ Ⓓ Ⓔ
25 Ⓐ Ⓑ Ⓒ Ⓓ Ⓔ

26 Ⓐ Ⓑ Ⓒ Ⓓ Ⓔ
27 Ⓐ Ⓑ Ⓒ Ⓓ Ⓔ
28 Ⓐ Ⓑ Ⓒ Ⓓ Ⓔ
29 Ⓐ Ⓑ Ⓒ Ⓓ Ⓔ
30 Ⓐ Ⓑ Ⓒ Ⓓ Ⓔ
31 Ⓐ Ⓑ Ⓒ Ⓓ Ⓔ
32 Ⓐ Ⓑ Ⓒ Ⓓ Ⓔ
33 Ⓐ Ⓑ Ⓒ Ⓓ Ⓔ
34 Ⓐ Ⓑ Ⓒ Ⓓ Ⓔ
35 Ⓐ Ⓑ Ⓒ Ⓓ Ⓔ
36 Ⓐ Ⓑ Ⓒ Ⓓ Ⓔ
37 Ⓐ Ⓑ Ⓒ Ⓓ Ⓔ
38 Ⓐ Ⓑ Ⓒ Ⓓ Ⓔ
39 Ⓐ Ⓑ Ⓒ Ⓓ Ⓔ
40 Ⓐ Ⓑ Ⓒ Ⓓ Ⓔ
41 Ⓐ Ⓑ Ⓒ Ⓓ Ⓔ
42 Ⓐ Ⓑ Ⓒ Ⓓ Ⓔ
43 Ⓐ Ⓑ Ⓒ Ⓓ Ⓔ
44 Ⓐ Ⓑ Ⓒ Ⓓ Ⓔ
45 Ⓐ Ⓑ Ⓒ Ⓓ Ⓔ
46 Ⓐ Ⓑ Ⓒ Ⓓ Ⓔ
47 Ⓐ Ⓑ Ⓒ Ⓓ Ⓔ
48 Ⓐ Ⓑ Ⓒ Ⓓ Ⓔ
49 Ⓐ Ⓑ Ⓒ Ⓓ Ⓔ
50 Ⓐ Ⓑ Ⓒ Ⓓ Ⓔ

51 Ⓐ Ⓑ Ⓒ Ⓓ Ⓔ
52 Ⓐ Ⓑ Ⓒ Ⓓ Ⓔ
53 Ⓐ Ⓑ Ⓒ Ⓓ Ⓔ
54 Ⓐ Ⓑ Ⓒ Ⓓ Ⓔ
55 Ⓐ Ⓑ Ⓒ Ⓓ Ⓔ
56 Ⓐ Ⓑ Ⓒ Ⓓ Ⓔ
57 Ⓐ Ⓑ Ⓒ Ⓓ Ⓔ
58 Ⓐ Ⓑ Ⓒ Ⓓ Ⓔ
59 Ⓐ Ⓑ Ⓒ Ⓓ Ⓔ
60 Ⓐ Ⓑ Ⓒ Ⓓ Ⓔ
61 Ⓐ Ⓑ Ⓒ Ⓓ Ⓔ
62 Ⓐ Ⓑ Ⓒ Ⓓ Ⓔ
63 Ⓐ Ⓑ Ⓒ Ⓓ Ⓔ
64 Ⓐ Ⓑ Ⓒ Ⓓ Ⓔ
65 Ⓐ Ⓑ Ⓒ Ⓓ Ⓔ
66 Ⓐ Ⓑ Ⓒ Ⓓ Ⓔ
67 Ⓐ Ⓑ Ⓒ Ⓓ Ⓔ
68 Ⓐ Ⓑ Ⓒ Ⓓ Ⓔ
69 Ⓐ Ⓑ Ⓒ Ⓓ Ⓔ
70 Ⓐ Ⓑ Ⓒ Ⓓ Ⓔ
71 Ⓐ Ⓑ Ⓒ Ⓓ Ⓔ
72 Ⓐ Ⓑ Ⓒ Ⓓ Ⓔ
73 Ⓐ Ⓑ Ⓒ Ⓓ Ⓔ
74 Ⓐ Ⓑ Ⓒ Ⓓ Ⓔ
75 Ⓐ Ⓑ Ⓒ Ⓓ Ⓔ

76 Ⓐ Ⓑ Ⓒ Ⓓ Ⓔ
77 Ⓐ Ⓑ Ⓒ Ⓓ Ⓔ
78 Ⓐ Ⓑ Ⓒ Ⓓ Ⓔ
79 Ⓐ Ⓑ Ⓒ Ⓓ Ⓔ
80 Ⓐ Ⓑ Ⓒ Ⓓ Ⓔ
81 Ⓐ Ⓑ Ⓒ Ⓓ Ⓔ
82 Ⓐ Ⓑ Ⓒ Ⓓ Ⓔ
83 Ⓐ Ⓑ Ⓒ Ⓓ Ⓔ
84 Ⓐ Ⓑ Ⓒ Ⓓ Ⓔ
85 Ⓐ Ⓑ Ⓒ Ⓓ Ⓔ
86 Ⓐ Ⓑ Ⓒ Ⓓ Ⓔ
87 Ⓐ Ⓑ Ⓒ Ⓓ Ⓔ
88 Ⓐ Ⓑ Ⓒ Ⓓ Ⓔ
89 Ⓐ Ⓑ Ⓒ Ⓓ Ⓔ
90 Ⓐ Ⓑ Ⓒ Ⓓ Ⓔ
91 Ⓐ Ⓑ Ⓒ Ⓓ Ⓔ
92 Ⓐ Ⓑ Ⓒ Ⓓ Ⓔ
93 Ⓐ Ⓑ Ⓒ Ⓓ Ⓔ
94 Ⓐ Ⓑ Ⓒ Ⓓ Ⓔ
95 Ⓐ Ⓑ Ⓒ Ⓓ Ⓔ
96 Ⓐ Ⓑ Ⓒ Ⓓ Ⓔ
97 Ⓐ Ⓑ Ⓒ Ⓓ Ⓔ
98 Ⓐ Ⓑ Ⓒ Ⓓ Ⓔ
99 Ⓐ Ⓑ Ⓒ Ⓓ Ⓔ
100 Ⓐ Ⓑ Ⓒ Ⓓ Ⓔ

Important: Fill in items 8 and 9 exactly as shown on the back of test book.

8 BOOK CODE (Copy and grid as on back of test book.)

9 BOOK ID (Copy from back of test book.)

10 TEST BOOK SERIAL NUMBER (Copy from front of test book.)

Quality ● Assurance Mark

Chemistry *Fill in circle CE only if II is correct explanation of I.

	I	II	CE*		I	II	CE*
101	Ⓣ Ⓕ	Ⓣ Ⓕ	○	109	Ⓣ Ⓕ	Ⓣ Ⓕ	○
102	Ⓣ Ⓕ	Ⓣ Ⓕ	○	110	Ⓣ Ⓕ	Ⓣ Ⓕ	○
103	Ⓣ Ⓕ	Ⓣ Ⓕ	○	111	Ⓣ Ⓕ	Ⓣ Ⓕ	○
104	Ⓣ Ⓕ	Ⓣ Ⓕ	○	112	Ⓣ Ⓕ	Ⓣ Ⓕ	○
105	Ⓣ Ⓕ	Ⓣ Ⓕ	○	113	Ⓣ Ⓕ	Ⓣ Ⓕ	○
106	Ⓣ Ⓕ	Ⓣ Ⓕ	○	114	Ⓣ Ⓕ	Ⓣ Ⓕ	○
107	Ⓣ Ⓕ	Ⓣ Ⓕ	○	115	Ⓣ Ⓕ	Ⓣ Ⓕ	○
108	Ⓣ Ⓕ	Ⓣ Ⓕ	○				

FOR OFFICIAL USE ONLY				
R/C	W/S1	FS/S2	CS/S3	WS

Page 4

PLEASE DO NOT WRITE IN THIS AREA

SERIAL #

2010-11 SAT Subject Tests™

You must use a No. 2 pencil. Do not use a mechanical pencil. It is very important that you fill in the entire circle darkly and completely. If you change your response, erase as completely as possible. Incomplete marks or erasures may affect your score. It is very important that you follow these instructions when filling out your answer sheet.

MARKS MUST BE COMPLETE

COMPLETE MARK ●

EXAMPLES OF INCOMPLETE MARKS

1 Your Name:
(Print)

Last   First   M.I.

I agree to the conditions on the front and back of the SAT Subject Tests™ book. I also agree to use only a No. 2 pencil to complete my answer sheet.

Signature: Date: / /
                         MM DD YY

Home Address:
(Print)
Number and Street   City   State   Zip Code

Home Phone: (   )   Test Center:
(Print)   City   State/Country

2 YOUR NAME
Last Name (First 6 Letters)   First Name (First 4 Letters)   Mid. Init.

3 DATE OF BIRTH
MONTH   DAY   YEAR
Jan
Feb
Mar
Apr
May
Jun
Jul
Aug
Sep
Oct
Nov
Dec

4 ZIP CODE

5 SEX
○ Female   ○ Male

6 REGISTRATION NUMBER
(Copy from Admission Ticket.)

○ I turned in my registration form today.

7 TEST CENTER
(Supplied by Test Center Supervisor.)

Important: Fill in items 8 and 9 exactly as shown on the back of test book.

8 BOOK CODE
(Copy and grid as on back of test book.)

9 BOOK ID
(Copy from back of test book.)

10 TEST BOOK SERIAL NUMBER
(Copy from front of test book.)

FOR OFFICIAL USE ONLY

83161-77191 • NS60C1285 • Printed in U.S.A.
755275

184596-001:321   Printed in the USA by Pearson   ISD0479

PLEASE DO NOT WRITE IN THIS AREA   **SERIAL #**

○ Literature
○ Biology E
○ Biology M
○ Chemistry
○ Physics

○ Mathematics Level 1
○ Mathematics Level 2
○ U.S. History
○ World History
○ French

○ German
○ Italian
○ Latin
○ Modern Hebrew
○ Spanish

○ Chinese Listening
○ French Listening
○ German Listening

○ Japanese Listening
○ Korean Listening
○ Spanish Listening

Background Questions: ① ② ③ ④ ⑤ ⑥ ⑦ ⑧ ⑨

1 Ⓐ Ⓑ Ⓒ Ⓓ Ⓔ   26 Ⓐ Ⓑ Ⓒ Ⓓ Ⓔ   51 Ⓐ Ⓑ Ⓒ Ⓓ Ⓔ   76 Ⓐ Ⓑ Ⓒ Ⓓ Ⓔ
2 Ⓐ Ⓑ Ⓒ Ⓓ Ⓔ   27 Ⓐ Ⓑ Ⓒ Ⓓ Ⓔ   52 Ⓐ Ⓑ Ⓒ Ⓓ Ⓔ   77 Ⓐ Ⓑ Ⓒ Ⓓ Ⓔ
3 Ⓐ Ⓑ Ⓒ Ⓓ Ⓔ   28 Ⓐ Ⓑ Ⓒ Ⓓ Ⓔ   53 Ⓐ Ⓑ Ⓒ Ⓓ Ⓔ   78 Ⓐ Ⓑ Ⓒ Ⓓ Ⓔ
4 Ⓐ Ⓑ Ⓒ Ⓓ Ⓔ   29 Ⓐ Ⓑ Ⓒ Ⓓ Ⓔ   54 Ⓐ Ⓑ Ⓒ Ⓓ Ⓔ   79 Ⓐ Ⓑ Ⓒ Ⓓ Ⓔ
5 Ⓐ Ⓑ Ⓒ Ⓓ Ⓔ   30 Ⓐ Ⓑ Ⓒ Ⓓ Ⓔ   55 Ⓐ Ⓑ Ⓒ Ⓓ Ⓔ   80 Ⓐ Ⓑ Ⓒ Ⓓ Ⓔ
6 Ⓐ Ⓑ Ⓒ Ⓓ Ⓔ   31 Ⓐ Ⓑ Ⓒ Ⓓ Ⓔ   56 Ⓐ Ⓑ Ⓒ Ⓓ Ⓔ   81 Ⓐ Ⓑ Ⓒ Ⓓ Ⓔ
7 Ⓐ Ⓑ Ⓒ Ⓓ Ⓔ   32 Ⓐ Ⓑ Ⓒ Ⓓ Ⓔ   57 Ⓐ Ⓑ Ⓒ Ⓓ Ⓔ   82 Ⓐ Ⓑ Ⓒ Ⓓ Ⓔ
8 Ⓐ Ⓑ Ⓒ Ⓓ Ⓔ   33 Ⓐ Ⓑ Ⓒ Ⓓ Ⓔ   58 Ⓐ Ⓑ Ⓒ Ⓓ Ⓔ   83 Ⓐ Ⓑ Ⓒ Ⓓ Ⓔ
9 Ⓐ Ⓑ Ⓒ Ⓓ Ⓔ   34 Ⓐ Ⓑ Ⓒ Ⓓ Ⓔ   59 Ⓐ Ⓑ Ⓒ Ⓓ Ⓔ   84 Ⓐ Ⓑ Ⓒ Ⓓ Ⓔ
10 Ⓐ Ⓑ Ⓒ Ⓓ Ⓔ   35 Ⓐ Ⓑ Ⓒ Ⓓ Ⓔ   60 Ⓐ Ⓑ Ⓒ Ⓓ Ⓔ   85 Ⓐ Ⓑ Ⓒ Ⓓ Ⓔ
11 Ⓐ Ⓑ Ⓒ Ⓓ Ⓔ   36 Ⓐ Ⓑ Ⓒ Ⓓ Ⓔ   61 Ⓐ Ⓑ Ⓒ Ⓓ Ⓔ   86 Ⓐ Ⓑ Ⓒ Ⓓ Ⓔ
12 Ⓐ Ⓑ Ⓒ Ⓓ Ⓔ   37 Ⓐ Ⓑ Ⓒ Ⓓ Ⓔ   62 Ⓐ Ⓑ Ⓒ Ⓓ Ⓔ   87 Ⓐ Ⓑ Ⓒ Ⓓ Ⓔ
13 Ⓐ Ⓑ Ⓒ Ⓓ Ⓔ   38 Ⓐ Ⓑ Ⓒ Ⓓ Ⓔ   63 Ⓐ Ⓑ Ⓒ Ⓓ Ⓔ   88 Ⓐ Ⓑ Ⓒ Ⓓ Ⓔ
14 Ⓐ Ⓑ Ⓒ Ⓓ Ⓔ   39 Ⓐ Ⓑ Ⓒ Ⓓ Ⓔ   64 Ⓐ Ⓑ Ⓒ Ⓓ Ⓔ   89 Ⓐ Ⓑ Ⓒ Ⓓ Ⓔ
15 Ⓐ Ⓑ Ⓒ Ⓓ Ⓔ   40 Ⓐ Ⓑ Ⓒ Ⓓ Ⓔ   65 Ⓐ Ⓑ Ⓒ Ⓓ Ⓔ   90 Ⓐ Ⓑ Ⓒ Ⓓ Ⓔ
16 Ⓐ Ⓑ Ⓒ Ⓓ Ⓔ   41 Ⓐ Ⓑ Ⓒ Ⓓ Ⓔ   66 Ⓐ Ⓑ Ⓒ Ⓓ Ⓔ   91 Ⓐ Ⓑ Ⓒ Ⓓ Ⓔ
17 Ⓐ Ⓑ Ⓒ Ⓓ Ⓔ   42 Ⓐ Ⓑ Ⓒ Ⓓ Ⓔ   67 Ⓐ Ⓑ Ⓒ Ⓓ Ⓔ   92 Ⓐ Ⓑ Ⓒ Ⓓ Ⓔ
18 Ⓐ Ⓑ Ⓒ Ⓓ Ⓔ   43 Ⓐ Ⓑ Ⓒ Ⓓ Ⓔ   68 Ⓐ Ⓑ Ⓒ Ⓓ Ⓔ   93 Ⓐ Ⓑ Ⓒ Ⓓ Ⓔ
19 Ⓐ Ⓑ Ⓒ Ⓓ Ⓔ   44 Ⓐ Ⓑ Ⓒ Ⓓ Ⓔ   69 Ⓐ Ⓑ Ⓒ Ⓓ Ⓔ   94 Ⓐ Ⓑ Ⓒ Ⓓ Ⓔ
20 Ⓐ Ⓑ Ⓒ Ⓓ Ⓔ   45 Ⓐ Ⓑ Ⓒ Ⓓ Ⓔ   70 Ⓐ Ⓑ Ⓒ Ⓓ Ⓔ   95 Ⓐ Ⓑ Ⓒ Ⓓ Ⓔ
21 Ⓐ Ⓑ Ⓒ Ⓓ Ⓔ   46 Ⓐ Ⓑ Ⓒ Ⓓ Ⓔ   71 Ⓐ Ⓑ Ⓒ Ⓓ Ⓔ   96 Ⓐ Ⓑ Ⓒ Ⓓ Ⓔ
22 Ⓐ Ⓑ Ⓒ Ⓓ Ⓔ   47 Ⓐ Ⓑ Ⓒ Ⓓ Ⓔ   72 Ⓐ Ⓑ Ⓒ Ⓓ Ⓔ   97 Ⓐ Ⓑ Ⓒ Ⓓ Ⓔ
23 Ⓐ Ⓑ Ⓒ Ⓓ Ⓔ   48 Ⓐ Ⓑ Ⓒ Ⓓ Ⓔ   73 Ⓐ Ⓑ Ⓒ Ⓓ Ⓔ   98 Ⓐ Ⓑ Ⓒ Ⓓ Ⓔ
24 Ⓐ Ⓑ Ⓒ Ⓓ Ⓔ   49 Ⓐ Ⓑ Ⓒ Ⓓ Ⓔ   74 Ⓐ Ⓑ Ⓒ Ⓓ Ⓔ   99 Ⓐ Ⓑ Ⓒ Ⓓ Ⓔ
25 Ⓐ Ⓑ Ⓒ Ⓓ Ⓔ   50 Ⓐ Ⓑ Ⓒ Ⓓ Ⓔ   75 Ⓐ Ⓑ Ⓒ Ⓓ Ⓔ   100 Ⓐ Ⓑ Ⓒ Ⓓ Ⓔ

Important: Fill in items 8 and 9 exactly as shown on the back of test book.

8 BOOK CODE
(Copy and grid as on back of test book.)

9 BOOK ID
(Copy from back of test book.)

10 TEST BOOK SERIAL NUMBER
(Copy from front of test book.)

Quality Assurance Mark ●

Chemistry *Fill in circle CE only if II is correct explanation of I.

	I	II	CE*		I	II	CE*
101	Ⓣ Ⓕ	Ⓣ Ⓕ	○	109	Ⓣ Ⓕ	Ⓣ Ⓕ	○
102	Ⓣ Ⓕ	Ⓣ Ⓕ	○	110	Ⓣ Ⓕ	Ⓣ Ⓕ	○
103	Ⓣ Ⓕ	Ⓣ Ⓕ	○	111	Ⓣ Ⓕ	Ⓣ Ⓕ	○
104	Ⓣ Ⓕ	Ⓣ Ⓕ	○	112	Ⓣ Ⓕ	Ⓣ Ⓕ	○
105	Ⓣ Ⓕ	Ⓣ Ⓕ	○	113	Ⓣ Ⓕ	Ⓣ Ⓕ	○
106	Ⓣ Ⓕ	Ⓣ Ⓕ	○	114	Ⓣ Ⓕ	Ⓣ Ⓕ	○
107	Ⓣ Ⓕ	Ⓣ Ⓕ	○	115	Ⓣ Ⓕ	Ⓣ Ⓕ	○
108	Ⓣ Ⓕ	Ⓣ Ⓕ	○				

FOR OFFICIAL USE ONLY				
R/C	W/S1	FS/S2	CS/S3	WS

CERTIFICATION STATEMENT Copy the statement below (do not print) and sign your name as you would an official document.

I hereby agree to the conditions set forth online at sat.collegeboard.com and in any paper registration materials given to me and certify that I am the person whose name and address appear on this answer sheet.

Signature _____   Date _____

By registering, you agreed not to share any specific test question with anyone by any form of communication, including, but not limited to: email, text messages, or use of the Internet. Doing so can result in score cancellation and other possible sanctions.

Page 2

○ Literature ○ Mathematics Level 1 ○ German
○ Biology E ○ Mathematics Level 2 ○ Italian
○ Biology M ○ U.S. History ○ Latin
○ Chemistry ○ World History ○ Modern Hebrew
○ Physics ○ French ○ Spanish

Background Questions: ① ② ③ ④ ⑤ ⑥ ⑦ ⑧ ⑨

1 Ⓐ Ⓑ Ⓒ Ⓓ Ⓔ   26 Ⓐ Ⓑ Ⓒ Ⓓ Ⓔ   51 Ⓐ Ⓑ Ⓒ Ⓓ Ⓔ   76 Ⓐ Ⓑ Ⓒ Ⓓ Ⓔ
2 Ⓐ Ⓑ Ⓒ Ⓓ Ⓔ   27 Ⓐ Ⓑ Ⓒ Ⓓ Ⓔ   52 Ⓐ Ⓑ Ⓒ Ⓓ Ⓔ   77 Ⓐ Ⓑ Ⓒ Ⓓ Ⓔ
3 Ⓐ Ⓑ Ⓒ Ⓓ Ⓔ   28 Ⓐ Ⓑ Ⓒ Ⓓ Ⓔ   53 Ⓐ Ⓑ Ⓒ Ⓓ Ⓔ   78 Ⓐ Ⓑ Ⓒ Ⓓ Ⓔ
4 Ⓐ Ⓑ Ⓒ Ⓓ Ⓔ   29 Ⓐ Ⓑ Ⓒ Ⓓ Ⓔ   54 Ⓐ Ⓑ Ⓒ Ⓓ Ⓔ   79 Ⓐ Ⓑ Ⓒ Ⓓ Ⓔ
5 Ⓐ Ⓑ Ⓒ Ⓓ Ⓔ   30 Ⓐ Ⓑ Ⓒ Ⓓ Ⓔ   55 Ⓐ Ⓑ Ⓒ Ⓓ Ⓔ   80 Ⓐ Ⓑ Ⓒ Ⓓ Ⓔ
6 Ⓐ Ⓑ Ⓒ Ⓓ Ⓔ   31 Ⓐ Ⓑ Ⓒ Ⓓ Ⓔ   56 Ⓐ Ⓑ Ⓒ Ⓓ Ⓔ   81 Ⓐ Ⓑ Ⓒ Ⓓ Ⓔ
7 Ⓐ Ⓑ Ⓒ Ⓓ Ⓔ   32 Ⓐ Ⓑ Ⓒ Ⓓ Ⓔ   57 Ⓐ Ⓑ Ⓒ Ⓓ Ⓔ   82 Ⓐ Ⓑ Ⓒ Ⓓ Ⓔ
8 Ⓐ Ⓑ Ⓒ Ⓓ Ⓔ   33 Ⓐ Ⓑ Ⓒ Ⓓ Ⓔ   58 Ⓐ Ⓑ Ⓒ Ⓓ Ⓔ   83 Ⓐ Ⓑ Ⓒ Ⓓ Ⓔ
9 Ⓐ Ⓑ Ⓒ Ⓓ Ⓔ   34 Ⓐ Ⓑ Ⓒ Ⓓ Ⓔ   59 Ⓐ Ⓑ Ⓒ Ⓓ Ⓔ   84 Ⓐ Ⓑ Ⓒ Ⓓ Ⓔ
10 Ⓐ Ⓑ Ⓒ Ⓓ Ⓔ   35 Ⓐ Ⓑ Ⓒ Ⓓ Ⓔ   60 Ⓐ Ⓑ Ⓒ Ⓓ Ⓔ   85 Ⓐ Ⓑ Ⓒ Ⓓ Ⓔ
11 Ⓐ Ⓑ Ⓒ Ⓓ Ⓔ   36 Ⓐ Ⓑ Ⓒ Ⓓ Ⓔ   61 Ⓐ Ⓑ Ⓒ Ⓓ Ⓔ   86 Ⓐ Ⓑ Ⓒ Ⓓ Ⓔ
12 Ⓐ Ⓑ Ⓒ Ⓓ Ⓔ   37 Ⓐ Ⓑ Ⓒ Ⓓ Ⓔ   62 Ⓐ Ⓑ Ⓒ Ⓓ Ⓔ   87 Ⓐ Ⓑ Ⓒ Ⓓ Ⓔ
13 Ⓐ Ⓑ Ⓒ Ⓓ Ⓔ   38 Ⓐ Ⓑ Ⓒ Ⓓ Ⓔ   63 Ⓐ Ⓑ Ⓒ Ⓓ Ⓔ   88 Ⓐ Ⓑ Ⓒ Ⓓ Ⓔ
14 Ⓐ Ⓑ Ⓒ Ⓓ Ⓔ   39 Ⓐ Ⓑ Ⓒ Ⓓ Ⓔ   64 Ⓐ Ⓑ Ⓒ Ⓓ Ⓔ   89 Ⓐ Ⓑ Ⓒ Ⓓ Ⓔ
15 Ⓐ Ⓑ Ⓒ Ⓓ Ⓔ   40 Ⓐ Ⓑ Ⓒ Ⓓ Ⓔ   65 Ⓐ Ⓑ Ⓒ Ⓓ Ⓔ   90 Ⓐ Ⓑ Ⓒ Ⓓ Ⓔ
16 Ⓐ Ⓑ Ⓒ Ⓓ Ⓔ   41 Ⓐ Ⓑ Ⓒ Ⓓ Ⓔ   66 Ⓐ Ⓑ Ⓒ Ⓓ Ⓔ   91 Ⓐ Ⓑ Ⓒ Ⓓ Ⓔ
17 Ⓐ Ⓑ Ⓒ Ⓓ Ⓔ   42 Ⓐ Ⓑ Ⓒ Ⓓ Ⓔ   67 Ⓐ Ⓑ Ⓒ Ⓓ Ⓔ   92 Ⓐ Ⓑ Ⓒ Ⓓ Ⓔ
18 Ⓐ Ⓑ Ⓒ Ⓓ Ⓔ   43 Ⓐ Ⓑ Ⓒ Ⓓ Ⓔ   68 Ⓐ Ⓑ Ⓒ Ⓓ Ⓔ   93 Ⓐ Ⓑ Ⓒ Ⓓ Ⓔ
19 Ⓐ Ⓑ Ⓒ Ⓓ Ⓔ   44 Ⓐ Ⓑ Ⓒ Ⓓ Ⓔ   69 Ⓐ Ⓑ Ⓒ Ⓓ Ⓔ   94 Ⓐ Ⓑ Ⓒ Ⓓ Ⓔ
20 Ⓐ Ⓑ Ⓒ Ⓓ Ⓔ   45 Ⓐ Ⓑ Ⓒ Ⓓ Ⓔ   70 Ⓐ Ⓑ Ⓒ Ⓓ Ⓔ   95 Ⓐ Ⓑ Ⓒ Ⓓ Ⓔ
21 Ⓐ Ⓑ Ⓒ Ⓓ Ⓔ   46 Ⓐ Ⓑ Ⓒ Ⓓ Ⓔ   71 Ⓐ Ⓑ Ⓒ Ⓓ Ⓔ   96 Ⓐ Ⓑ Ⓒ Ⓓ Ⓔ
22 Ⓐ Ⓑ Ⓒ Ⓓ Ⓔ   47 Ⓐ Ⓑ Ⓒ Ⓓ Ⓔ   72 Ⓐ Ⓑ Ⓒ Ⓓ Ⓔ   97 Ⓐ Ⓑ Ⓒ Ⓓ Ⓔ
23 Ⓐ Ⓑ Ⓒ Ⓓ Ⓔ   48 Ⓐ Ⓑ Ⓒ Ⓓ Ⓔ   73 Ⓐ Ⓑ Ⓒ Ⓓ Ⓔ   98 Ⓐ Ⓑ Ⓒ Ⓓ Ⓔ
24 Ⓐ Ⓑ Ⓒ Ⓓ Ⓔ   49 Ⓐ Ⓑ Ⓒ Ⓓ Ⓔ   74 Ⓐ Ⓑ Ⓒ Ⓓ Ⓔ   99 Ⓐ Ⓑ Ⓒ Ⓓ Ⓔ
25 Ⓐ Ⓑ Ⓒ Ⓓ Ⓔ   50 Ⓐ Ⓑ Ⓒ Ⓓ Ⓔ   75 Ⓐ Ⓑ Ⓒ Ⓓ Ⓔ   100 Ⓐ Ⓑ Ⓒ Ⓓ Ⓔ

Quality Assurance Mark ●

Important: Fill in items 8 and 9 exactly as shown on the back of test book.

8 BOOK CODE (Copy and grid as on back of test book.)

9 BOOK ID (Copy from back of test book.)

10 TEST BOOK SERIAL NUMBER (Copy from front of test book.)

Chemistry *Fill in circle CE only if II is correct explanation of I.

	I	II	CE*		I	II	CE*
101	Ⓣ Ⓕ	Ⓣ Ⓕ	○	109	Ⓣ Ⓕ	Ⓣ Ⓕ	○
102	Ⓣ Ⓕ	Ⓣ Ⓕ	○	110	Ⓣ Ⓕ	Ⓣ Ⓕ	○
103	Ⓣ Ⓕ	Ⓣ Ⓕ	○	111	Ⓣ Ⓕ	Ⓣ Ⓕ	○
104	Ⓣ Ⓕ	Ⓣ Ⓕ	○	112	Ⓣ Ⓕ	Ⓣ Ⓕ	○
105	Ⓣ Ⓕ	Ⓣ Ⓕ	○	113	Ⓣ Ⓕ	Ⓣ Ⓕ	○
106	Ⓣ Ⓕ	Ⓣ Ⓕ	○	114	Ⓣ Ⓕ	Ⓣ Ⓕ	○
107	Ⓣ Ⓕ	Ⓣ Ⓕ	○	115	Ⓣ Ⓕ	Ⓣ Ⓕ	○
108	Ⓣ Ⓕ	Ⓣ Ⓕ	○				

FOR OFFICIAL USE ONLY				
R/C	W/S1	FS/S2	CS/S3	WS

Page 3

○ Literature
○ Biology E
○ Biology M
○ Chemistry
○ Physics

○ Mathematics Level 1
○ Mathematics Level 2
○ U.S. History
○ World History
○ French

○ German
○ Italian
○ Latin
○ Modern Hebrew
○ Spanish

Background Questions: ① ② ③ ④ ⑤ ⑥ ⑦ ⑧ ⑨

1 Ⓐ Ⓑ Ⓒ Ⓓ Ⓔ   26 Ⓐ Ⓑ Ⓒ Ⓓ Ⓔ   51 Ⓐ Ⓑ Ⓒ Ⓓ Ⓔ   76 Ⓐ Ⓑ Ⓒ Ⓓ Ⓔ
2 Ⓐ Ⓑ Ⓒ Ⓓ Ⓔ   27 Ⓐ Ⓑ Ⓒ Ⓓ Ⓔ   52 Ⓐ Ⓑ Ⓒ Ⓓ Ⓔ   77 Ⓐ Ⓑ Ⓒ Ⓓ Ⓔ
3 Ⓐ Ⓑ Ⓒ Ⓓ Ⓔ   28 Ⓐ Ⓑ Ⓒ Ⓓ Ⓔ   53 Ⓐ Ⓑ Ⓒ Ⓓ Ⓔ   78 Ⓐ Ⓑ Ⓒ Ⓓ Ⓔ
4 Ⓐ Ⓑ Ⓒ Ⓓ Ⓔ   29 Ⓐ Ⓑ Ⓒ Ⓓ Ⓔ   54 Ⓐ Ⓑ Ⓒ Ⓓ Ⓔ   79 Ⓐ Ⓑ Ⓒ Ⓓ Ⓔ
5 Ⓐ Ⓑ Ⓒ Ⓓ Ⓔ   30 Ⓐ Ⓑ Ⓒ Ⓓ Ⓔ   55 Ⓐ Ⓑ Ⓒ Ⓓ Ⓔ   80 Ⓐ Ⓑ Ⓒ Ⓓ Ⓔ
6 Ⓐ Ⓑ Ⓒ Ⓓ Ⓔ   31 Ⓐ Ⓑ Ⓒ Ⓓ Ⓔ   56 Ⓐ Ⓑ Ⓒ Ⓓ Ⓔ   81 Ⓐ Ⓑ Ⓒ Ⓓ Ⓔ
7 Ⓐ Ⓑ Ⓒ Ⓓ Ⓔ   32 Ⓐ Ⓑ Ⓒ Ⓓ Ⓔ   57 Ⓐ Ⓑ Ⓒ Ⓓ Ⓔ   82 Ⓐ Ⓑ Ⓒ Ⓓ Ⓔ
8 Ⓐ Ⓑ Ⓒ Ⓓ Ⓔ   33 Ⓐ Ⓑ Ⓒ Ⓓ Ⓔ   58 Ⓐ Ⓑ Ⓒ Ⓓ Ⓔ   83 Ⓐ Ⓑ Ⓒ Ⓓ Ⓔ
9 Ⓐ Ⓑ Ⓒ Ⓓ Ⓔ   34 Ⓐ Ⓑ Ⓒ Ⓓ Ⓔ   59 Ⓐ Ⓑ Ⓒ Ⓓ Ⓔ   84 Ⓐ Ⓑ Ⓒ Ⓓ Ⓔ
10 Ⓐ Ⓑ Ⓒ Ⓓ Ⓔ   35 Ⓐ Ⓑ Ⓒ Ⓓ Ⓔ   60 Ⓐ Ⓑ Ⓒ Ⓓ Ⓔ   85 Ⓐ Ⓑ Ⓒ Ⓓ Ⓔ
11 Ⓐ Ⓑ Ⓒ Ⓓ Ⓔ   36 Ⓐ Ⓑ Ⓒ Ⓓ Ⓔ   61 Ⓐ Ⓑ Ⓒ Ⓓ Ⓔ   86 Ⓐ Ⓑ Ⓒ Ⓓ Ⓔ
12 Ⓐ Ⓑ Ⓒ Ⓓ Ⓔ   37 Ⓐ Ⓑ Ⓒ Ⓓ Ⓔ   62 Ⓐ Ⓑ Ⓒ Ⓓ Ⓔ   87 Ⓐ Ⓑ Ⓒ Ⓓ Ⓔ
13 Ⓐ Ⓑ Ⓒ Ⓓ Ⓔ   38 Ⓐ Ⓑ Ⓒ Ⓓ Ⓔ   63 Ⓐ Ⓑ Ⓒ Ⓓ Ⓔ   88 Ⓐ Ⓑ Ⓒ Ⓓ Ⓔ
14 Ⓐ Ⓑ Ⓒ Ⓓ Ⓔ   39 Ⓐ Ⓑ Ⓒ Ⓓ Ⓔ   64 Ⓐ Ⓑ Ⓒ Ⓓ Ⓔ   89 Ⓐ Ⓑ Ⓒ Ⓓ Ⓔ
15 Ⓐ Ⓑ Ⓒ Ⓓ Ⓔ   40 Ⓐ Ⓑ Ⓒ Ⓓ Ⓔ   65 Ⓐ Ⓑ Ⓒ Ⓓ Ⓔ   90 Ⓐ Ⓑ Ⓒ Ⓓ Ⓔ
16 Ⓐ Ⓑ Ⓒ Ⓓ Ⓔ   41 Ⓐ Ⓑ Ⓒ Ⓓ Ⓔ   66 Ⓐ Ⓑ Ⓒ Ⓓ Ⓔ   91 Ⓐ Ⓑ Ⓒ Ⓓ Ⓔ
17 Ⓐ Ⓑ Ⓒ Ⓓ Ⓔ   42 Ⓐ Ⓑ Ⓒ Ⓓ Ⓔ   67 Ⓐ Ⓑ Ⓒ Ⓓ Ⓔ   92 Ⓐ Ⓑ Ⓒ Ⓓ Ⓔ
18 Ⓐ Ⓑ Ⓒ Ⓓ Ⓔ   43 Ⓐ Ⓑ Ⓒ Ⓓ Ⓔ   68 Ⓐ Ⓑ Ⓒ Ⓓ Ⓔ   93 Ⓐ Ⓑ Ⓒ Ⓓ Ⓔ
19 Ⓐ Ⓑ Ⓒ Ⓓ Ⓔ   44 Ⓐ Ⓑ Ⓒ Ⓓ Ⓔ   69 Ⓐ Ⓑ Ⓒ Ⓓ Ⓔ   94 Ⓐ Ⓑ Ⓒ Ⓓ Ⓔ
20 Ⓐ Ⓑ Ⓒ Ⓓ Ⓔ   45 Ⓐ Ⓑ Ⓒ Ⓓ Ⓔ   70 Ⓐ Ⓑ Ⓒ Ⓓ Ⓔ   95 Ⓐ Ⓑ Ⓒ Ⓓ Ⓔ
21 Ⓐ Ⓑ Ⓒ Ⓓ Ⓔ   46 Ⓐ Ⓑ Ⓒ Ⓓ Ⓔ   71 Ⓐ Ⓑ Ⓒ Ⓓ Ⓔ   96 Ⓐ Ⓑ Ⓒ Ⓓ Ⓔ
22 Ⓐ Ⓑ Ⓒ Ⓓ Ⓔ   47 Ⓐ Ⓑ Ⓒ Ⓓ Ⓔ   72 Ⓐ Ⓑ Ⓒ Ⓓ Ⓔ   97 Ⓐ Ⓑ Ⓒ Ⓓ Ⓔ
23 Ⓐ Ⓑ Ⓒ Ⓓ Ⓔ   48 Ⓐ Ⓑ Ⓒ Ⓓ Ⓔ   73 Ⓐ Ⓑ Ⓒ Ⓓ Ⓔ   98 Ⓐ Ⓑ Ⓒ Ⓓ Ⓔ
24 Ⓐ Ⓑ Ⓒ Ⓓ Ⓔ   49 Ⓐ Ⓑ Ⓒ Ⓓ Ⓔ   74 Ⓐ Ⓑ Ⓒ Ⓓ Ⓔ   99 Ⓐ Ⓑ Ⓒ Ⓓ Ⓔ
25 Ⓐ Ⓑ Ⓒ Ⓓ Ⓔ   50 Ⓐ Ⓑ Ⓒ Ⓓ Ⓔ   75 Ⓐ Ⓑ Ⓒ Ⓓ Ⓔ   100 Ⓐ Ⓑ Ⓒ Ⓓ Ⓔ

Important: Fill in items 8 and 9 exactly as shown on the back of test book.

8 BOOK CODE (Copy and grid as on back of test book.)

9 BOOK ID (Copy from back of test book.)

10 TEST BOOK SERIAL NUMBER (Copy from front of test book.)

Quality Assurance Mark

Chemistry *Fill in circle CE only if II is correct explanation of I.

	I	II	CE*		I	II	CE*
101	Ⓣ Ⓕ	Ⓣ Ⓕ	○	109	Ⓣ Ⓕ	Ⓣ Ⓕ	○
102	Ⓣ Ⓕ	Ⓣ Ⓕ	○	110	Ⓣ Ⓕ	Ⓣ Ⓕ	○
103	Ⓣ Ⓕ	Ⓣ Ⓕ	○	111	Ⓣ Ⓕ	Ⓣ Ⓕ	○
104	Ⓣ Ⓕ	Ⓣ Ⓕ	○	112	Ⓣ Ⓕ	Ⓣ Ⓕ	○
105	Ⓣ Ⓕ	Ⓣ Ⓕ	○	113	Ⓣ Ⓕ	Ⓣ Ⓕ	○
106	Ⓣ Ⓕ	Ⓣ Ⓕ	○	114	Ⓣ Ⓕ	Ⓣ Ⓕ	○
107	Ⓣ Ⓕ	Ⓣ Ⓕ	○	115	Ⓣ Ⓕ	Ⓣ Ⓕ	○
108	Ⓣ Ⓕ	Ⓣ Ⓕ	○				

FOR OFFICIAL USE ONLY				
R/C	W/S1	FS/S2	CS/S3	WS

Page 4

PLEASE DO NOT WRITE IN THIS AREA

SERIAL #

1 Your Name:
(Print)

Last   First   M.I.

I agree to the conditions on the front and back of the SAT Subject Tests™ book. I also agree to use only a No. 2 pencil to complete my answer sheet.

Signature: _____ Date: ___/___/___
                                          MM DD YY

Home Address: _____
(Print)   Number and Street   City   State   Zip Code

Home Phone: (   )   Test Center: _____
                           (Print)   City   State/Country

2 YOUR NAME
Last Name (First 6 Letters) First Name (First 4 Letters) Mid. Init.

3 DATE OF BIRTH
MONTH DAY YEAR
Jan Feb Mar Apr May Jun Jul Aug Sep Oct Nov Dec

5 SEX
○ Female ○ Male

6 REGISTRATION NUMBER
(Copy from Admission Ticket.)

○ I turned in my registration form today.

Important: Fill in items 8 and 9 exactly as shown on the back of test book.

9 BOOK ID
(Copy from back of test book.)

8 BOOK CODE
(Copy and grid as on back of test book.)

10 TEST BOOK SERIAL NUMBER
(Copy from front of test book.)

4 ZIP CODE

7 TEST CENTER
(Supplied by Test Center Supervisor.)

FOR OFFICIAL USE ONLY

PLEASE DO NOT WRITE IN THIS AREA   SERIAL #

○ Literature
○ Biology E
○ Biology M
○ Chemistry
○ Physics

○ Mathematics Level 1
○ Mathematics Level 2
○ U.S. History
○ World History
○ French

○ German
○ Italian
○ Latin
○ Modern Hebrew
○ Spanish

○ Chinese Listening
○ French Listening
○ German Listening

○ Japanese Listening
○ Korean Listening
○ Spanish Listening

Background Questions: ① ② ③ ④ ⑤ ⑥ ⑦ ⑧ ⑨

1–100 answer grid, each A B C D E

Important: Fill in items 8 and 9 exactly as shown on the back of test book.

8 BOOK CODE (Copy and grid as on back of test book.)

9 BOOK ID (Copy from back of test book.)

10 TEST BOOK SERIAL NUMBER (Copy from front of test book.)

Quality Assurance Mark

Chemistry *Fill in circle CE only if II is correct explanation of I.

	I	II	CE*		I	II	CE*
101	T F	T F	○	109	T F	T F	○
102	T F	T F	○	110	T F	T F	○
103	T F	T F	○	111	T F	T F	○
104	T F	T F	○	112	T F	T F	○
105	T F	T F	○	113	T F	T F	○
106	T F	T F	○	114	T F	T F	○
107	T F	T F	○	115	T F	T F	○
108	T F	T F	○				

FOR OFFICIAL USE ONLY

R/C	W/S1	FS/S2	CS/S3	WS

CERTIFICATION STATEMENT   Copy the statement below (do not print) and sign your name as you would an official document.

I hereby agree to the conditions set forth online at sat.collegeboard.com and in any paper registration materials given to me and certify that I am the person whose name and address appear on this answer sheet.

Signature _____   Date _____

By registering, you agreed not to share any specific test question with anyone by any form of communication, including, but not limited to: email, text messages, or use of the Internet. Doing so can result in score cancellation and other possible sanctions.

Page 2

COMPLETE MARK ● EXAMPLES OF INCOMPLETE MARKS Ⓐ ⊗ ⊖ ⊙ ◉ ⊘ ⬚ ⬤

You must use a No. 2 pencil and marks must be complete. Do not use a mechanical pencil. It is very important that you fill in the entire circle darkly and completely. If you change your response, erase as completely as possible. Incomplete marks or erasures may affect your score.

○ Literature
○ Biology E
○ Biology M
○ Chemistry
○ Physics

○ Mathematics Level 1
○ Mathematics Level 2
○ U.S. History
○ World History
○ French

○ German
○ Italian
○ Latin
○ Modern Hebrew
○ Spanish

Background Questions: ① ② ③ ④ ⑤ ⑥ ⑦ ⑧ ⑨

Important: Fill in items 8 and 9 exactly as shown on the back of test book.

8 BOOK CODE (Copy and grid as on back of test book.)

9 BOOK ID (Copy from back of test book.)

10 TEST BOOK SERIAL NUMBER (Copy from front of test book.)

Quality Assurance Mark ●

Chemistry *Fill in circle CE only if II is correct explanation of I.

	I	II	CE*		I	II	CE*
101	Ⓣ Ⓕ	Ⓣ Ⓕ	○	109	Ⓣ Ⓕ	Ⓣ Ⓕ	○
102	Ⓣ Ⓕ	Ⓣ Ⓕ	○	110	Ⓣ Ⓕ	Ⓣ Ⓕ	○
103	Ⓣ Ⓕ	Ⓣ Ⓕ	○	111	Ⓣ Ⓕ	Ⓣ Ⓕ	○
104	Ⓣ Ⓕ	Ⓣ Ⓕ	○	112	Ⓣ Ⓕ	Ⓣ Ⓕ	○
105	Ⓣ Ⓕ	Ⓣ Ⓕ	○	113	Ⓣ Ⓕ	Ⓣ Ⓕ	○
106	Ⓣ Ⓕ	Ⓣ Ⓕ	○	114	Ⓣ Ⓕ	Ⓣ Ⓕ	○
107	Ⓣ Ⓕ	Ⓣ Ⓕ	○	115	Ⓣ Ⓕ	Ⓣ Ⓕ	○
108	Ⓣ Ⓕ	Ⓣ Ⓕ	○				

FOR OFFICIAL USE ONLY

R/C	W/S1	FS/S2	CS/S3	WS

Page 3

○ Literature   ○ Mathematics Level 1   ○ German
○ Biology E   ○ Mathematics Level 2   ○ Italian
○ Biology M   ○ U.S. History   ○ Latin
○ Chemistry   ○ World History   ○ Modern Hebrew
○ Physics   ○ French   ○ Spanish

Background Questions: ① ② ③ ④ ⑤ ⑥ ⑦ ⑧ ⑨

1–100 answer grid (A B C D E for each)

Important: Fill in items 8 and 9 exactly as shown on the back of test book.

8 BOOK CODE (Copy and grid as on back of test book.)

9 BOOK ID (Copy from back of test book.)

10 TEST BOOK SERIAL NUMBER (Copy from front of test book.)

Quality Assurance Mark ●

Chemistry *Fill in circle CE only if II is correct explanation of I.

	I	II	CE*		I	II	CE*
101	T F	T F	○	109	T F	T F	○
102	T F	T F	○	110	T F	T F	○
103	T F	T F	○	111	T F	T F	○
104	T F	T F	○	112	T F	T F	○
105	T F	T F	○	113	T F	T F	○
106	T F	T F	○	114	T F	T F	○
107	T F	T F	○	115	T F	T F	○
108	T F	T F	○				

FOR OFFICIAL USE ONLY

R/C	W/S1	FS/S2	CS/S3	WS

Page 4

PLEASE DO NOT WRITE IN THIS AREA

SERIAL #

CollegeBoard SAT

2010-11 SAT Subject Tests™

MARKS MUST BE COMPLETE

COMPLETE MARK ●

EXAMPLES OF INCOMPLETE MARKS

You must use a No. 2 pencil. Do not use a mechanical pencil. It is very important that you fill in the entire circle darkly and completely. If you change your response, erase as completely as possible. Incomplete marks or erasures may affect your score. It is very important that you follow these instructions when filling out your answer sheet.

1 Your Name:
(Print)

Last   First   M.I.

I agree to the conditions on the front and back of the SAT Subject Tests™ book. I also agree to use only a No. 2 pencil to complete my answer sheet.

Signature: _____

Date: ___/___/___
MM   DD   YY

Home Address: _____
(Print)   Number and Street   City   State   Zip Code

Home Phone: ( ) _____

Test Center: _____
(Print)   City   State/Country

2 YOUR NAME

Last Name (First 6 Letters)   First Name (First 4 Letters)   Mid. Init.

3 DATE OF BIRTH

MONTH | DAY | YEAR
Jan, Feb, Mar, Apr, May, Jun, Jul, Aug, Sep, Oct, Nov, Dec

5 SEX

○ Female   ○ Male

6 REGISTRATION NUMBER

(Copy from Admission Ticket.)

○ I turned in my registration form today.

4 ZIP CODE

7 TEST CENTER

(Supplied by Test Center Supervisor.)

Important: Fill in items 8 and 9 exactly as shown on the back of test book.

8 BOOK CODE

(Copy and grid as on back of test book.)

9 BOOK ID

(Copy from back of test book.)

10 TEST BOOK SERIAL NUMBER

(Copy from front of test book.)

FOR OFFICIAL USE ONLY

83161-77191 • NS60C1285 • Printed in U.S.A.

755275

184596-001:321   Printed in the USA by Pearson   ISD0479

PLEASE DO NOT WRITE IN THIS AREA

SERIAL #

You must use a No. 2 pencil and marks must be complete. Do not use a mechanical pencil. It is very important that you fill in the entire circle darkly and completely. If you change your response, erase as completely as possible. Incomplete marks or erasures may affect your score.

- ○ Literature
- ○ Biology E
- ○ Biology M
- ○ Chemistry
- ○ Physics
- ○ Mathematics Level 1
- ○ Mathematics Level 2
- ○ U.S. History
- ○ World History
- ○ French
- ○ German
- ○ Italian
- ○ Latin
- ○ Modern Hebrew
- ○ Spanish
- ○ Chinese Listening
- ○ French Listening
- ○ German Listening
- ○ Japanese Listening
- ○ Korean Listening
- ○ Spanish Listening

Background Questions: ① ② ③ ④ ⑤ ⑥ ⑦ ⑧ ⑨

Questions 1–100: each with answer bubbles A B C D E

Important: Fill in items 8 and 9 exactly as shown on the back of test book.

8 BOOK CODE (Copy and grid as on back of test book.)

9 BOOK ID (Copy from back of test book.)

10 TEST BOOK SERIAL NUMBER (Copy from front of test book.)

Quality Assurance Mark ●

Chemistry *Fill in circle CE only if II is correct explanation of I.

	I	II	CE*		I	II	CE*
101	T F	T F	○	109	T F	T F	○
102	T F	T F	○	110	T F	T F	○
103	T F	T F	○	111	T F	T F	○
104	T F	T F	○	112	T F	T F	○
105	T F	T F	○	113	T F	T F	○
106	T F	T F	○	114	T F	T F	○
107	T F	T F	○	115	T F	T F	○
108	T F	T F	○				

FOR OFFICIAL USE ONLY

R/C	W/S1	FS/S2	CS/S3	WS

CERTIFICATION STATEMENT Copy the statement below (do not print) and sign your name as you would an official document.

I hereby agree to the conditions set forth online at sat.collegeboard.com and in any paper registration materials given to me and certify that I am the person whose name and address appear on this answer sheet.

_____

_____

_____

Signature _____   Date _____

By registering, you agreed not to share any specific test question with anyone by any form of communication, including, but not limited to: email, text messages, or use of the Internet. Doing so can result in score cancellation and other possible sanctions.

COMPLETE MARK ● EXAMPLES OF INCOMPLETE MARKS Ⓐ ⊗ ⊖ ⓒ ⦿ ∅ ⊘ ⊛

You must use a No. 2 pencil and marks must be complete. Do not use a mechanical pencil. It is very important that you fill in the entire circle darkly and completely. If you change your response, erase as completely as possible. Incomplete marks or erasures may affect your score.

○ Literature
○ Biology E
○ Biology M
○ Chemistry
○ Physics

○ Mathematics Level 1
○ Mathematics Level 2
○ U.S. History
○ World History
○ French

○ German
○ Italian
○ Latin
○ Modern Hebrew
○ Spanish

Background Questions: ① ② ③ ④ ⑤ ⑥ ⑦ ⑧ ⑨

1–100 answer grid with options A B C D E for each question.

Important: Fill in items 8 and 9 exactly as shown on the back of test book.

8 BOOK CODE (Copy and grid as on back of test book.)

9 BOOK ID (Copy from back of test book.)

10 TEST BOOK SERIAL NUMBER (Copy from front of test book.)

Quality Assurance Mark ●

Chemistry *Fill in circle CE only if II is correct explanation of I.

	I	II	CE*		I	II	CE*
101	T F	T F	○	109	T F	T F	○
102	T F	T F	○	110	T F	T F	○
103	T F	T F	○	111	T F	T F	○
104	T F	T F	○	112	T F	T F	○
105	T F	T F	○	113	T F	T F	○
106	T F	T F	○	114	T F	T F	○
107	T F	T F	○	115	T F	T F	○
108	T F	T F	○				

FOR OFFICIAL USE ONLY				
R/C	W/S1	FS/S2	CS/S3	WS

○ Literature   ○ Mathematics Level 1   ○ German
○ Biology E   ○ Mathematics Level 2   ○ Italian
○ Biology M   ○ U.S. History   ○ Latin
○ Chemistry   ○ World History   ○ Modern Hebrew
○ Physics   ○ French   ○ Spanish

Background Questions: ① ② ③ ④ ⑤ ⑥ ⑦ ⑧ ⑨

1 Ⓐ Ⓑ Ⓒ Ⓓ Ⓔ   26 Ⓐ Ⓑ Ⓒ Ⓓ Ⓔ   51 Ⓐ Ⓑ Ⓒ Ⓓ Ⓔ   76 Ⓐ Ⓑ Ⓒ Ⓓ Ⓔ
2 Ⓐ Ⓑ Ⓒ Ⓓ Ⓔ   27 Ⓐ Ⓑ Ⓒ Ⓓ Ⓔ   52 Ⓐ Ⓑ Ⓒ Ⓓ Ⓔ   77 Ⓐ Ⓑ Ⓒ Ⓓ Ⓔ
3 Ⓐ Ⓑ Ⓒ Ⓓ Ⓔ   28 Ⓐ Ⓑ Ⓒ Ⓓ Ⓔ   53 Ⓐ Ⓑ Ⓒ Ⓓ Ⓔ   78 Ⓐ Ⓑ Ⓒ Ⓓ Ⓔ
4 Ⓐ Ⓑ Ⓒ Ⓓ Ⓔ   29 Ⓐ Ⓑ Ⓒ Ⓓ Ⓔ   54 Ⓐ Ⓑ Ⓒ Ⓓ Ⓔ   79 Ⓐ Ⓑ Ⓒ Ⓓ Ⓔ
5 Ⓐ Ⓑ Ⓒ Ⓓ Ⓔ   30 Ⓐ Ⓑ Ⓒ Ⓓ Ⓔ   55 Ⓐ Ⓑ Ⓒ Ⓓ Ⓔ   80 Ⓐ Ⓑ Ⓒ Ⓓ Ⓔ
6 Ⓐ Ⓑ Ⓒ Ⓓ Ⓔ   31 Ⓐ Ⓑ Ⓒ Ⓓ Ⓔ   56 Ⓐ Ⓑ Ⓒ Ⓓ Ⓔ   81 Ⓐ Ⓑ Ⓒ Ⓓ Ⓔ
7 Ⓐ Ⓑ Ⓒ Ⓓ Ⓔ   32 Ⓐ Ⓑ Ⓒ Ⓓ Ⓔ   57 Ⓐ Ⓑ Ⓒ Ⓓ Ⓔ   82 Ⓐ Ⓑ Ⓒ Ⓓ Ⓔ
8 Ⓐ Ⓑ Ⓒ Ⓓ Ⓔ   33 Ⓐ Ⓑ Ⓒ Ⓓ Ⓔ   58 Ⓐ Ⓑ Ⓒ Ⓓ Ⓔ   83 Ⓐ Ⓑ Ⓒ Ⓓ Ⓔ
9 Ⓐ Ⓑ Ⓒ Ⓓ Ⓔ   34 Ⓐ Ⓑ Ⓒ Ⓓ Ⓔ   59 Ⓐ Ⓑ Ⓒ Ⓓ Ⓔ   84 Ⓐ Ⓑ Ⓒ Ⓓ Ⓔ
10 Ⓐ Ⓑ Ⓒ Ⓓ Ⓔ   35 Ⓐ Ⓑ Ⓒ Ⓓ Ⓔ   60 Ⓐ Ⓑ Ⓒ Ⓓ Ⓔ   85 Ⓐ Ⓑ Ⓒ Ⓓ Ⓔ
11 Ⓐ Ⓑ Ⓒ Ⓓ Ⓔ   36 Ⓐ Ⓑ Ⓒ Ⓓ Ⓔ   61 Ⓐ Ⓑ Ⓒ Ⓓ Ⓔ   86 Ⓐ Ⓑ Ⓒ Ⓓ Ⓔ
12 Ⓐ Ⓑ Ⓒ Ⓓ Ⓔ   37 Ⓐ Ⓑ Ⓒ Ⓓ Ⓔ   62 Ⓐ Ⓑ Ⓒ Ⓓ Ⓔ   87 Ⓐ Ⓑ Ⓒ Ⓓ Ⓔ
13 Ⓐ Ⓑ Ⓒ Ⓓ Ⓔ   38 Ⓐ Ⓑ Ⓒ Ⓓ Ⓔ   63 Ⓐ Ⓑ Ⓒ Ⓓ Ⓔ   88 Ⓐ Ⓑ Ⓒ Ⓓ Ⓔ
14 Ⓐ Ⓑ Ⓒ Ⓓ Ⓔ   39 Ⓐ Ⓑ Ⓒ Ⓓ Ⓔ   64 Ⓐ Ⓑ Ⓒ Ⓓ Ⓔ   89 Ⓐ Ⓑ Ⓒ Ⓓ Ⓔ
15 Ⓐ Ⓑ Ⓒ Ⓓ Ⓔ   40 Ⓐ Ⓑ Ⓒ Ⓓ Ⓔ   65 Ⓐ Ⓑ Ⓒ Ⓓ Ⓔ   90 Ⓐ Ⓑ Ⓒ Ⓓ Ⓔ
16 Ⓐ Ⓑ Ⓒ Ⓓ Ⓔ   41 Ⓐ Ⓑ Ⓒ Ⓓ Ⓔ   66 Ⓐ Ⓑ Ⓒ Ⓓ Ⓔ   91 Ⓐ Ⓑ Ⓒ Ⓓ Ⓔ
17 Ⓐ Ⓑ Ⓒ Ⓓ Ⓔ   42 Ⓐ Ⓑ Ⓒ Ⓓ Ⓔ   67 Ⓐ Ⓑ Ⓒ Ⓓ Ⓔ   92 Ⓐ Ⓑ Ⓒ Ⓓ Ⓔ
18 Ⓐ Ⓑ Ⓒ Ⓓ Ⓔ   43 Ⓐ Ⓑ Ⓒ Ⓓ Ⓔ   68 Ⓐ Ⓑ Ⓒ Ⓓ Ⓔ   93 Ⓐ Ⓑ Ⓒ Ⓓ Ⓔ
19 Ⓐ Ⓑ Ⓒ Ⓓ Ⓔ   44 Ⓐ Ⓑ Ⓒ Ⓓ Ⓔ   69 Ⓐ Ⓑ Ⓒ Ⓓ Ⓔ   94 Ⓐ Ⓑ Ⓒ Ⓓ Ⓔ
20 Ⓐ Ⓑ Ⓒ Ⓓ Ⓔ   45 Ⓐ Ⓑ Ⓒ Ⓓ Ⓔ   70 Ⓐ Ⓑ Ⓒ Ⓓ Ⓔ   95 Ⓐ Ⓑ Ⓒ Ⓓ Ⓔ
21 Ⓐ Ⓑ Ⓒ Ⓓ Ⓔ   46 Ⓐ Ⓑ Ⓒ Ⓓ Ⓔ   71 Ⓐ Ⓑ Ⓒ Ⓓ Ⓔ   96 Ⓐ Ⓑ Ⓒ Ⓓ Ⓔ
22 Ⓐ Ⓑ Ⓒ Ⓓ Ⓔ   47 Ⓐ Ⓑ Ⓒ Ⓓ Ⓔ   72 Ⓐ Ⓑ Ⓒ Ⓓ Ⓔ   97 Ⓐ Ⓑ Ⓒ Ⓓ Ⓔ
23 Ⓐ Ⓑ Ⓒ Ⓓ Ⓔ   48 Ⓐ Ⓑ Ⓒ Ⓓ Ⓔ   73 Ⓐ Ⓑ Ⓒ Ⓓ Ⓔ   98 Ⓐ Ⓑ Ⓒ Ⓓ Ⓔ
24 Ⓐ Ⓑ Ⓒ Ⓓ Ⓔ   49 Ⓐ Ⓑ Ⓒ Ⓓ Ⓔ   74 Ⓐ Ⓑ Ⓒ Ⓓ Ⓔ   99 Ⓐ Ⓑ Ⓒ Ⓓ Ⓔ
25 Ⓐ Ⓑ Ⓒ Ⓓ Ⓔ   50 Ⓐ Ⓑ Ⓒ Ⓓ Ⓔ   75 Ⓐ Ⓑ Ⓒ Ⓓ Ⓔ   100 Ⓐ Ⓑ Ⓒ Ⓓ Ⓔ

Important: Fill in items 8 and 9 exactly as shown on the back of test book.

8 BOOK CODE (Copy and grid as on back of test book.)

9 BOOK ID (Copy from back of test book.)

10 TEST BOOK SERIAL NUMBER (Copy from front of test book.)

Quality Assurance Mark ●

Chemistry *Fill in circle CE only if II is correct explanation of I.

	I	II	CE*		I	II	CE*
101	Ⓣ Ⓕ	Ⓣ Ⓕ	○	109	Ⓣ Ⓕ	Ⓣ Ⓕ	○
102	Ⓣ Ⓕ	Ⓣ Ⓕ	○	110	Ⓣ Ⓕ	Ⓣ Ⓕ	○
103	Ⓣ Ⓕ	Ⓣ Ⓕ	○	111	Ⓣ Ⓕ	Ⓣ Ⓕ	○
104	Ⓣ Ⓕ	Ⓣ Ⓕ	○	112	Ⓣ Ⓕ	Ⓣ Ⓕ	○
105	Ⓣ Ⓕ	Ⓣ Ⓕ	○	113	Ⓣ Ⓕ	Ⓣ Ⓕ	○
106	Ⓣ Ⓕ	Ⓣ Ⓕ	○	114	Ⓣ Ⓕ	Ⓣ Ⓕ	○
107	Ⓣ Ⓕ	Ⓣ Ⓕ	○	115	Ⓣ Ⓕ	Ⓣ Ⓕ	○
108	Ⓣ Ⓕ	Ⓣ Ⓕ	○				

FOR OFFICIAL USE ONLY				
R/C	W/S1	FS/S2	CS/S3	WS

Page 4

SERIAL #